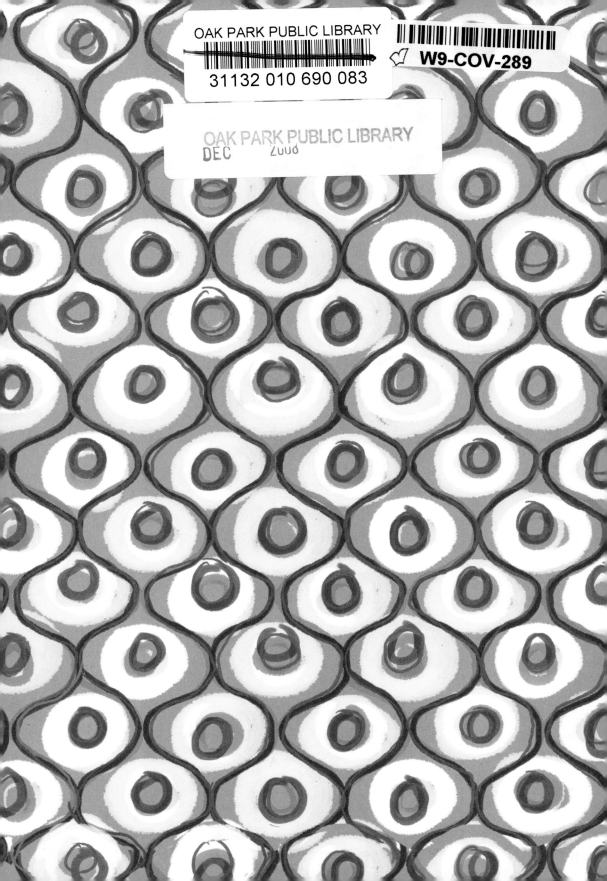

For Saga Odje Isaac
M.A.
For Catherine and Juju
C.O.

A big thank you goes to Antoine Delesvaux for his invaluable and indispensable help.

Thanks also to Ernest Odje, Nicolas Merki, Patrick Chapatte, Reynold Leclercq, Mendozza, Christian Ronget, Guillaume Boilève, 1 Jour 2 Mai and Beybson for their beautiful color photos, without forgetting the participation of the Grezaud family.

And lastly our gratitude to Hyppolite B. for the music!

Marguerite Abouet and Clément Oubrerie

Translation by Dag Dascher.
With great thanks to Helge Dascher for wielding the word-machete and editing the translation, and to Herman Koutouan for his invaluable assistance in explaining aspects of Ivorian culture.
Lettering by Rich Tomasso, with thanks to John Kuramoto.

Previously published in French by Gallimard Jeunesse (ISBN 2-07-057588-8) as part of the Joann Sfar edited Bayou collection.

Library and Archives Canada Cataloguing in Publication
Abouet, Marguerite, 1971-
Aya of Yop City / Marguerite Abouet & Clément Oubrerie; translator: Dag Dascher.
Sequel to *Aya*.
ISBN 978-1-897299-41-8
1. Teenage girls--Côte d'Ivoire--Comic books, strips, etc. 2. Côte d'Ivoire--Comic books, strips, etc. I. Oubrerie, Clément II. Dascher, Dag, 1962- III. Title.
PN6790.I93A26 2008 741.5'96668 C2008-901254-2

Drawn & Quarterly, Post Office Box 48056, Montreal, Quebec, Canada H2V 4S8
www.drawnandquarterly.com

First hardcover edition: September 2008.
Printed in Singapore.
10 9 8 7 6 5 4 3 2 1

Distributed in the USA and abroad by:
Farrar, Straus and Giroux
18 West 18th street, New York, NY 10011
Orders: 888.330.8477

Distributed in Canada by:
Raincoast Books
9050 Shaughnessy Street, Vancouver, BC V6P 6E5
Orders: 800.663.5714

The first volume of Aya *(ISBN 978-1-894937-90-0) is also available from many fine book and comic stores.*

MARGUERITE ABOUET   CLÉMENT OUBRERIE

AYA
OF YOP CITY

DRAWN & QUARTERLY
MONTREAL

The characters

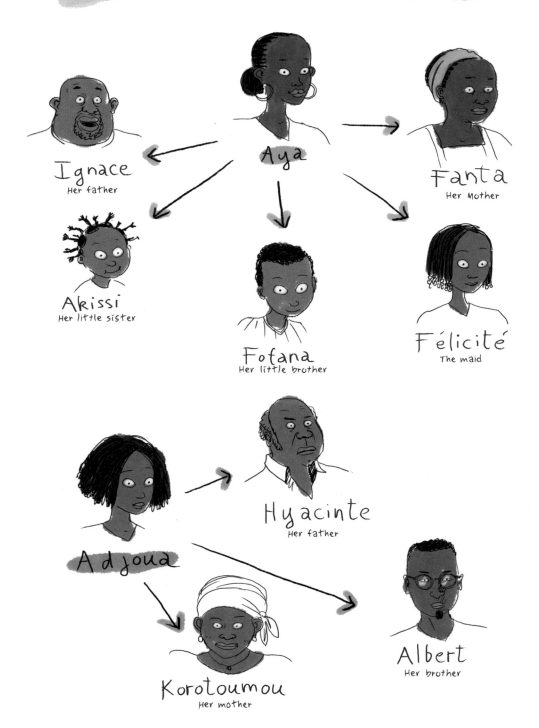

Ignace
Her father

Aya

Fanta
Her Mother

Akissi
Her little sister

Fofana
Her little brother

Félicité
The maid

Adjoua

Hyacinte
Her father

Korotoumou
Her mother

Albert
Her brother

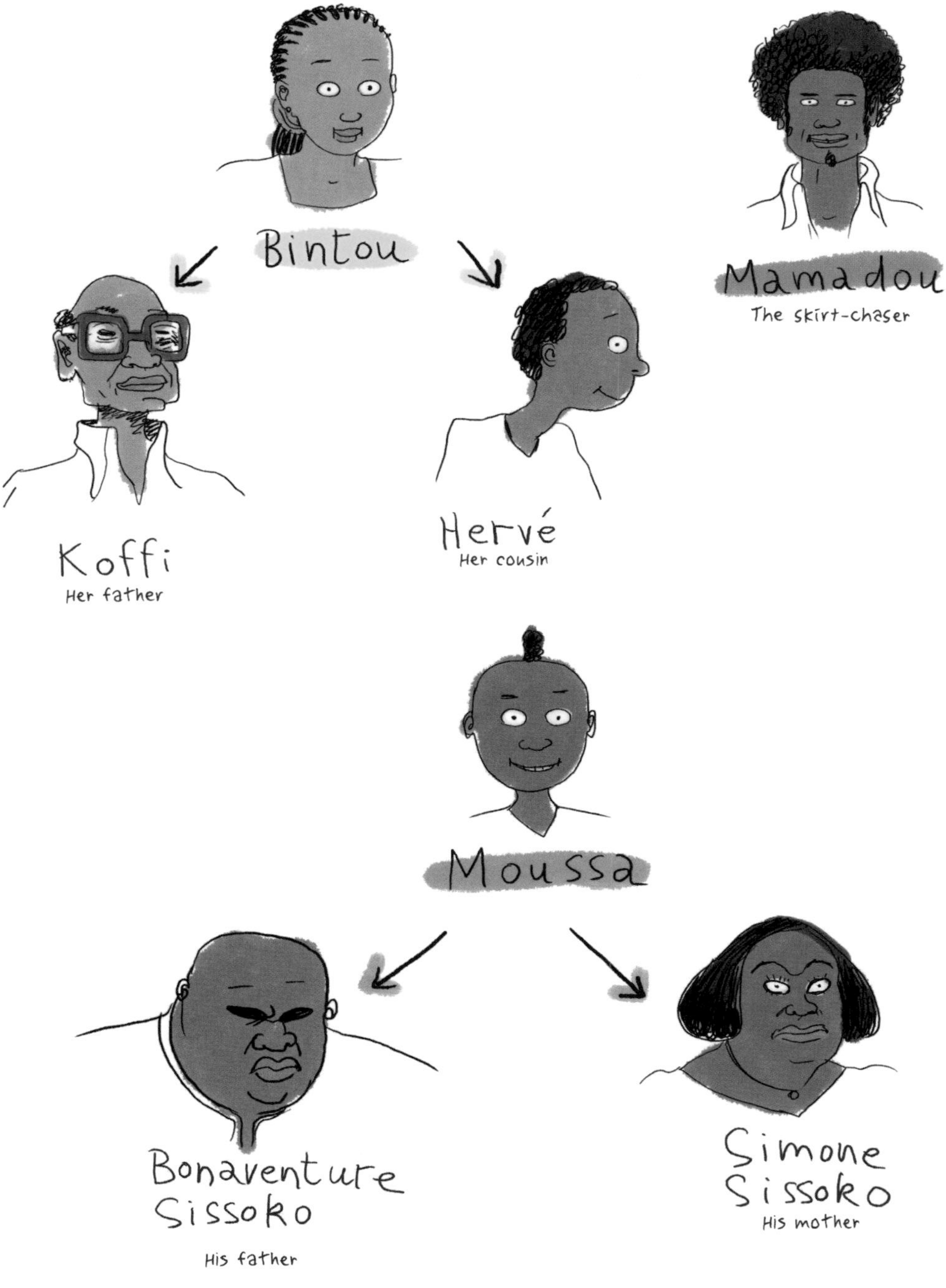
Bintou
Mamadou
The skirt-chaser
Koffi
Her father
Hervé
Her cousin
Moussa
Bonaventure Sissoko
His father
Simone Sissoko
His mother

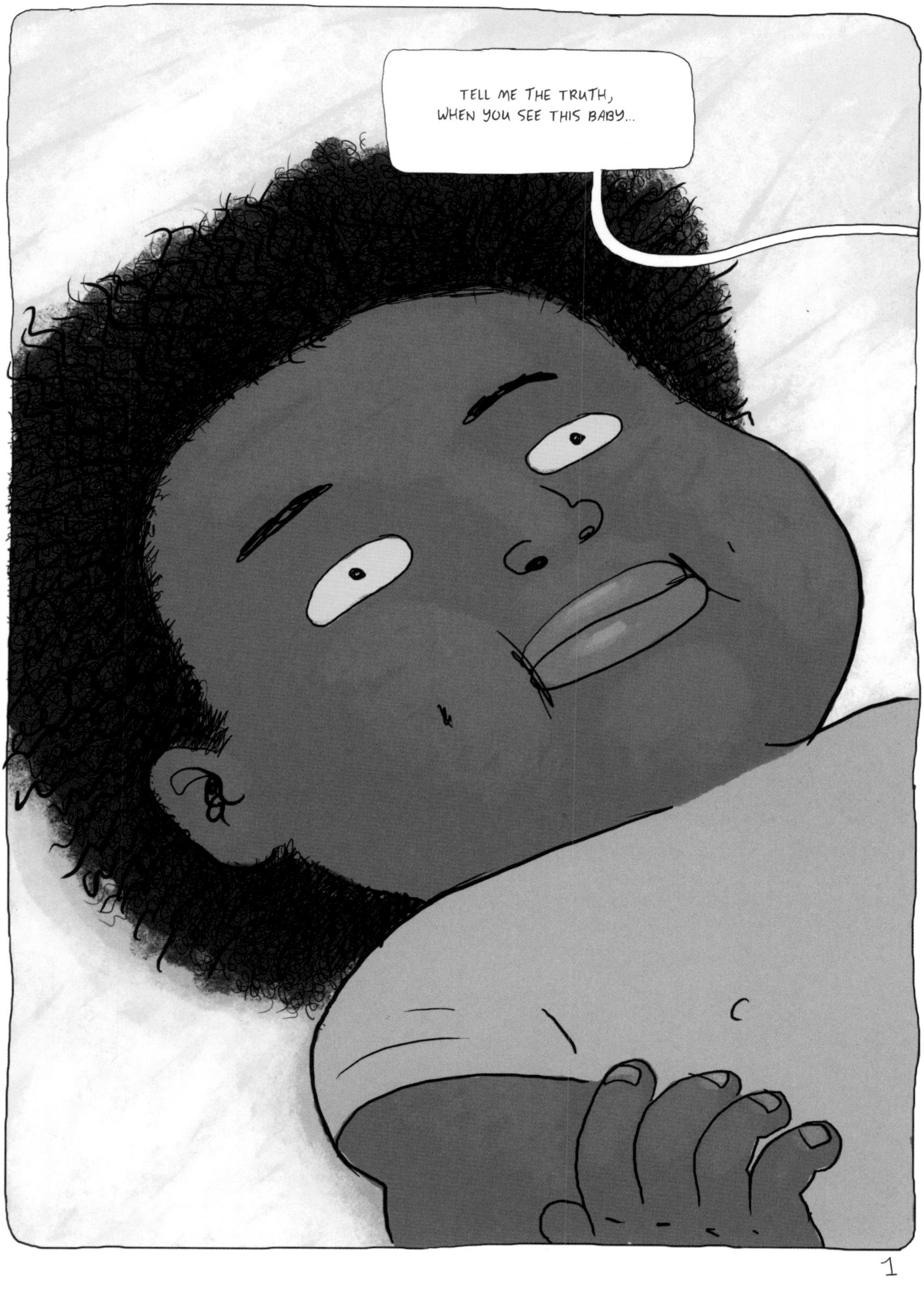
TELL ME THE TRUTH, WHEN YOU SEE THIS BABY...

DOES HE LOOK LIKE MY SON MOUSSA?
LOOKING CLOSELY AT HIS EYES, MR. SISSOKO...
ENOUGH!
HE DOESN'T LOOK MUCH LIKE YOU EITHER.
BUT HE DOES LOOK LIKE MY BROTHER'S KIDS...RIGHT, KORO?
YES, YES...A SPITTING IMAGE OF OUR COUSINS IN THE VILLAGE.
THEY SAY LOOKS CAN SKIP GENERATIONS... AND EVEN PASS RIGHT BY THE PARENTS SOMETIMES!
WHICH IS WHY YOUR SON MOUSSA DOESN'T LOOK LIKE YOUR CHARMING WIFE.
BUT THAT DOESN'T EXPLAIN WHY HE LOOKS LIKE OUR NEIGHBOR.
YOUR DAUGHTER ADJOUA HAD BETTER TELL THE TRUTH!

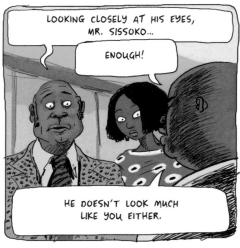

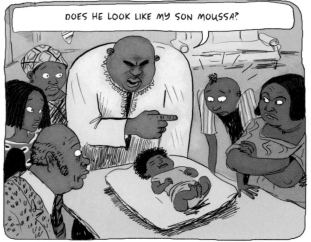

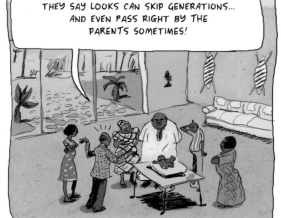

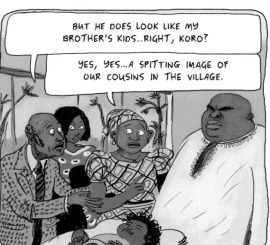

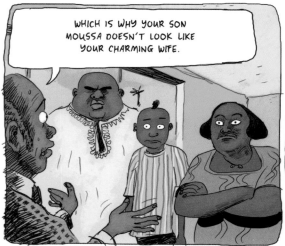

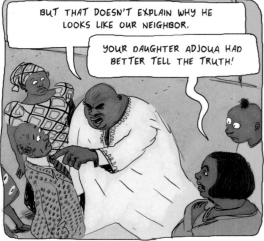

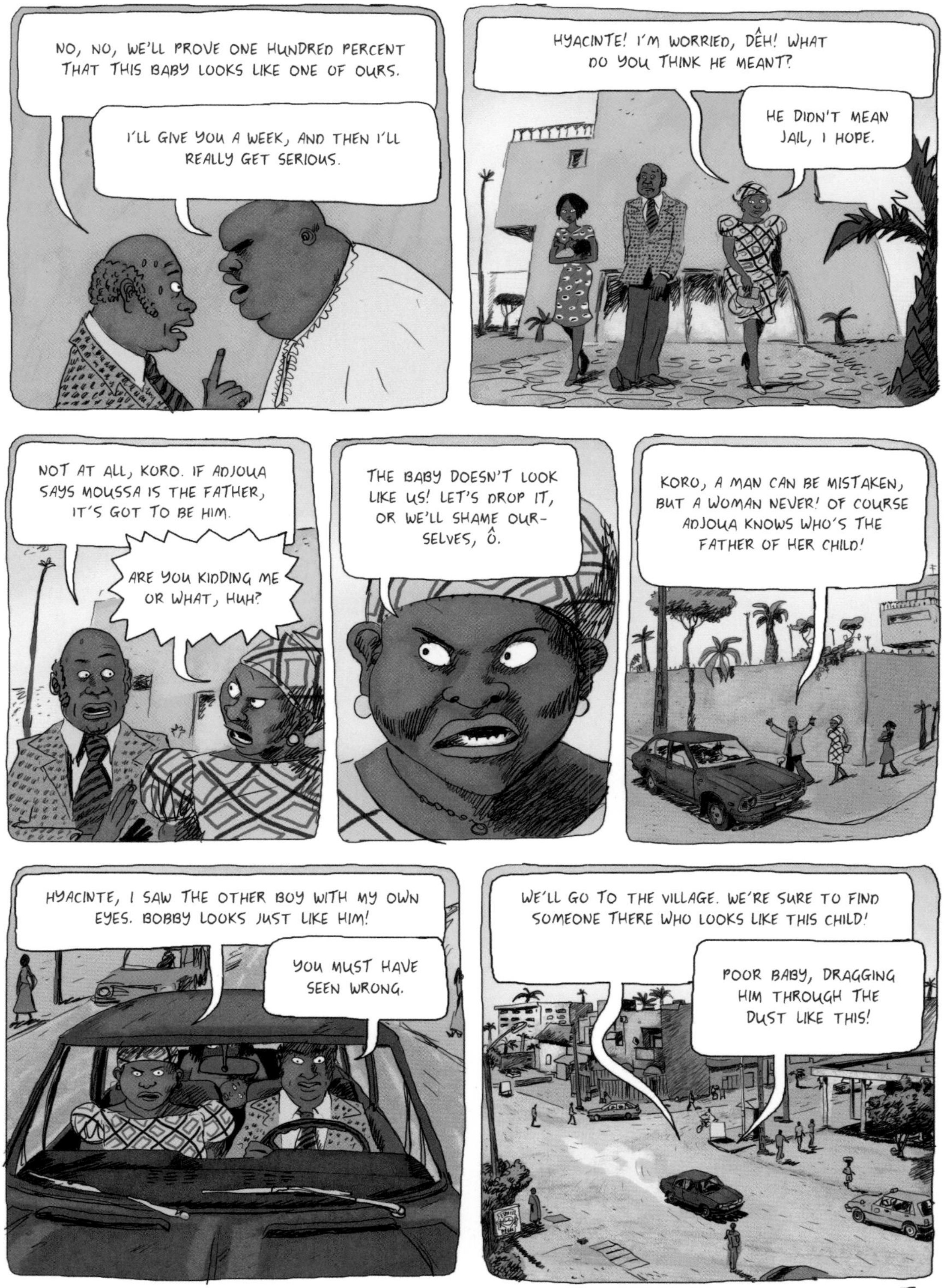
NO, NO, WE'LL PROVE ONE HUNDRED PERCENT THAT THIS BABY LOOKS LIKE ONE OF OURS.
I'LL GIVE YOU A WEEK, AND THEN I'LL REALLY GET SERIOUS.
HYACINTE! I'M WORRIED, DÊH! WHAT DO YOU THINK HE MEANT?
HE DIDN'T MEAN JAIL, I HOPE.
NOT AT ALL, KORO. IF ADJOUA SAYS MOUSSA IS THE FATHER, IT'S GOT TO BE HIM.
ARE YOU KIDDING ME OR WHAT, HUH?
THE BABY DOESN'T LOOK LIKE US! LET'S DROP IT, OR WE'LL SHAME OURSELVES, Ô.
KORO, A MAN CAN BE MISTAKEN, BUT A WOMAN NEVER! OF COURSE ADJOUA KNOWS WHO'S THE FATHER OF HER CHILD!
HYACINTE, I SAW THE OTHER BOY WITH MY OWN EYES. BOBBY LOOKS JUST LIKE HIM!
YOU MUST HAVE SEEN WRONG.
WE'LL GO TO THE VILLAGE. WE'RE SURE TO FIND SOMEONE THERE WHO LOOKS LIKE THIS CHILD!
POOR BABY, DRAGGING HIM THROUGH THE DUST LIKE THIS!

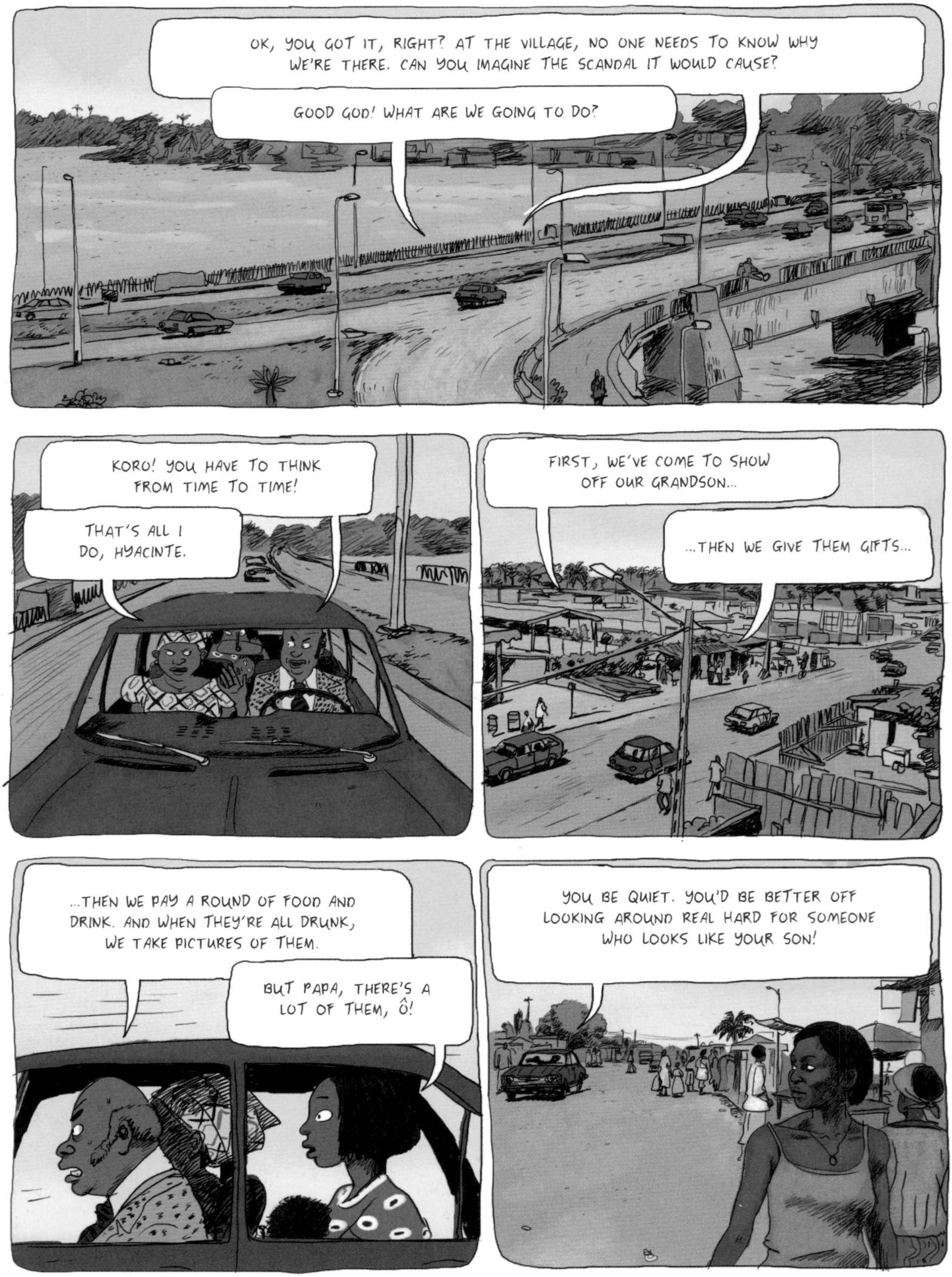
OK, YOU GOT IT, RIGHT? AT THE VILLAGE, NO ONE NEEDS TO KNOW WHY WE'RE THERE. CAN YOU IMAGINE THE SCANDAL IT WOULD CAUSE?
GOOD GOD! WHAT ARE WE GOING TO DO?
KORO! YOU HAVE TO THINK FROM TIME TO TIME!
THAT'S ALL I DO, HYACINTE.
FIRST, WE'VE COME TO SHOW OFF OUR GRANDSON...
...THEN WE GIVE THEM GIFTS...
...THEN WE PAY A ROUND OF FOOD AND DRINK. AND WHEN THEY'RE ALL DRUNK, WE TAKE PICTURES OF THEM.
BUT PAPA, THERE'S A LOT OF THEM, Ô!
YOU BE QUIET. YOU'D BE BETTER OFF LOOKING AROUND REAL HARD FOR SOMEONE WHO LOOKS LIKE YOUR SON!

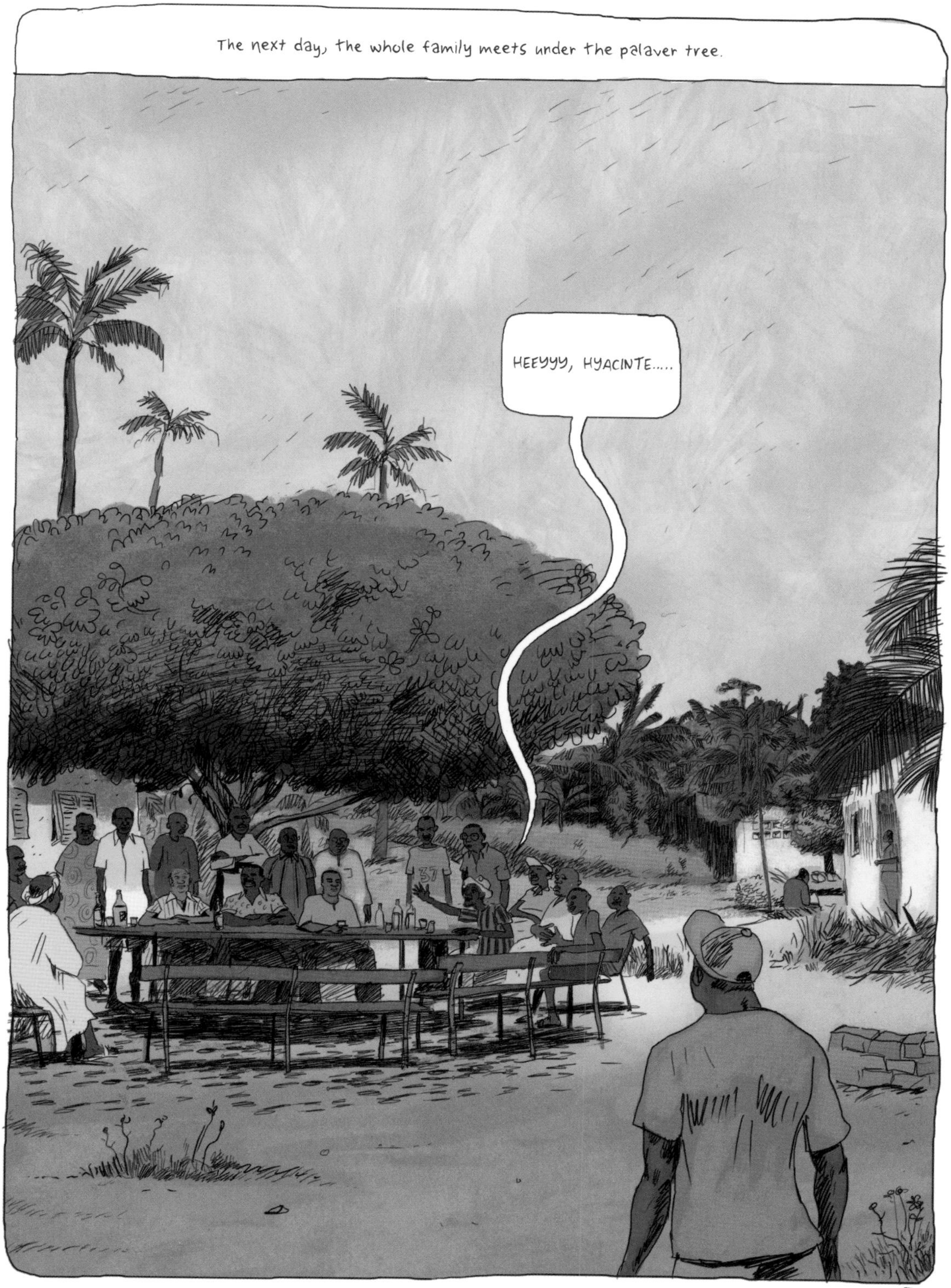
The next day, the whole family meets under the palaver tree.
HEEYYY, HYACINTE.....

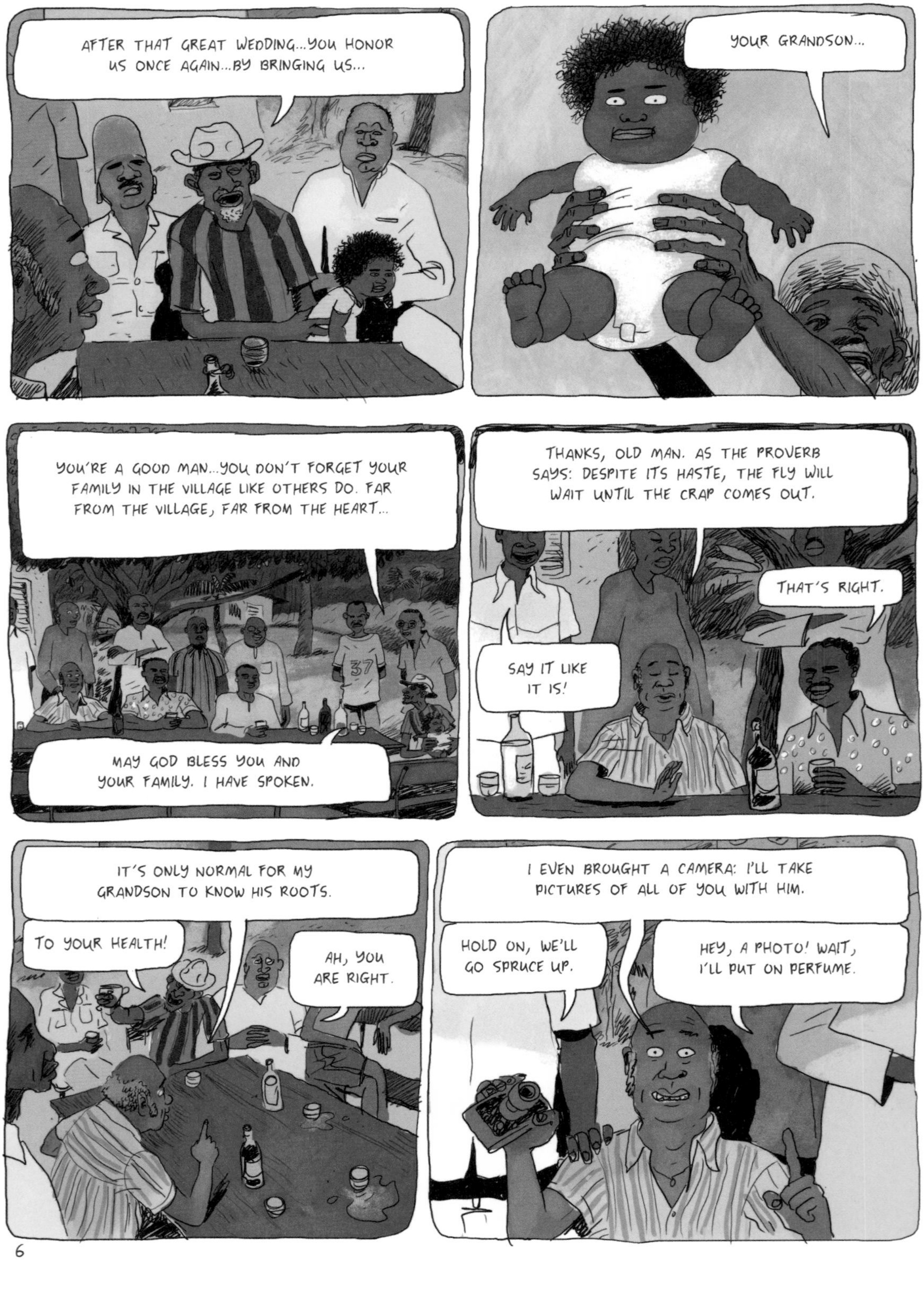
AFTER THAT GREAT WEDDING...YOU HONOR US ONCE AGAIN...BY BRINGING US...
YOUR GRANDSON...
YOU'RE A GOOD MAN...YOU DON'T FORGET YOUR FAMILY IN THE VILLAGE LIKE OTHERS DO. FAR FROM THE VILLAGE, FAR FROM THE HEART...
37
MAY GOD BLESS YOU AND YOUR FAMILY. I HAVE SPOKEN.
THANKS, OLD MAN. AS THE PROVERB SAYS: DESPITE ITS HASTE, THE FLY WILL WAIT UNTIL THE CRAP COMES OUT.
THAT'S RIGHT.
SAY IT LIKE IT IS!
IT'S ONLY NORMAL FOR MY GRANDSON TO KNOW HIS ROOTS.
TO YOUR HEALTH!
AH, YOU ARE RIGHT.
I EVEN BROUGHT A CAMERA: I'LL TAKE PICTURES OF ALL OF YOU WITH HIM.
HOLD ON, WE'LL GO SPRUCE UP.
HEY, A PHOTO! WAIT, I'LL PUT ON PERFUME.

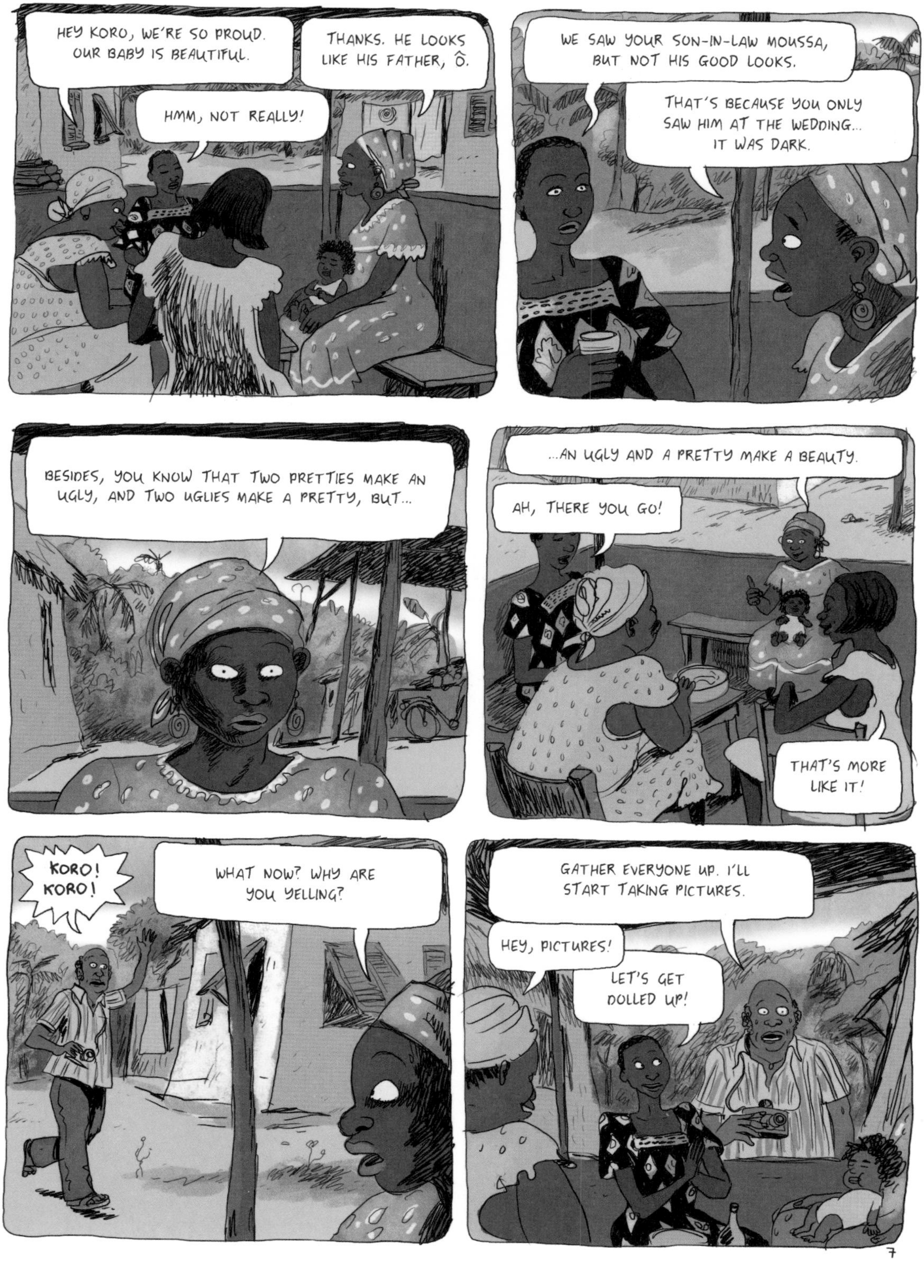
HEY KORO, WE'RE SO PROUD. OUR BABY IS BEAUTIFUL.
THANKS. HE LOOKS LIKE HIS FATHER, Ô.
HMM, NOT REALLY!
WE SAW YOUR SON-IN-LAW MOUSSA, BUT NOT HIS GOOD LOOKS.
THAT'S BECAUSE YOU ONLY SAW HIM AT THE WEDDING... IT WAS DARK.
BESIDES, YOU KNOW THAT TWO PRETTIES MAKE AN UGLY, AND TWO UGLIES MAKE A PRETTY, BUT...
...AN UGLY AND A PRETTY MAKE A BEAUTY.
AH, THERE YOU GO!
THAT'S MORE LIKE IT!
KORO! KORO!
WHAT NOW? WHY ARE YOU YELLING?
GATHER EVERYONE UP. I'LL START TAKING PICTURES.
HEY, PICTURES!
LET'S GET DOLLED UP!

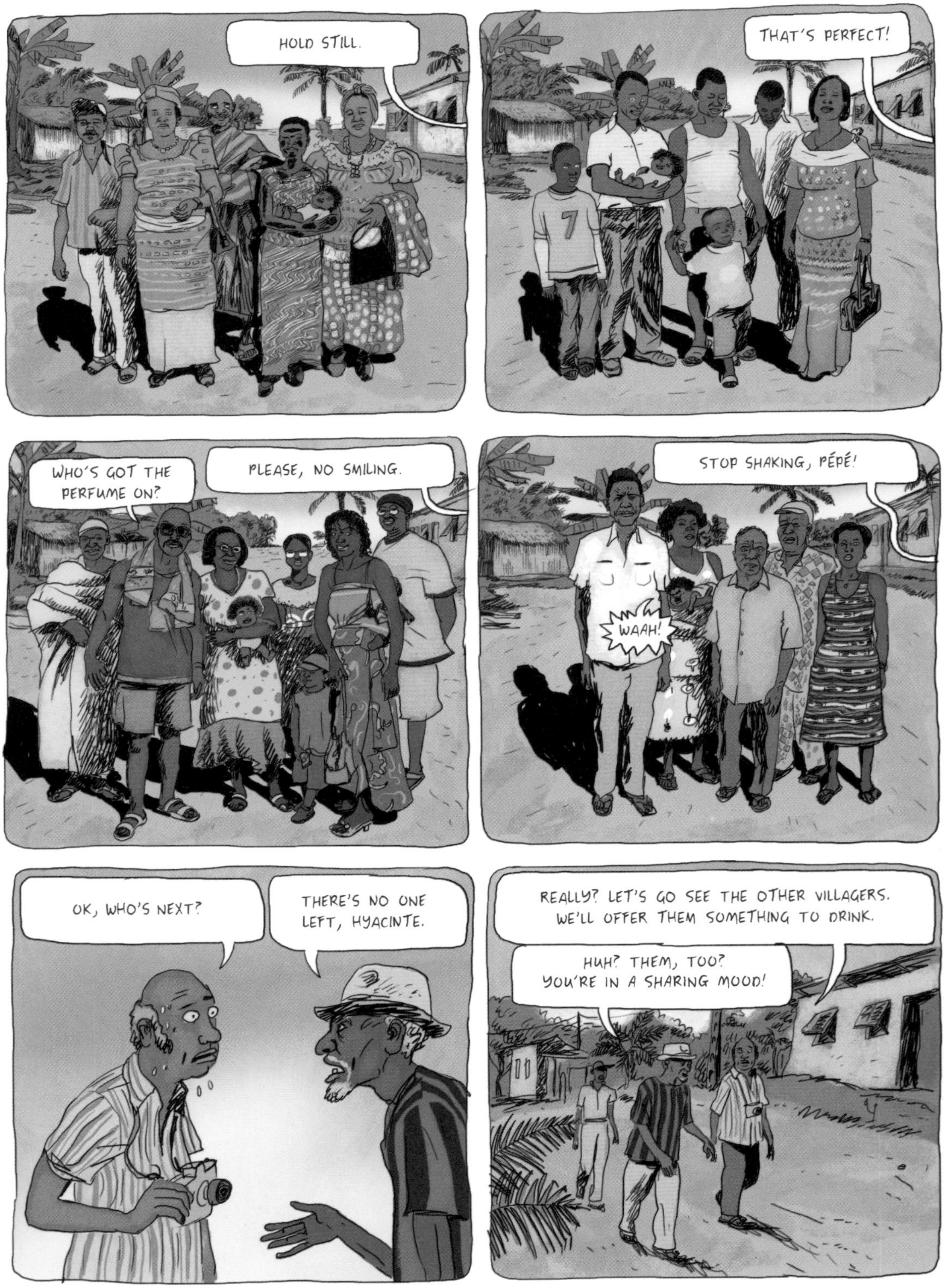
HOLD STILL.
THAT'S PERFECT!
WHO'S GOT THE PERFUME ON?
PLEASE, NO SMILING.
STOP SHAKING, PÉPÉ!
WAAH!
OK, WHO'S NEXT?
THERE'S NO ONE LEFT, HYACINTE.
REALLY? LET'S GO SEE THE OTHER VILLAGERS. WE'LL OFFER THEM SOMETHING TO DRINK.
HUH? THEM, TOO? YOU'RE IN A SHARING MOOD!

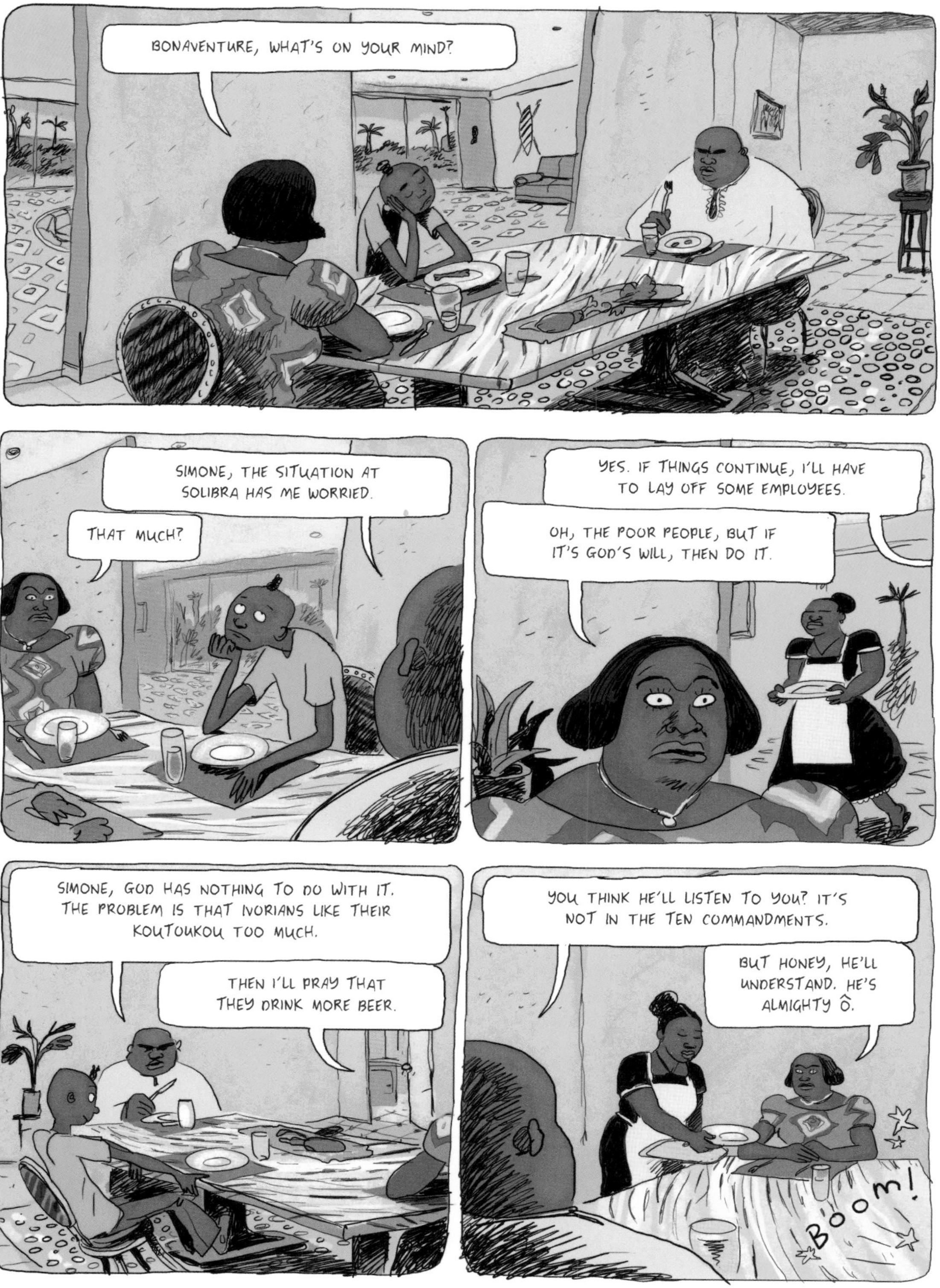

BONAVENTURE, WHAT'S ON YOUR MIND?
SIMONE, THE SITUATION AT SOLIBRA HAS ME WORRIED.
THAT MUCH?
YES. IF THINGS CONTINUE, I'LL HAVE TO LAY OFF SOME EMPLOYEES.
OH, THE POOR PEOPLE, BUT IF IT'S GOD'S WILL, THEN DO IT.
SIMONE, GOD HAS NOTHING TO DO WITH IT. THE PROBLEM IS THAT IVORIANS LIKE THEIR KOUTOUKOU TOO MUCH.
THEN I'LL PRAY THAT THEY DRINK MORE BEER.
YOU THINK HE'LL LISTEN TO YOU? IT'S NOT IN THE TEN COMMANDMENTS.
BUT HONEY, HE'LL UNDERSTAND. HE'S ALMIGHTY Ô.
BOOM!

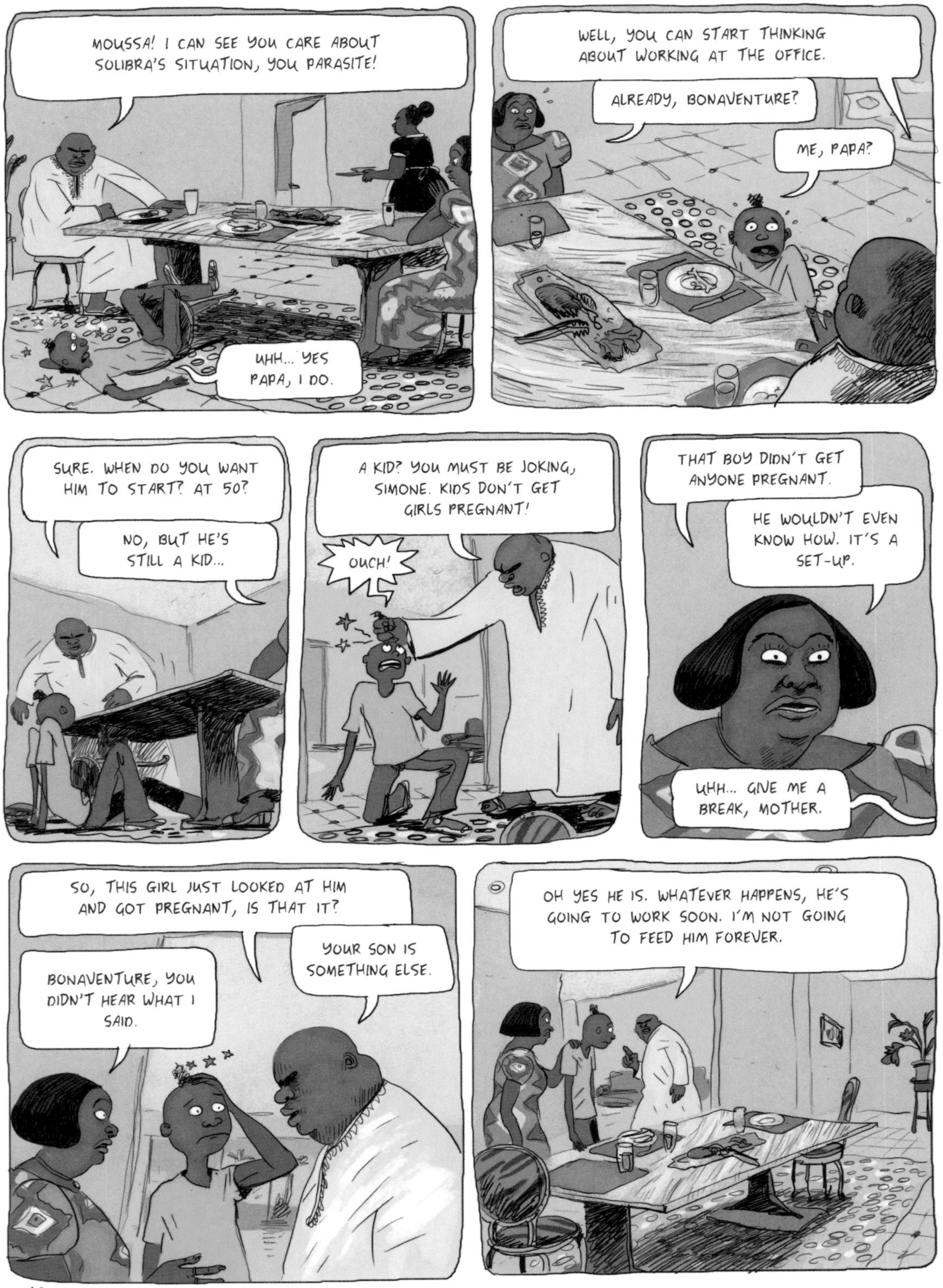
MOUSSA! I CAN SEE YOU CARE ABOUT SOLIBRA'S SITUATION, YOU PARASITE!
UHH... YES PAPA, I DO.
WELL, YOU CAN START THINKING ABOUT WORKING AT THE OFFICE.
ALREADY, BONAVENTURE?
ME, PAPA?
SURE. WHEN DO YOU WANT HIM TO START? AT 50?
NO, BUT HE'S STILL A KID...
A KID? YOU MUST BE JOKING, SIMONE. KIDS DON'T GET GIRLS PREGNANT!
OUCH!
THAT BOY DIDN'T GET ANYONE PREGNANT.
HE WOULDN'T EVEN KNOW HOW. IT'S A SET-UP.
UHH... GIVE ME A BREAK, MOTHER.
SO, THIS GIRL JUST LOOKED AT HIM AND GOT PREGNANT, IS THAT IT?
YOUR SON IS SOMETHING ELSE.
BONAVENTURE, YOU DIDN'T HEAR WHAT I SAID.
OH YES HE IS. WHATEVER HAPPENS, HE'S GOING TO WORK SOON. I'M NOT GOING TO FEED HIM FOREVER.

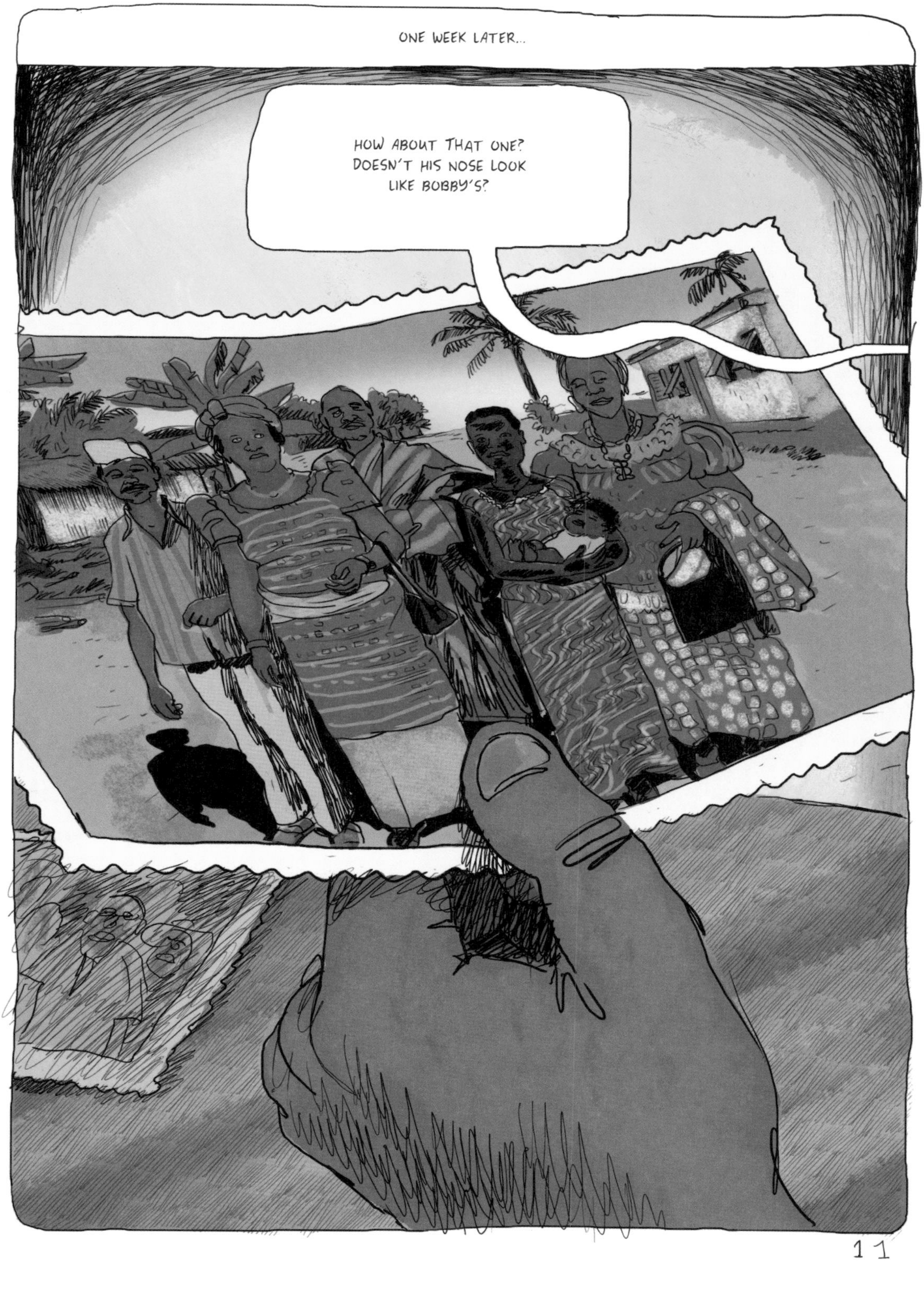
ONE WEEK LATER...
HOW ABOUT THAT ONE? DOESN'T HIS NOSE LOOK LIKE BOBBY'S?

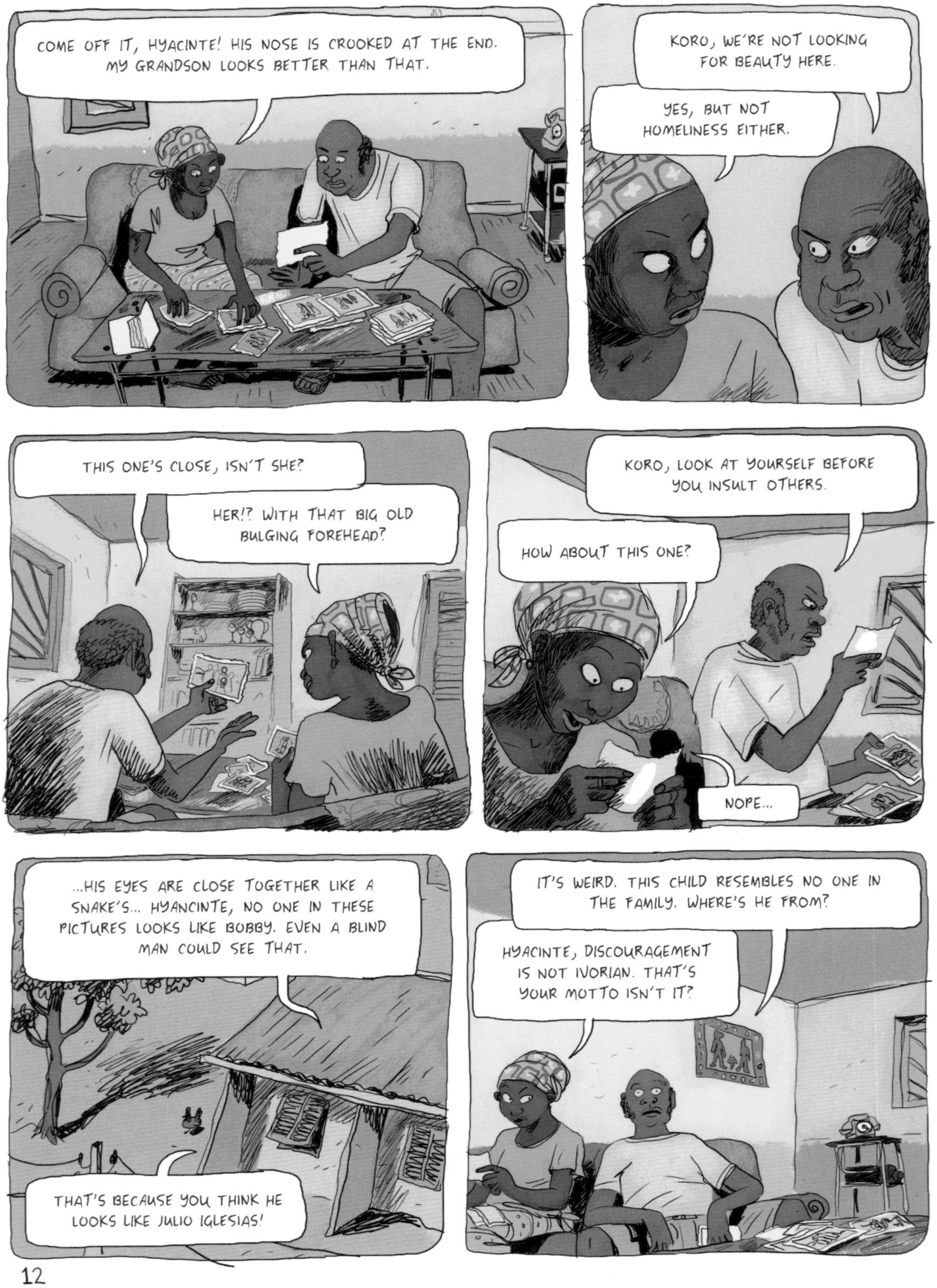
COME OFF IT, HYACINTE! HIS NOSE IS CROOKED AT THE END. MY GRANDSON LOOKS BETTER THAN THAT.
KORO, WE'RE NOT LOOKING FOR BEAUTY HERE.
YES, BUT NOT HOMELINESS EITHER.
THIS ONE'S CLOSE, ISN'T SHE?
HER!? WITH THAT BIG OLD BULGING FOREHEAD?
KORO, LOOK AT YOURSELF BEFORE YOU INSULT OTHERS.
HOW ABOUT THIS ONE?
NOPE...
...HIS EYES ARE CLOSE TOGETHER LIKE A SNAKE'S... HYANCINTE, NO ONE IN THESE PICTURES LOOKS LIKE BOBBY. EVEN A BLIND MAN COULD SEE THAT.
THAT'S BECAUSE YOU THINK HE LOOKS LIKE JULIO IGLESIAS!
IT'S WEIRD. THIS CHILD RESEMBLES NO ONE IN THE FAMILY. WHERE'S HE FROM?
HYACINTE, DISCOURAGEMENT IS NOT IVORIAN. THAT'S YOUR MOTTO ISN'T IT?

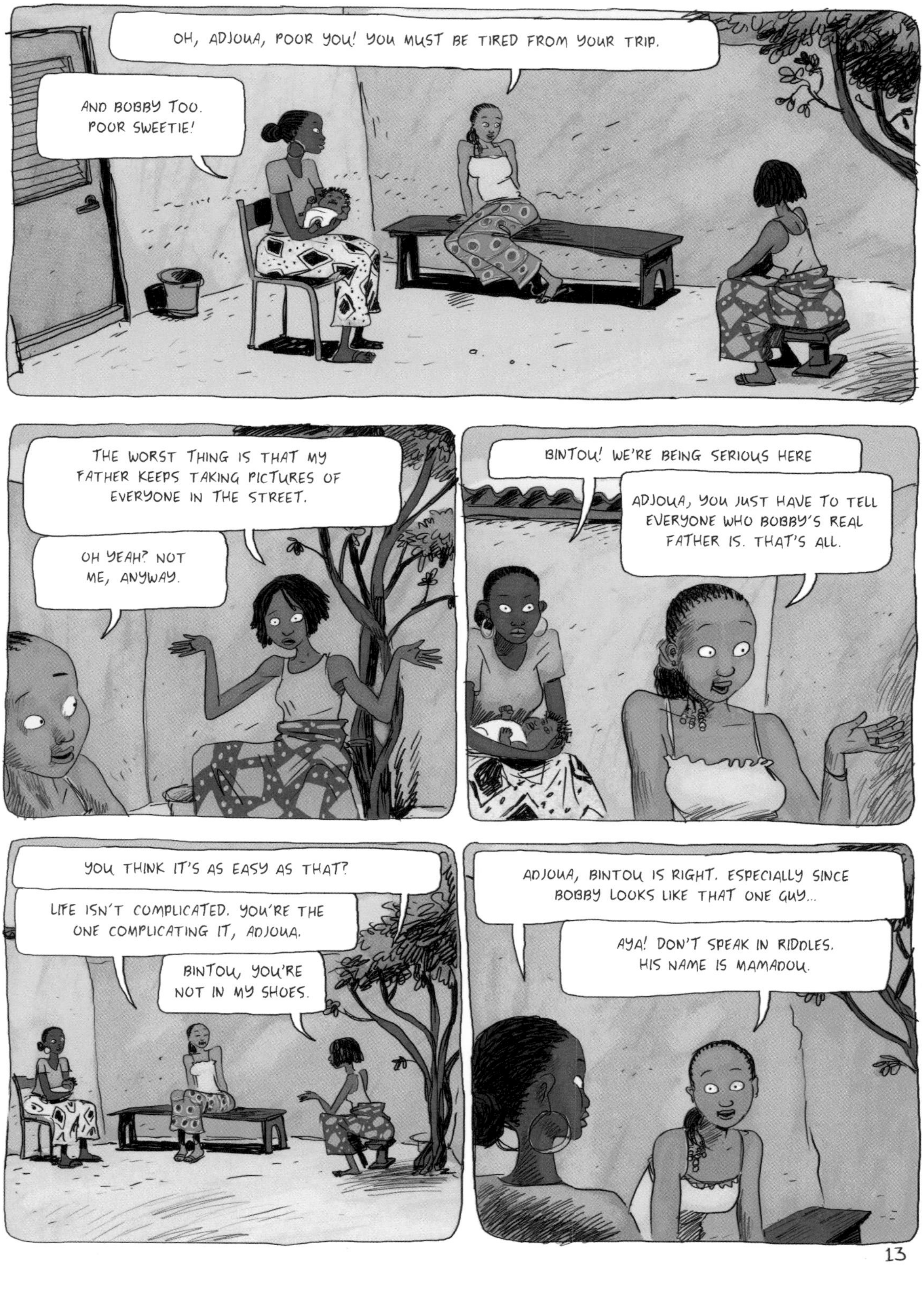
OH, ADJOUA, POOR YOU! YOU MUST BE TIRED FROM YOUR TRIP.
AND BOBBY TOO. POOR SWEETIE!
THE WORST THING IS THAT MY FATHER KEEPS TAKING PICTURES OF EVERYONE IN THE STREET.
OH YEAH? NOT ME, ANYWAY.
BINTOU! WE'RE BEING SERIOUS HERE
ADJOUA, YOU JUST HAVE TO TELL EVERYONE WHO BOBBY'S REAL FATHER IS. THAT'S ALL.
YOU THINK IT'S AS EASY AS THAT?
LIFE ISN'T COMPLICATED. YOU'RE THE ONE COMPLICATING IT, ADJOUA.
BINTOU, YOU'RE NOT IN MY SHOES.
ADJOUA, BINTOU IS RIGHT. ESPECIALLY SINCE BOBBY LOOKS LIKE THAT ONE GUY...
AYA! DON'T SPEAK IN RIDDLES. HIS NAME IS MAMADOU.

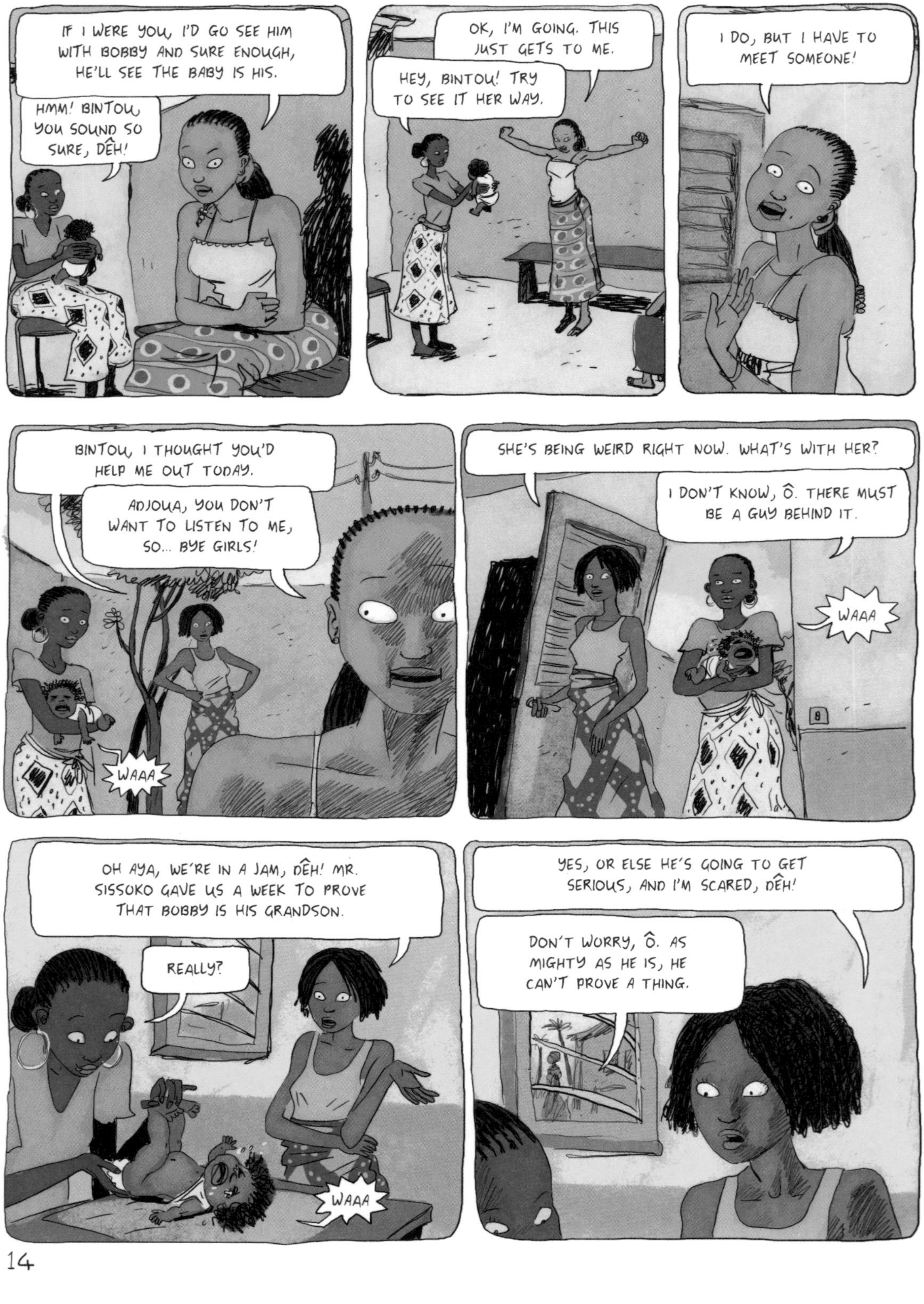
IF I WERE YOU, I'D GO SEE HIM WITH BOBBY AND SURE ENOUGH, HE'LL SEE THE BABY IS HIS.
HMM! BINTOU, YOU SOUND SO SURE, DÊH!
OK, I'M GOING. THIS JUST GETS TO ME.
HEY, BINTOU! TRY TO SEE IT HER WAY.
I DO, BUT I HAVE TO MEET SOMEONE!
BINTOU, I THOUGHT YOU'D HELP ME OUT TODAY.
ADJOUA, YOU DON'T WANT TO LISTEN TO ME, SO... BYE GIRLS!
WAAA
SHE'S BEING WEIRD RIGHT NOW. WHAT'S WITH HER?
I DON'T KNOW, Ô. THERE MUST BE A GUY BEHIND IT.
WAAA
OH AYA, WE'RE IN A JAM, DÊH! MR. SISSOKO GAVE US A WEEK TO PROVE THAT BOBBY IS HIS GRANDSON.
REALLY?
WAAA
YES, OR ELSE HE'S GOING TO GET SERIOUS, AND I'M SCARED, DÊH!
DON'T WORRY, Ô. AS MIGHTY AS HE IS, HE CAN'T PROVE A THING.

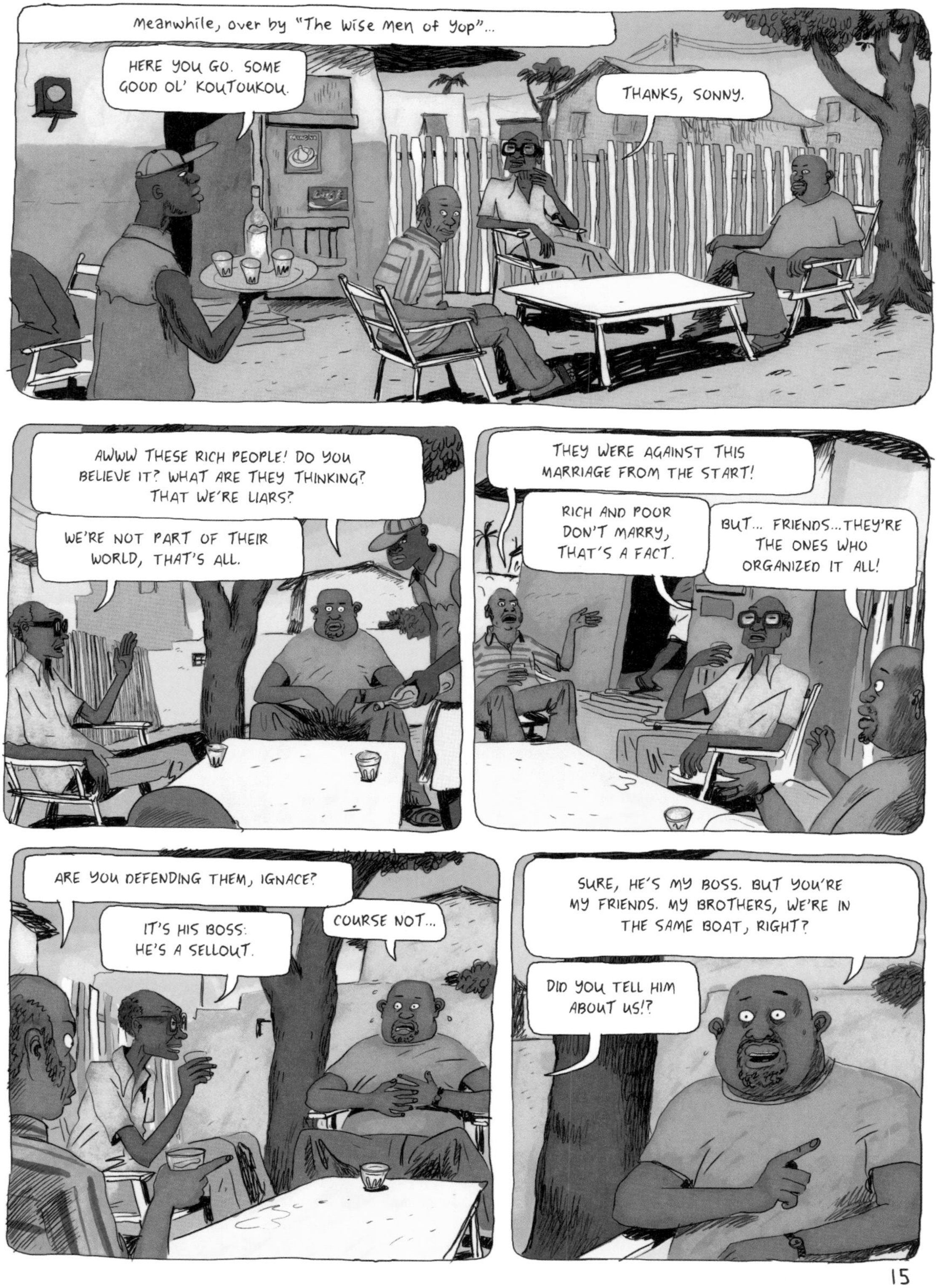
Meanwhile, over by "The Wise Men of Yop"...
HERE YOU GO. SOME GOOD OL' KOUTOUKOU.
THANKS, SONNY.
AWWW THESE RICH PEOPLE! DO YOU BELIEVE IT? WHAT ARE THEY THINKING? THAT WE'RE LIARS?
WE'RE NOT PART OF THEIR WORLD, THAT'S ALL.
THEY WERE AGAINST THIS MARRIAGE FROM THE START!
RICH AND POOR DON'T MARRY, THAT'S A FACT.
BUT... FRIENDS... THEY'RE THE ONES WHO ORGANIZED IT ALL!
ARE YOU DEFENDING THEM, IGNACE?
IT'S HIS BOSS: HE'S A SELLOUT.
COURSE NOT...
SURE, HE'S MY BOSS. BUT YOU'RE MY FRIENDS. MY BROTHERS, WE'RE IN THE SAME BOAT, RIGHT?
DID YOU TELL HIM ABOUT US!?

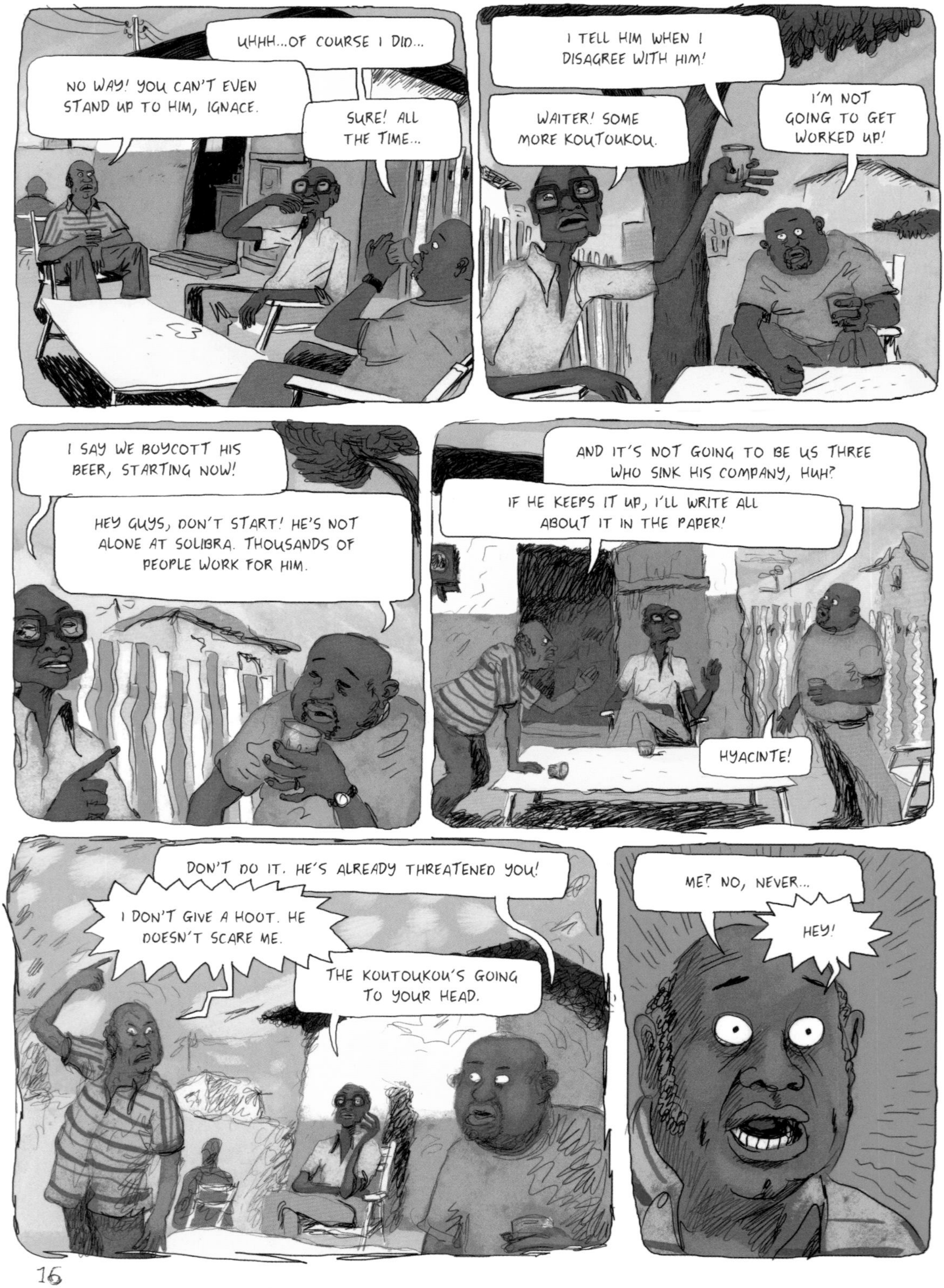
NO WAY! YOU CAN'T EVEN STAND UP TO HIM, IGNACE.
UHHH...OF COURSE I DID...
SURE! ALL THE TIME...
I TELL HIM WHEN I DISAGREE WITH HIM!
WAITER! SOME MORE KOUTOUKOU.
I'M NOT GOING TO GET WORKED UP!
I SAY WE BOYCOTT HIS BEER, STARTING NOW!
HEY GUYS, DON'T START! HE'S NOT ALONE AT SOLIBRA. THOUSANDS OF PEOPLE WORK FOR HIM.
AND IT'S NOT GOING TO BE US THREE WHO SINK HIS COMPANY, HUH?
IF HE KEEPS IT UP, I'LL WRITE ALL ABOUT IT IN THE PAPER!
HYACINTE!
DON'T DO IT. HE'S ALREADY THREATENED YOU!
I DON'T GIVE A HOOT. HE DOESN'T SCARE ME.
THE KOUTOUKOU'S GOING TO YOUR HEAD.
ME? NO, NEVER...
HEY!

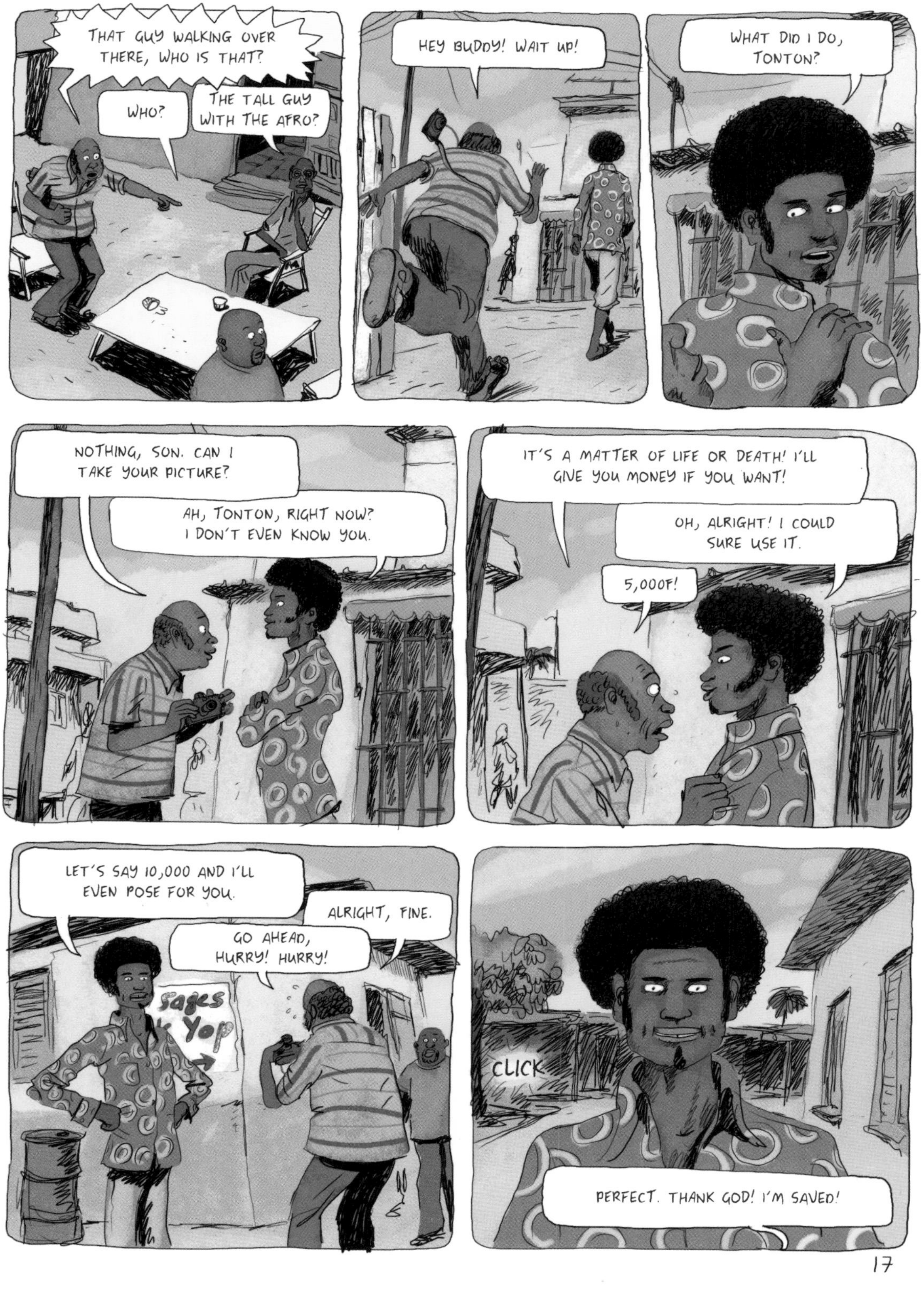
THAT GUY WALKING OVER THERE, WHO IS THAT?
WHO?
THE TALL GUY WITH THE AFRO?
HEY BUDDY! WAIT UP!
WHAT DID I DO, TONTON?
NOTHING, SON. CAN I TAKE YOUR PICTURE?
AH, TONTON, RIGHT NOW? I DON'T EVEN KNOW YOU.
IT'S A MATTER OF LIFE OR DEATH! I'LL GIVE YOU MONEY IF YOU WANT!
OH, ALRIGHT! I COULD SURE USE IT.
5,000F!
LET'S SAY 10,000 AND I'LL EVEN POSE FOR YOU.
ALRIGHT, FINE.
GO AHEAD, HURRY! HURRY!
CLICK
PERFECT. THANK GOD! I'M SAVED!

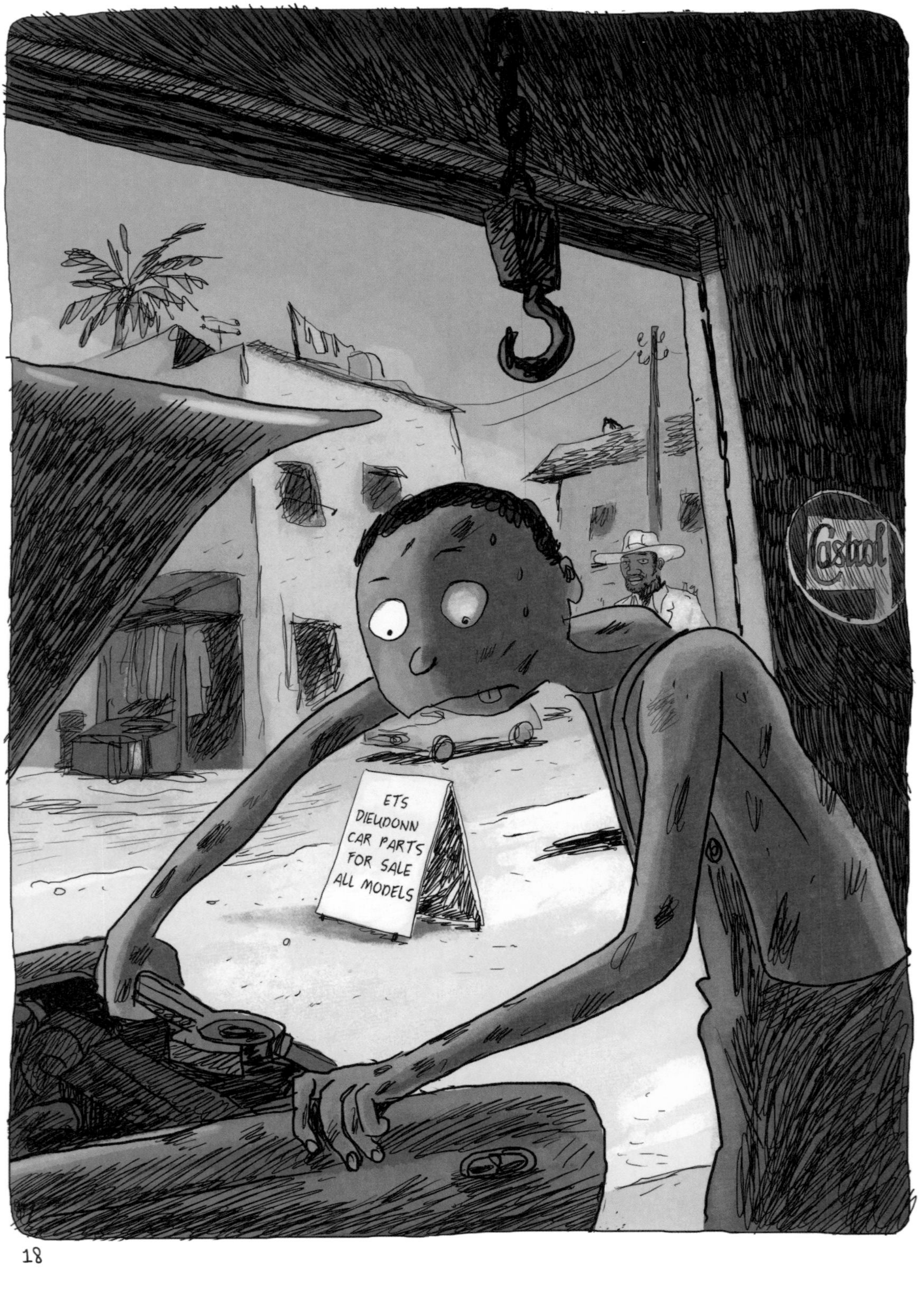
Castrol
ETS
DIEUDONN
CAR PARTS
FOR SALE
ALL MODELS

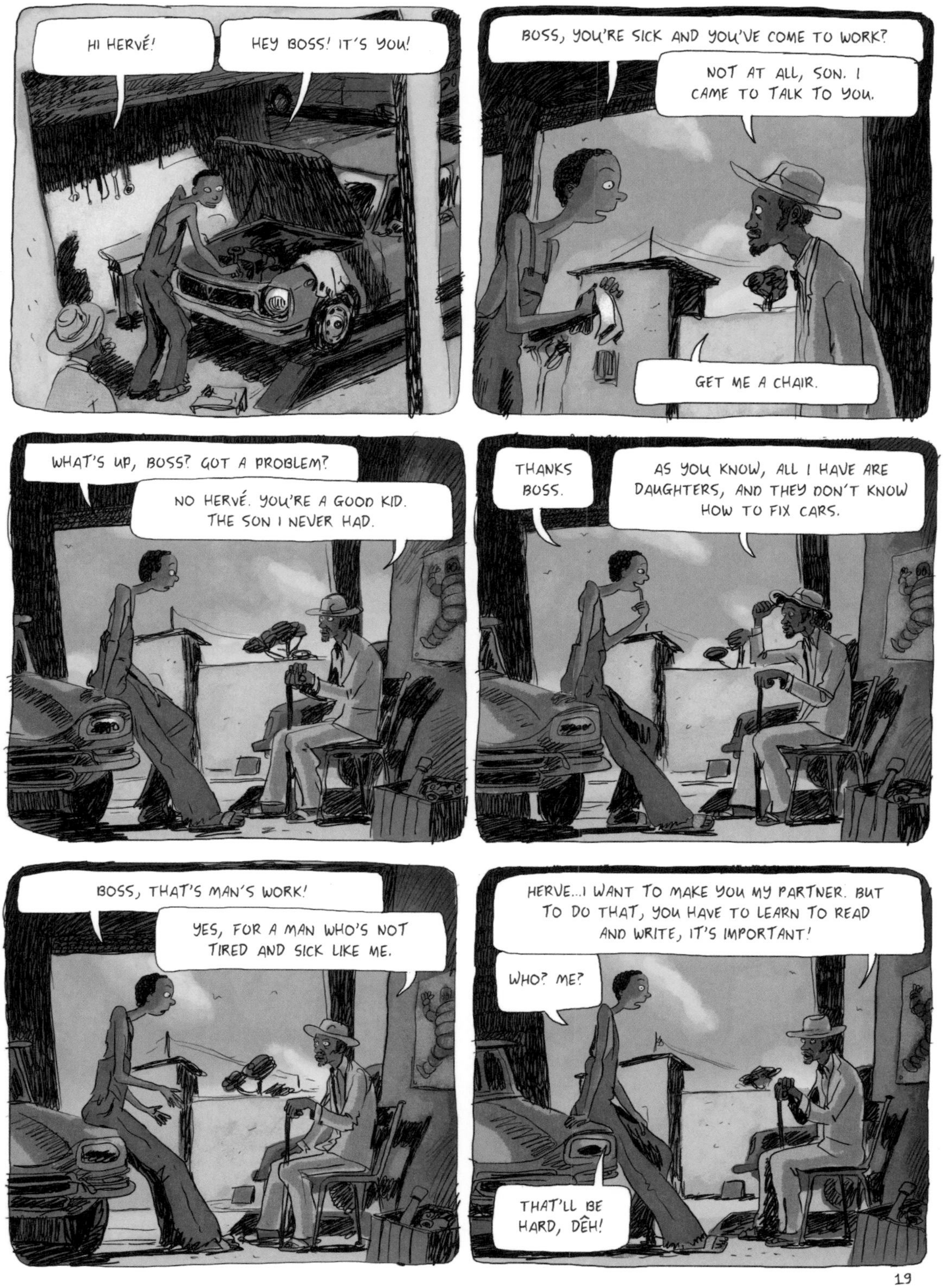
HI HERVÉ!
HEY BOSS! IT'S YOU!
BOSS, YOU'RE SICK AND YOU'VE COME TO WORK?
NOT AT ALL, SON. I CAME TO TALK TO YOU.
GET ME A CHAIR.
WHAT'S UP, BOSS? GOT A PROBLEM?
NO HERVÉ. YOU'RE A GOOD KID. THE SON I NEVER HAD.
THANKS BOSS.
AS YOU KNOW, ALL I HAVE ARE DAUGHTERS, AND THEY DON'T KNOW HOW TO FIX CARS.
BOSS, THAT'S MAN'S WORK!
YES, FOR A MAN WHO'S NOT TIRED AND SICK LIKE ME.
HERVE...I WANT TO MAKE YOU MY PARTNER. BUT TO DO THAT, YOU HAVE TO LEARN TO READ AND WRITE, IT'S IMPORTANT!
WHO? ME?
THAT'LL BE HARD, DÊH!

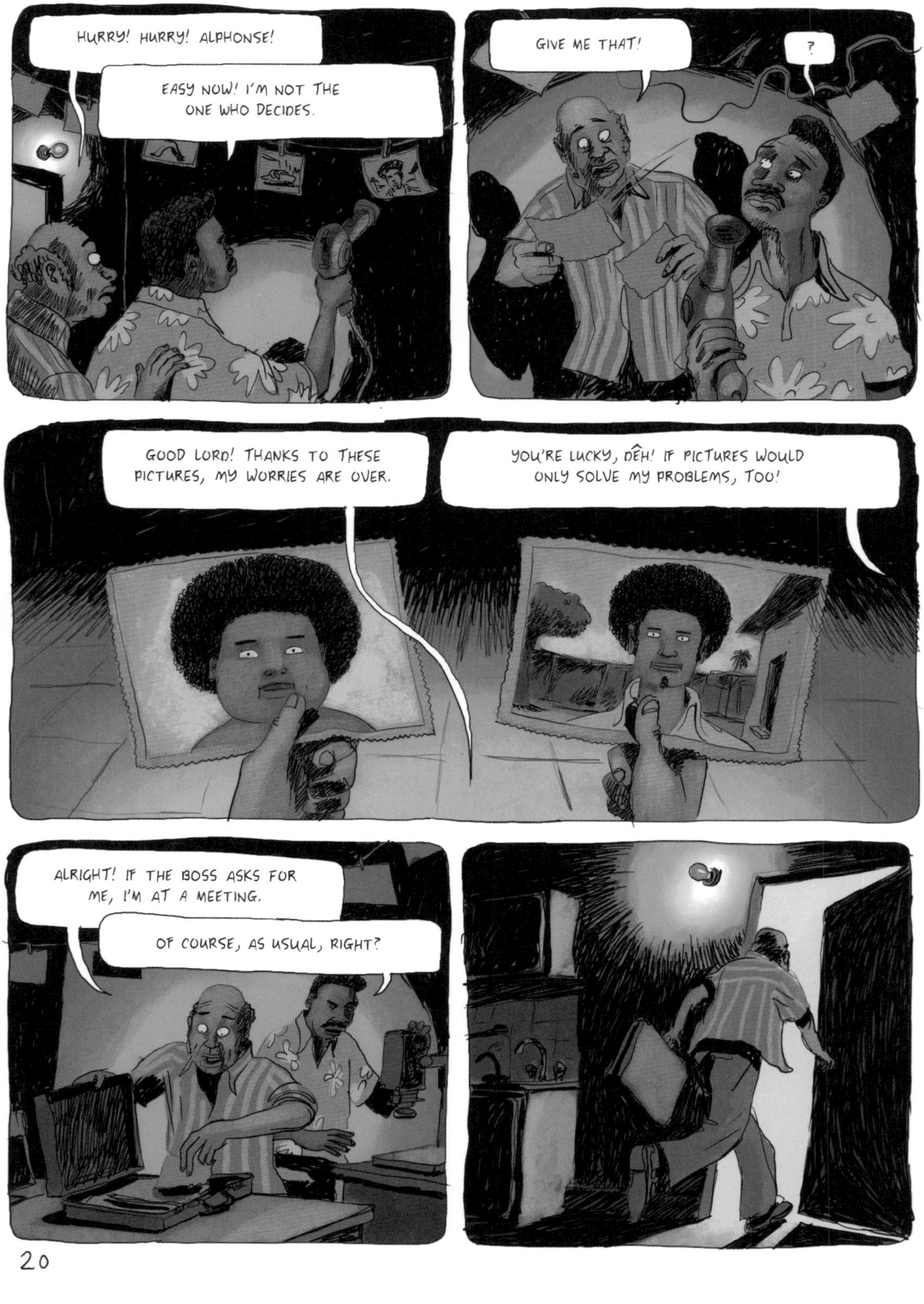
HURRY! HURRY! ALPHONSE!
EASY NOW! I'M NOT THE ONE WHO DECIDES.
GIVE ME THAT!
?
GOOD LORD! THANKS TO THESE PICTURES, MY WORRIES ARE OVER.
YOU'RE LUCKY, DÊH! IF PICTURES WOULD ONLY SOLVE MY PROBLEMS, TOO!
ALRIGHT! IF THE BOSS ASKS FOR ME, I'M AT A MEETING.
OF COURSE, AS USUAL, RIGHT?

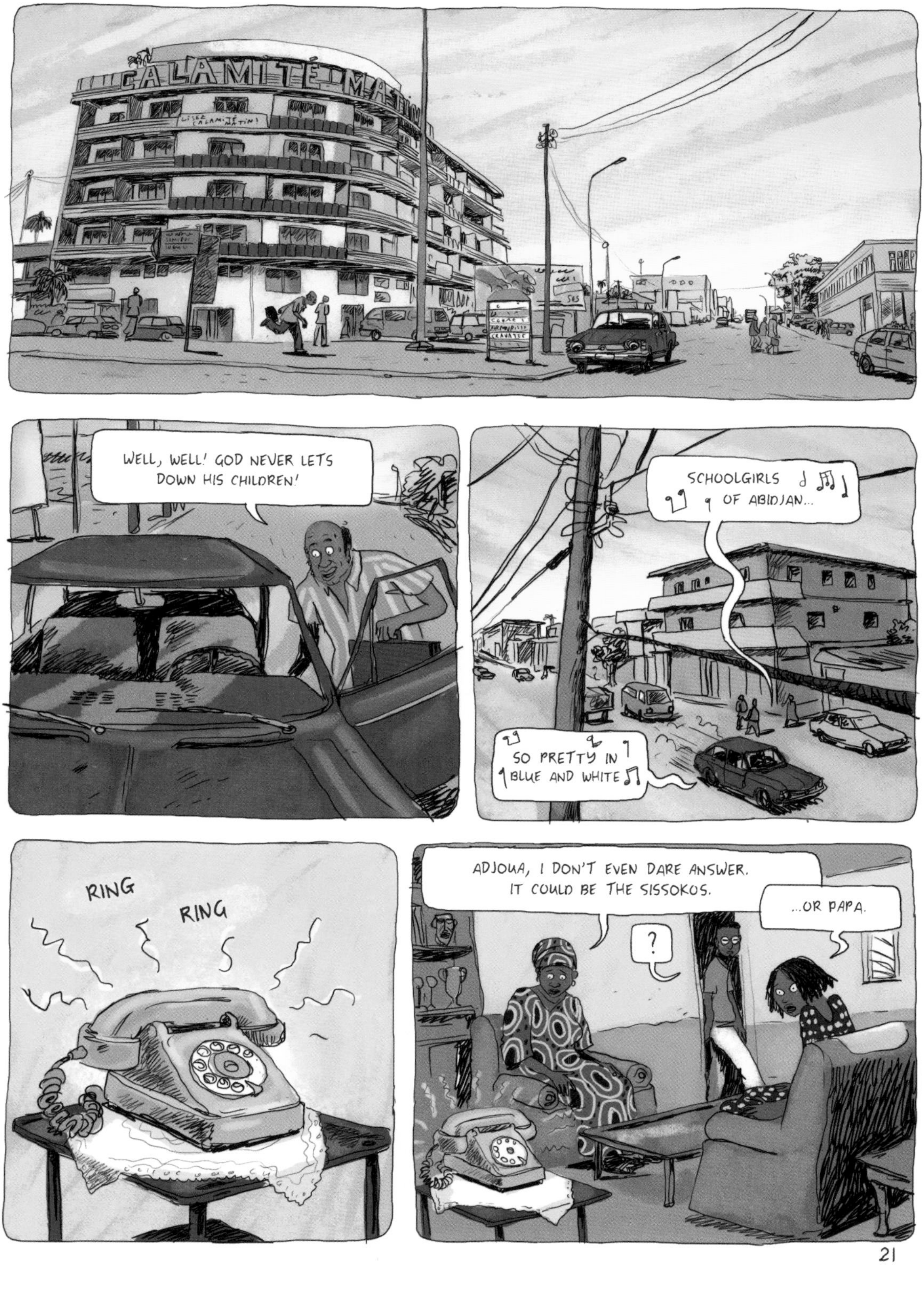
CALAMITÉ MATIN
WELL, WELL! GOD NEVER LETS DOWN HIS CHILDREN!
SCHOOLGIRLS OF ABIDJAN...
SO PRETTY IN BLUE AND WHITE
RING
RING
ADJOUA, I DON'T EVEN DARE ANSWER. IT COULD BE THE SISSOKOS.
?
...OR PAPA.

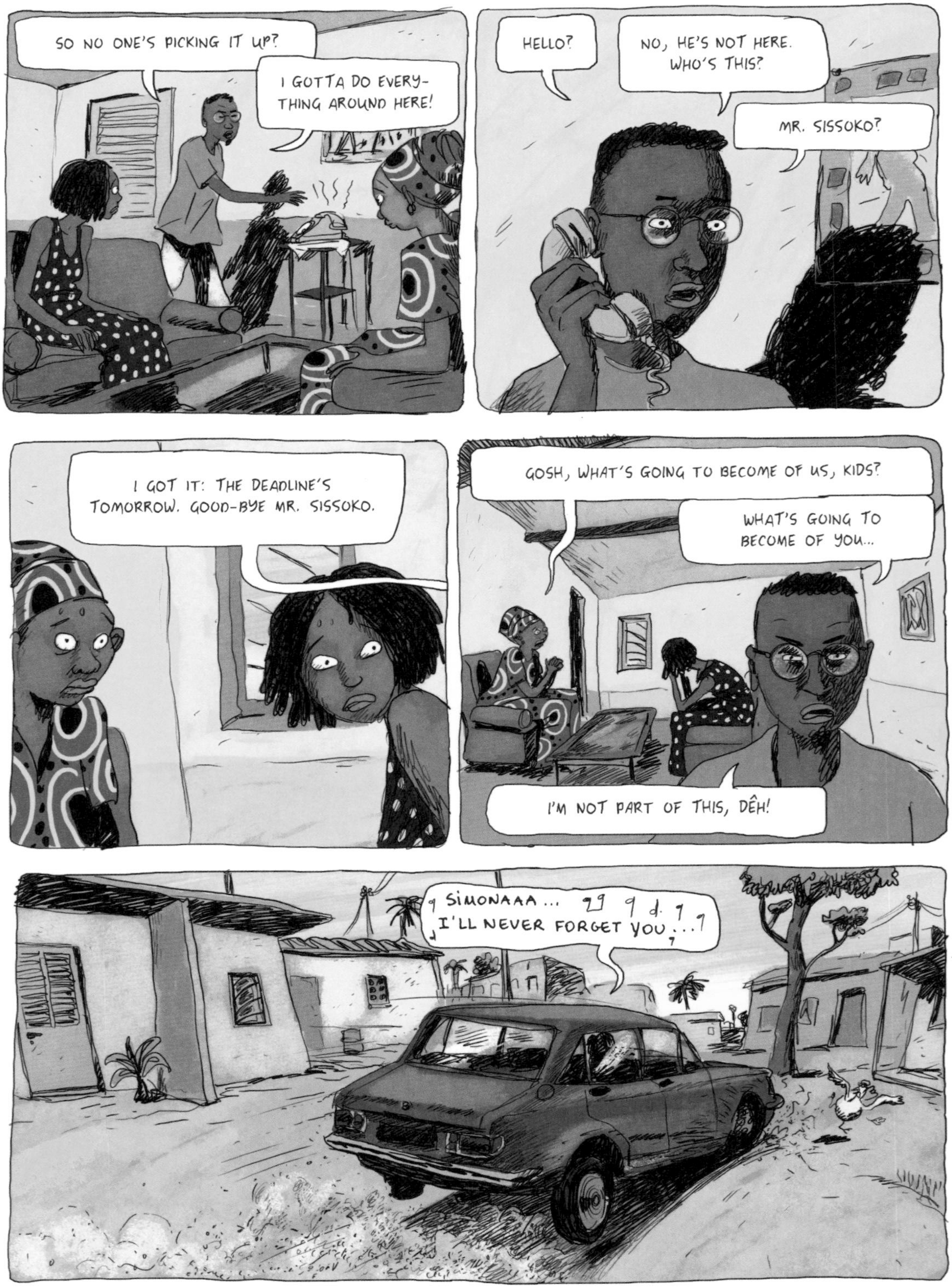
SO NO ONE'S PICKING IT UP?
I GOTTA DO EVERY-THING AROUND HERE!
HELLO?
NO, HE'S NOT HERE. WHO'S THIS?
MR. SISSOKO?
I GOT IT: THE DEADLINE'S TOMORROW. GOOD-BYE MR. SISSOKO.
GOSH, WHAT'S GOING TO BECOME OF US, KIDS?
WHAT'S GOING TO BECOME OF YOU...
I'M NOT PART OF THIS, DÊH!
SIMONAAA... I'LL NEVER FORGET YOU...

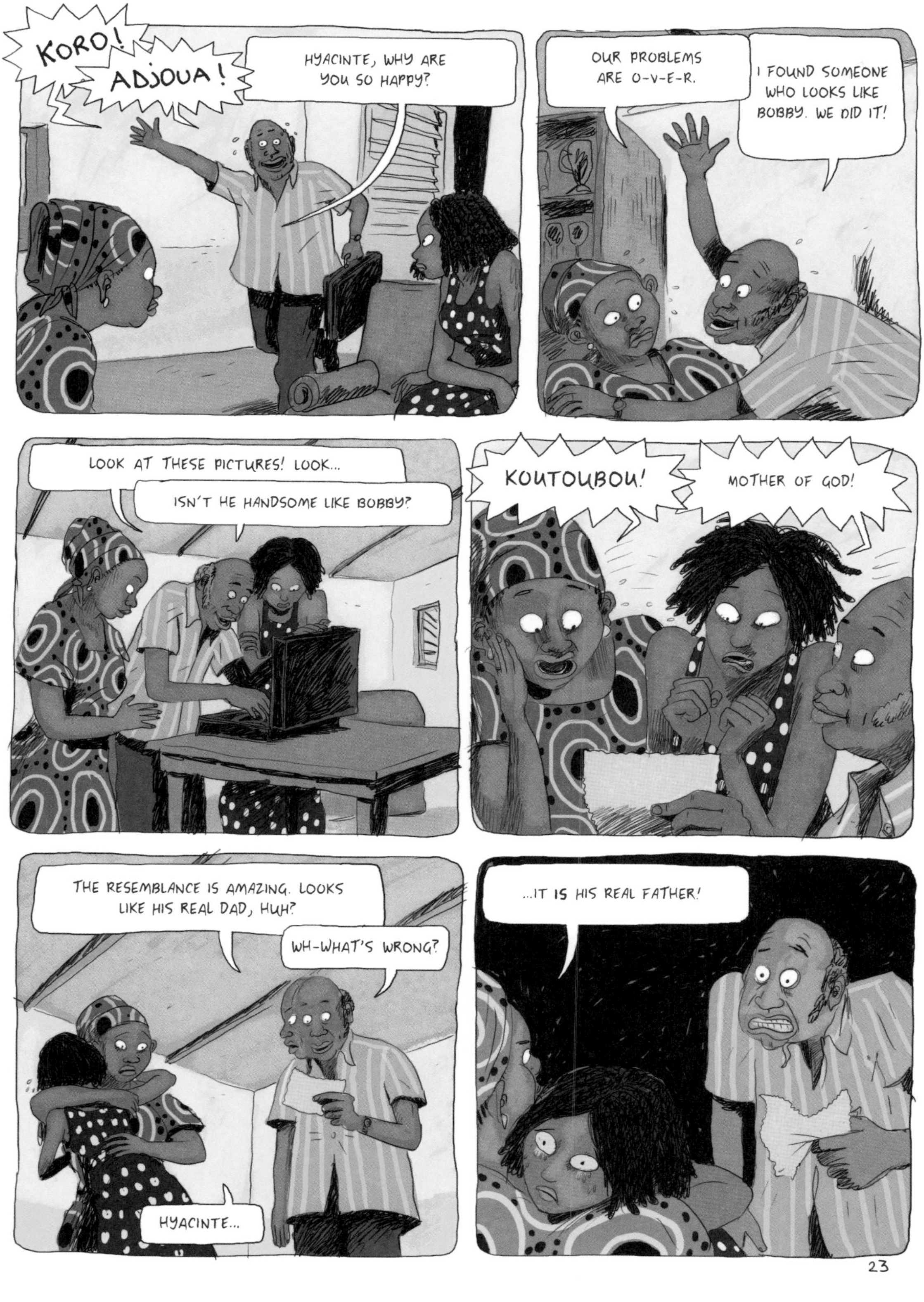
KORO!
ADJOUA!
HYACINTE, WHY ARE YOU SO HAPPY?
OUR PROBLEMS ARE O-V-E-R.
I FOUND SOMEONE WHO LOOKS LIKE BOBBY. WE DID IT!
LOOK AT THESE PICTURES! LOOK...
ISN'T HE HANDSOME LIKE BOBBY?
KOUTOUBOU!
MOTHER OF GOD!
THE RESEMBLANCE IS AMAZING. LOOKS LIKE HIS REAL DAD, HUH?
WH-WHAT'S WRONG?
HYACINTE...
...IT IS HIS REAL FATHER!

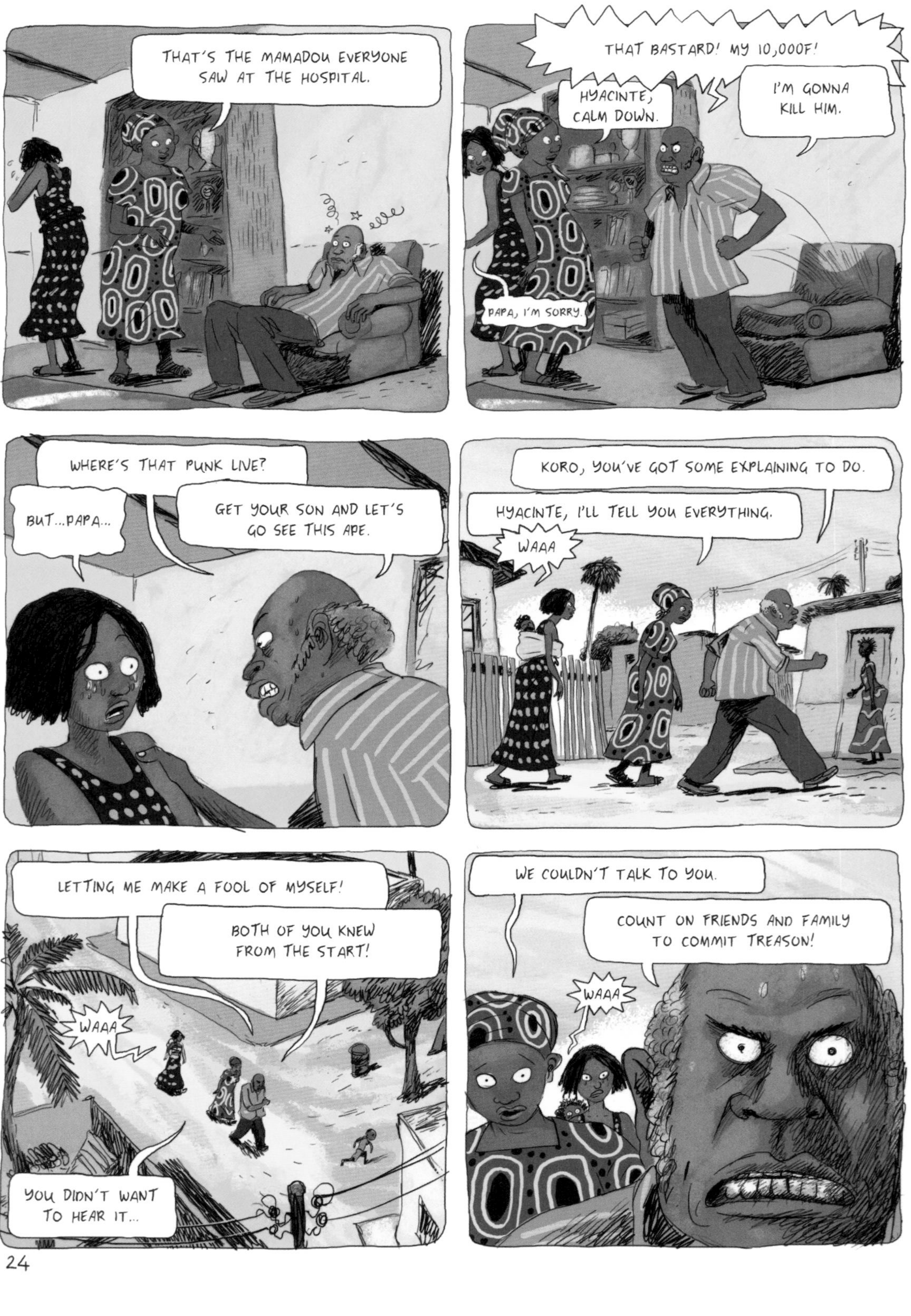
THAT'S THE MAMADOU EVERYONE SAW AT THE HOSPITAL.
THAT BASTARD! MY 10,000F!
HYACINTE, CALM DOWN.
I'M GONNA KILL HIM.
PAPA, I'M SORRY.
WHERE'S THAT PUNK LIVE?
BUT...PAPA...
GET YOUR SON AND LET'S GO SEE THIS APE.
KORO, YOU'VE GOT SOME EXPLAINING TO DO.
HYACINTE, I'LL TELL YOU EVERYTHING.
WAAA
LETTING ME MAKE A FOOL OF MYSELF!
BOTH OF YOU KNEW FROM THE START!
WAAA
YOU DIDN'T WANT TO HEAR IT...
WE COULDN'T TALK TO YOU.
COUNT ON FRIENDS AND FAMILY TO COMMIT TREASON!
WAAA

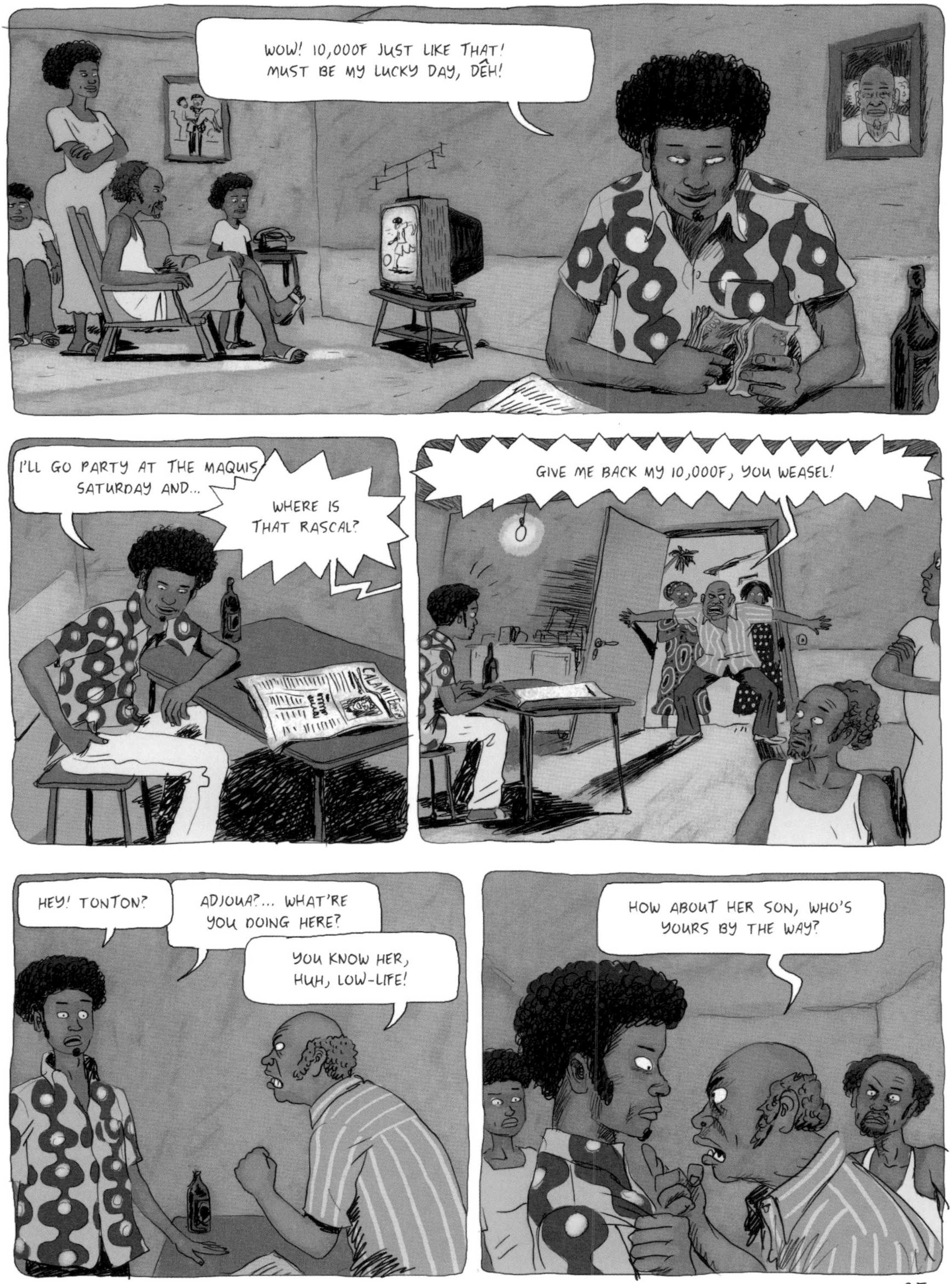
WOW! 10,000F JUST LIKE THAT! MUST BE MY LUCKY DAY, DÊH!
I'LL GO PARTY AT THE MAQUIS SATURDAY AND...
WHERE IS THAT RASCAL?
GIVE ME BACK MY 10,000F, YOU WEASEL!
HEY! TONTON?
ADJOUA?... WHAT'RE YOU DOING HERE?
YOU KNOW HER, HUH, LOW-LIFE!
HOW ABOUT HER SON, WHO'S YOURS BY THE WAY?

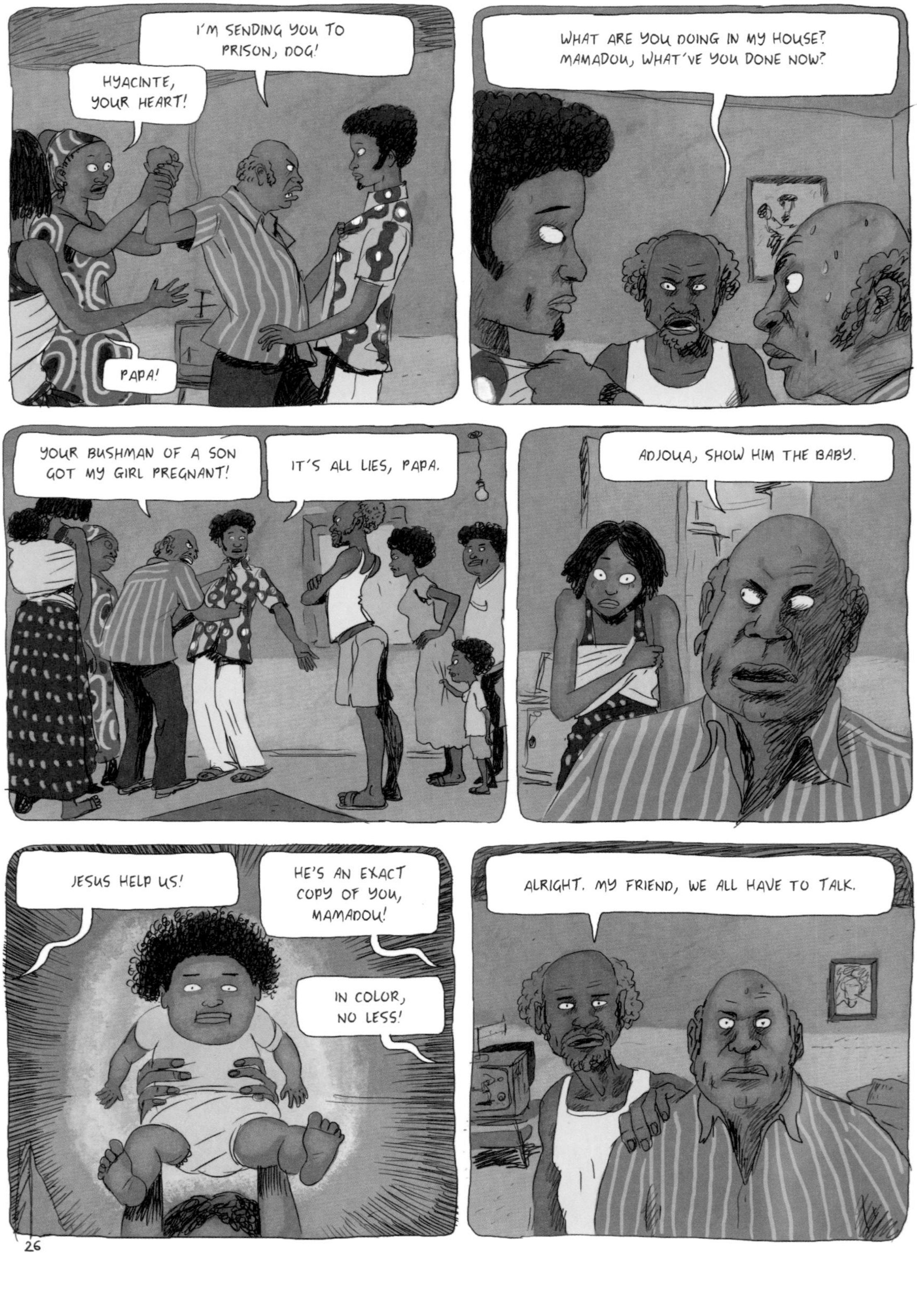

HYACINTE, YOUR HEART!
I'M SENDING YOU TO PRISON, DOG!
PAPA!
WHAT ARE YOU DOING IN MY HOUSE? MAMADOU, WHAT'VE YOU DONE NOW?
YOUR BUSHMAN OF A SON GOT MY GIRL PREGNANT!
IT'S ALL LIES, PAPA.
ADJOUA, SHOW HIM THE BABY.
JESUS HELP US!
HE'S AN EXACT COPY OF YOU, MAMADOU!
IN COLOR, NO LESS!
ALRIGHT. MY FRIEND, WE ALL HAVE TO TALK.

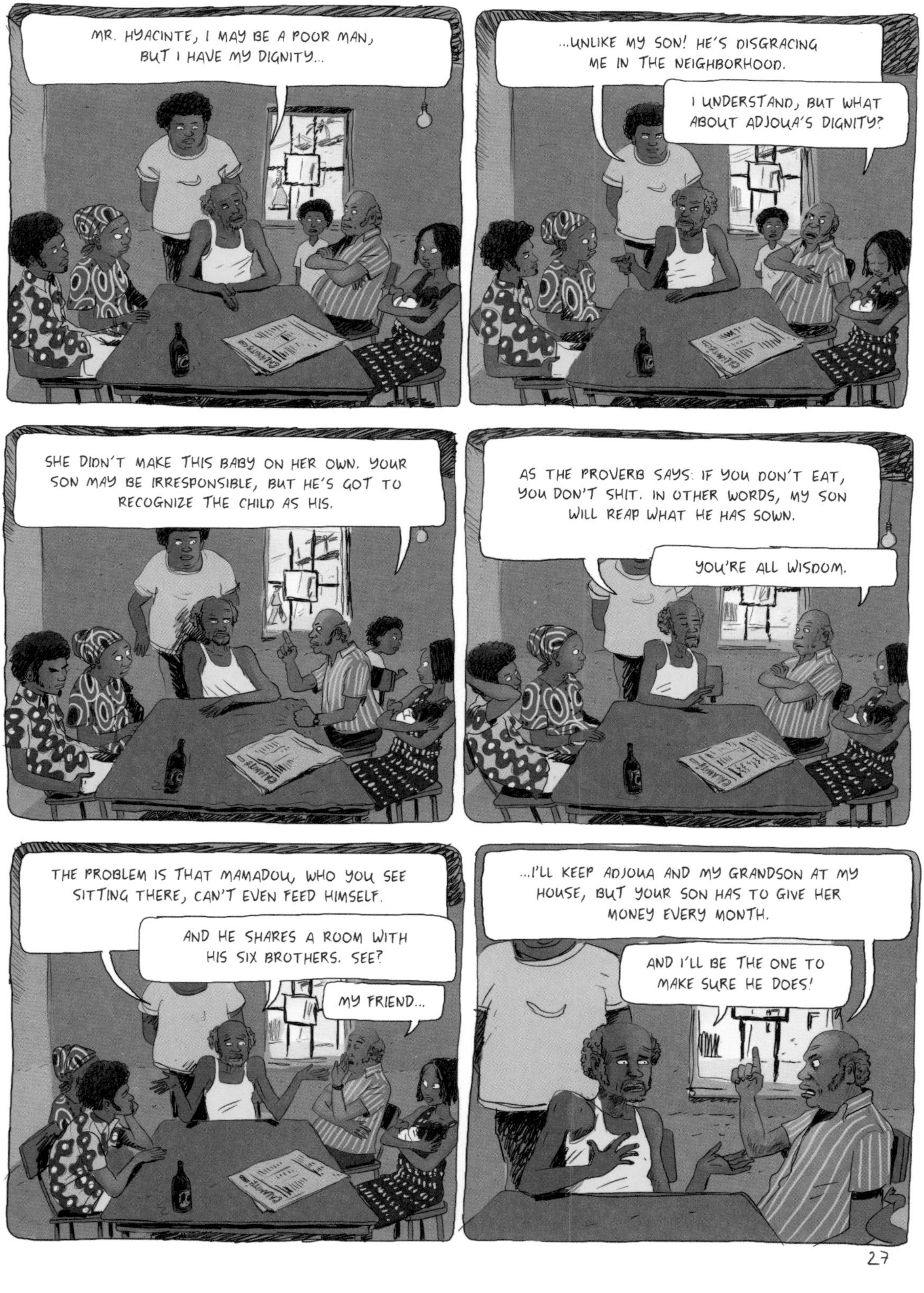
MR. HYACINTE, I MAY BE A POOR MAN, BUT I HAVE MY DIGNITY...
...UNLIKE MY SON! HE'S DISGRACING ME IN THE NEIGHBORHOOD.
I UNDERSTAND, BUT WHAT ABOUT ADJOUA'S DIGNITY?
SHE DIDN'T MAKE THIS BABY ON HER OWN. YOUR SON MAY BE IRRESPONSIBLE, BUT HE'S GOT TO RECOGNIZE THE CHILD AS HIS.
AS THE PROVERB SAYS: IF YOU DON'T EAT, YOU DON'T SHIT. IN OTHER WORDS, MY SON WILL REAP WHAT HE HAS SOWN.
YOU'RE ALL WISDOM.
THE PROBLEM IS THAT MAMADOU, WHO YOU SEE SITTING THERE, CAN'T EVEN FEED HIMSELF.
AND HE SHARES A ROOM WITH HIS SIX BROTHERS. SEE?
MY FRIEND...
...I'LL KEEP ADJOUA AND MY GRANDSON AT MY HOUSE, BUT YOUR SON HAS TO GIVE HER MONEY EVERY MONTH.
AND I'LL BE THE ONE TO MAKE SURE HE DOES!

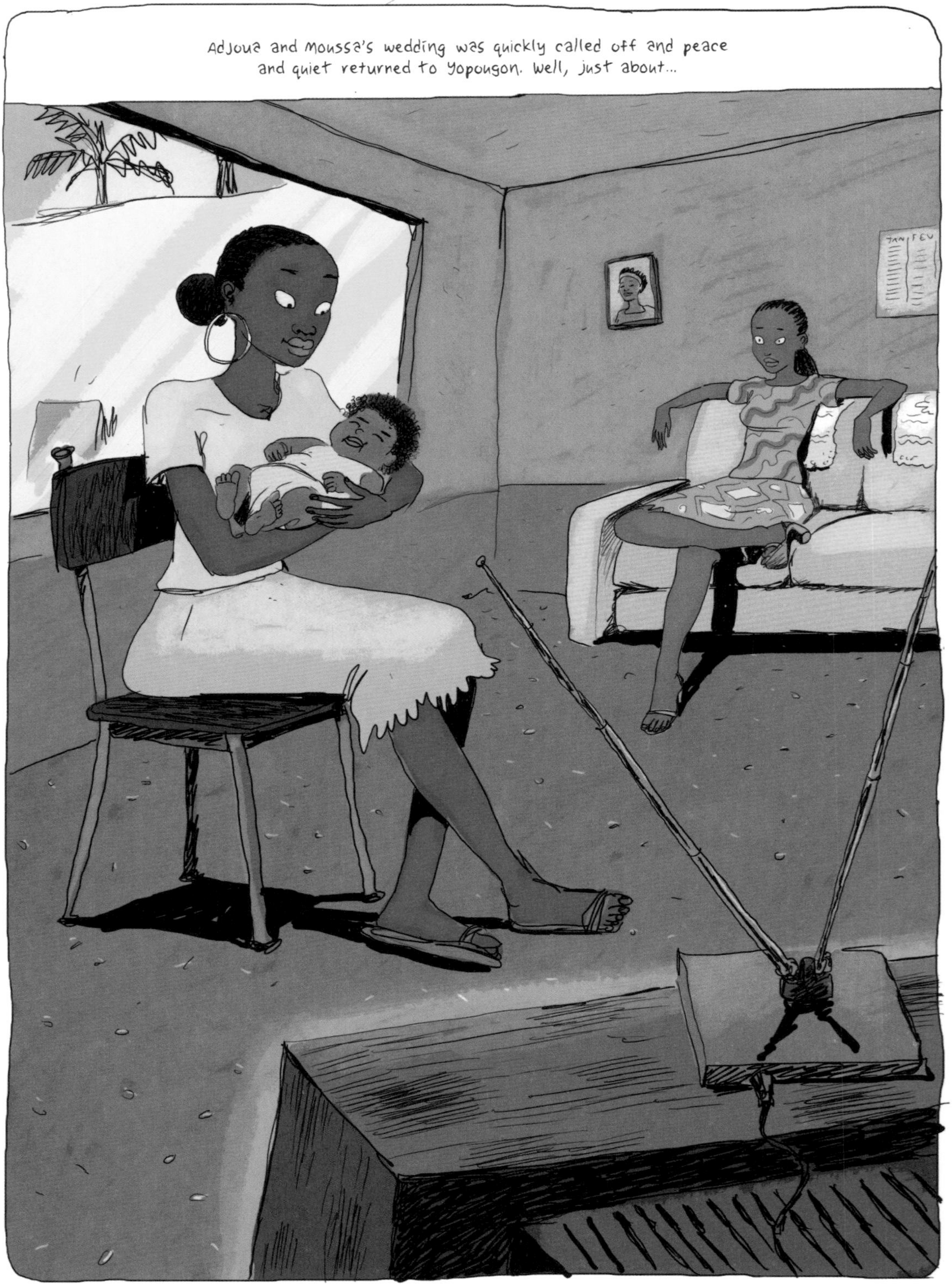
Adjoua and Moussa's wedding was quickly called off and peace and quiet returned to Yopougon. Well, just about...

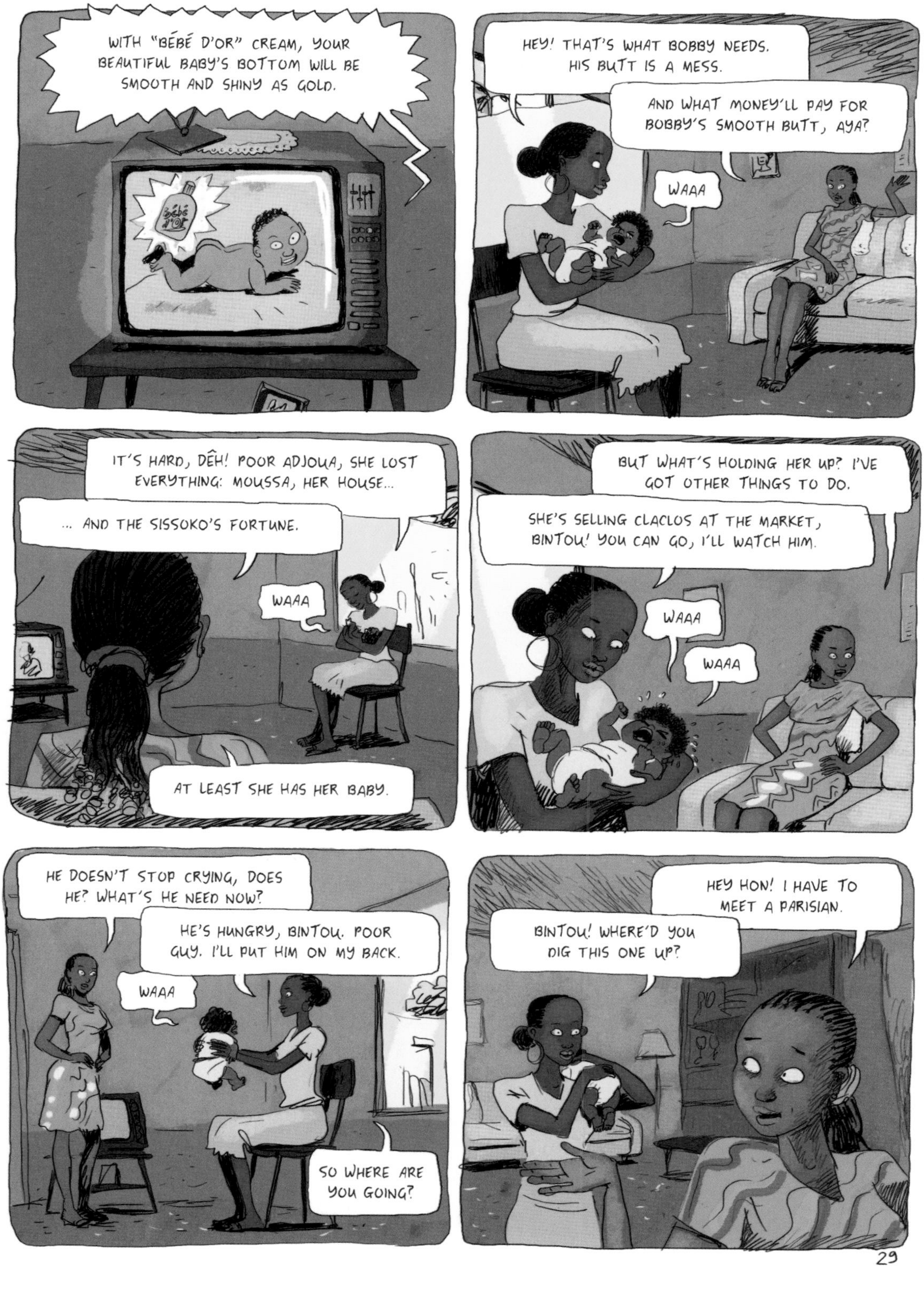
WITH "BÉBÉ D'OR" CREAM, YOUR BEAUTIFUL BABY'S BOTTOM WILL BE SMOOTH AND SHINY AS GOLD.
Bébé d'or
HEY! THAT'S WHAT BOBBY NEEDS. HIS BUTT IS A MESS.
AND WHAT MONEY'LL PAY FOR BOBBY'S SMOOTH BUTT, AYA?
WAAA
IT'S HARD, DÊH! POOR ADJOUA, SHE LOST EVERYTHING: MOUSSA, HER HOUSE...
... AND THE SISSOKO'S FORTUNE.
WAAA
AT LEAST SHE HAS HER BABY.
BUT WHAT'S HOLDING HER UP? I'VE GOT OTHER THINGS TO DO.
SHE'S SELLING CLACLOS AT THE MARKET, BINTOU! YOU CAN GO, I'LL WATCH HIM.
WAAA
WAAA
HE DOESN'T STOP CRYING, DOES HE? WHAT'S HE NEED NOW?
HE'S HUNGRY, BINTOU. POOR GUY. I'LL PUT HIM ON MY BACK.
WAAA
SO WHERE ARE YOU GOING?
HEY HON! I HAVE TO MEET A PARISIAN.
BINTOU! WHERE'D YOU DIG THIS ONE UP?

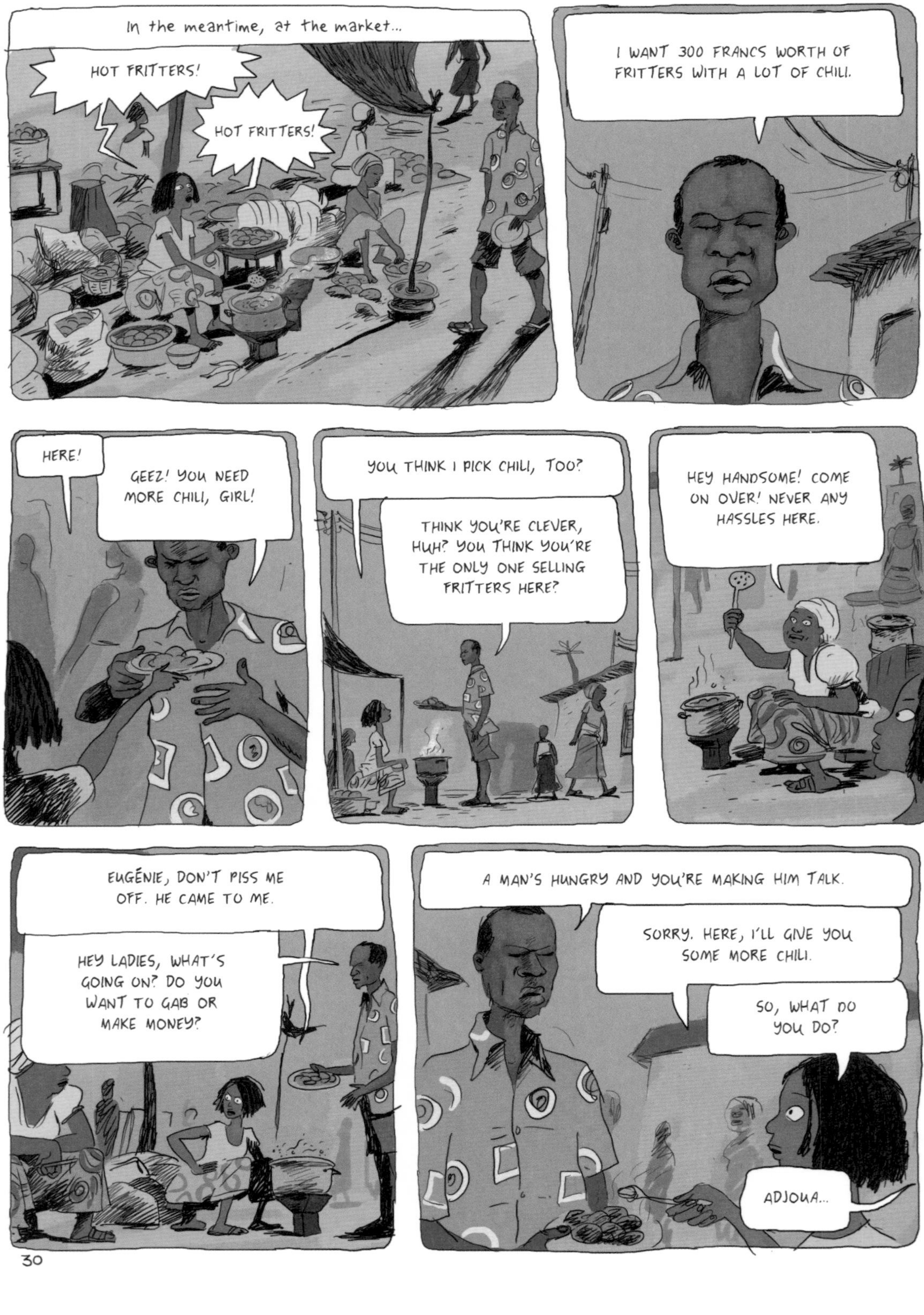
In the meantime, at the market...
HOT FRITTERS!
HOT FRITTERS!
I WANT 300 FRANCS WORTH OF FRITTERS WITH A LOT OF CHILI.
HERE!
GEEZ! YOU NEED MORE CHILI, GIRL!
YOU THINK I PICK CHILI, TOO?
THINK YOU'RE CLEVER, HUH? YOU THINK YOU'RE THE ONLY ONE SELLING FRITTERS HERE?
HEY HANDSOME! COME ON OVER! NEVER ANY HASSLES HERE.
EUGÉNIE, DON'T PISS ME OFF. HE CAME TO ME.
HEY LADIES, WHAT'S GOING ON? DO YOU WANT TO GAB OR MAKE MONEY?
A MAN'S HUNGRY AND YOU'RE MAKING HIM TALK.
SORRY. HERE, I'LL GIVE YOU SOME MORE CHILI.
SO, WHAT DO YOU DO?
ADJOUA...

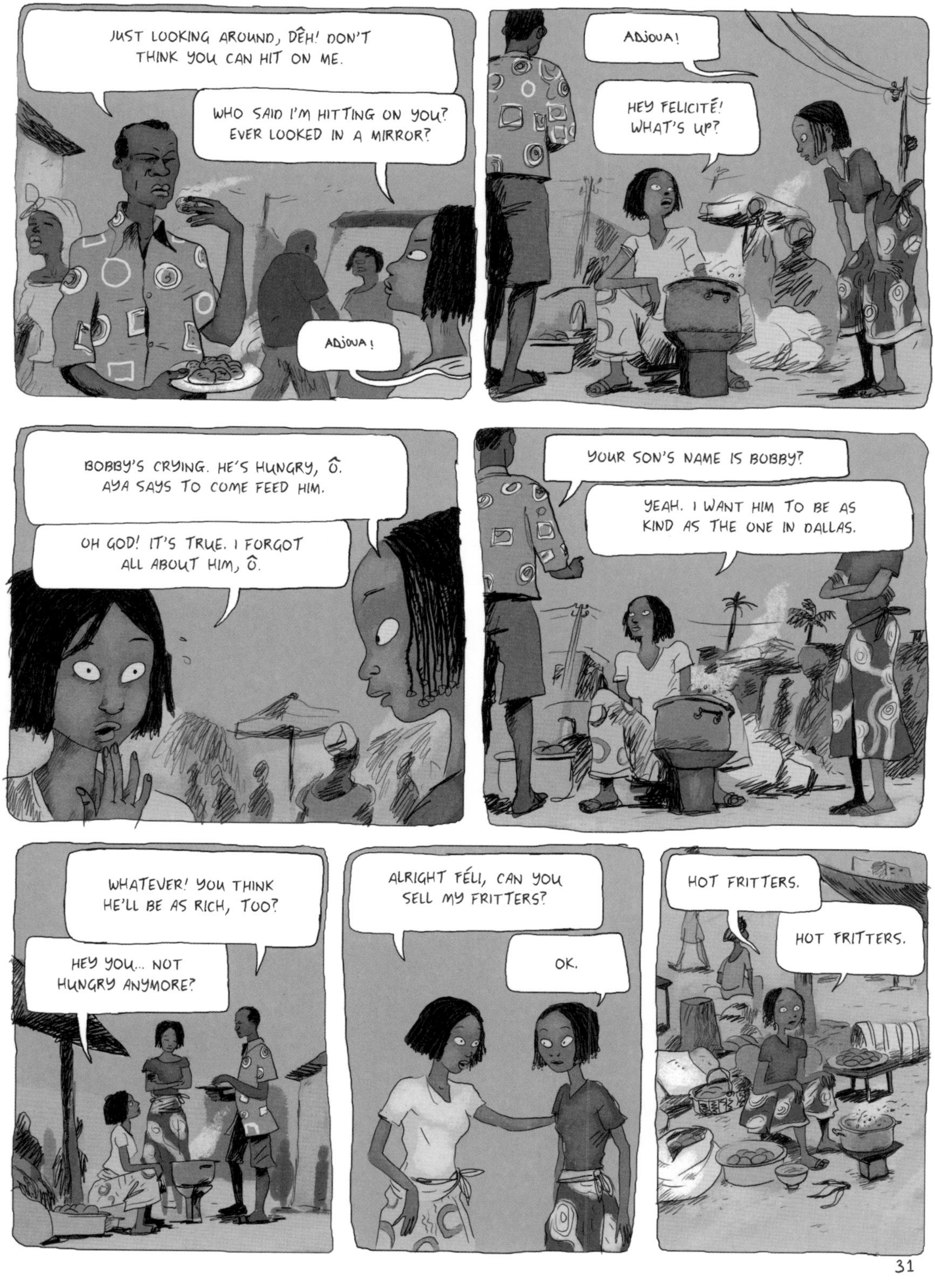
JUST LOOKING AROUND, DÊH! DON'T THINK YOU CAN HIT ON ME.
WHO SAID I'M HITTING ON YOU? EVER LOOKED IN A MIRROR?
ADJOUA!
ADJOUA!
HEY FELICITÉ! WHAT'S UP?
BOBBY'S CRYING. HE'S HUNGRY, Ô. AYA SAYS TO COME FEED HIM.
OH GOD! IT'S TRUE. I FORGOT ALL ABOUT HIM, Ô.
YOUR SON'S NAME IS BOBBY?
YEAH. I WANT HIM TO BE AS KIND AS THE ONE IN DALLAS.
WHATEVER! YOU THINK HE'LL BE AS RICH, TOO?
HEY YOU... NOT HUNGRY ANYMORE?
ALRIGHT FÉLI, CAN YOU SELL MY FRITTERS?
OK.
HOT FRITTERS.
HOT FRITTERS.

AH!

WOW, YOU ARE AWESOME, SON!

?

YOU FIXED MY HONDA! I THOUGHT IT WAS A GONER. HEY, THANK GOD.

NO, I'M HERVÉ, TONTON.

SURE, I KNOW!

OK

SO WHERE'S YOUR BOSS?

AT HOME, SICK. HE'S GETTING OLD.

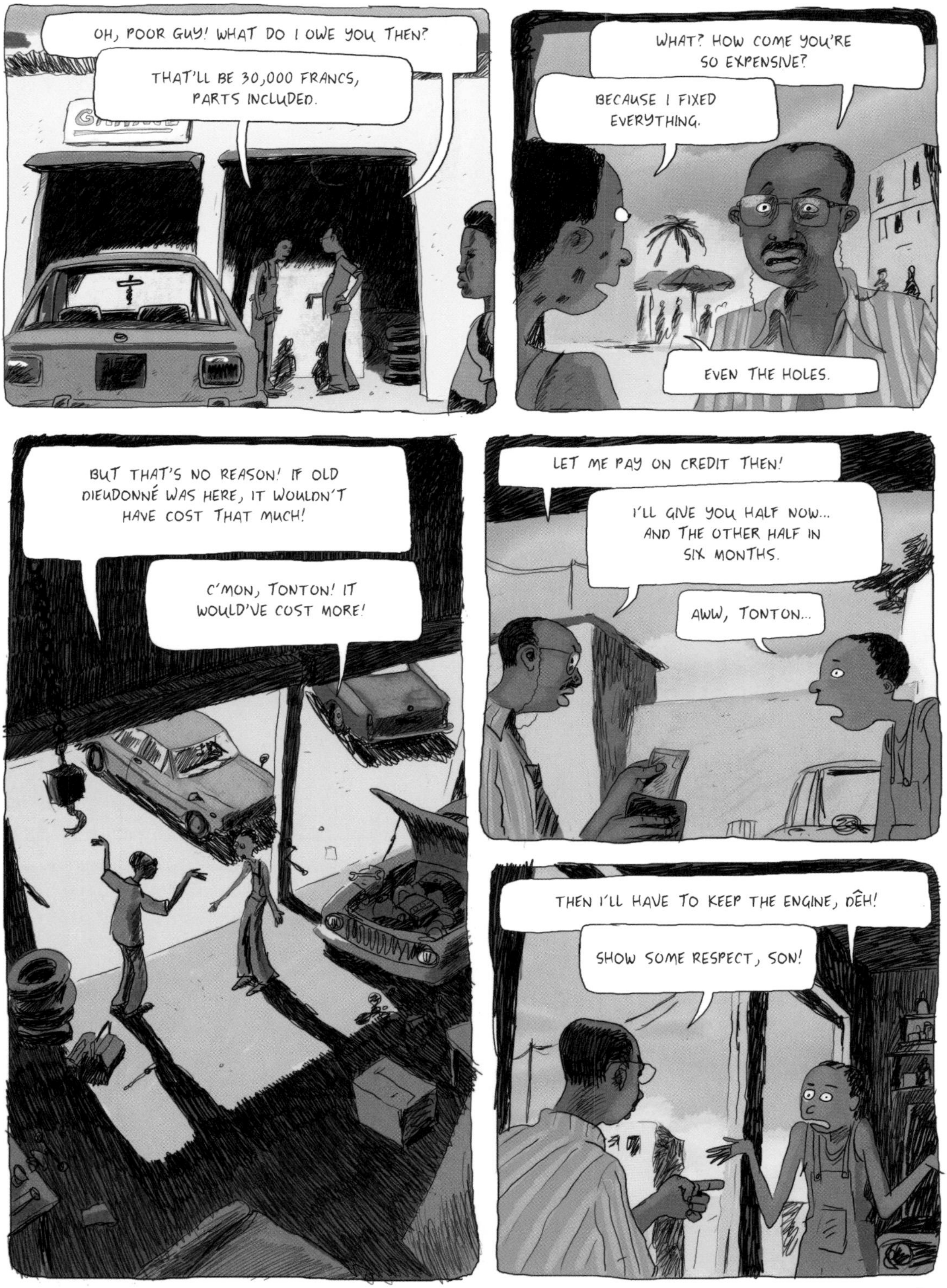
OH, POOR GUY! WHAT DO I OWE YOU THEN?
THAT'LL BE 30,000 FRANCS, PARTS INCLUDED.
WHAT? HOW COME YOU'RE SO EXPENSIVE?
BECAUSE I FIXED EVERYTHING.
EVEN THE HOLES.
BUT THAT'S NO REASON! IF OLD DIEUDONNÉ WAS HERE, IT WOULDN'T HAVE COST THAT MUCH!
C'MON, TONTON! IT WOULD'VE COST MORE!
LET ME PAY ON CREDIT THEN!
I'LL GIVE YOU HALF NOW... AND THE OTHER HALF IN SIX MONTHS.
AWW, TONTON...
THEN I'LL HAVE TO KEEP THE ENGINE, DÊH!
SHOW SOME RESPECT, SON!

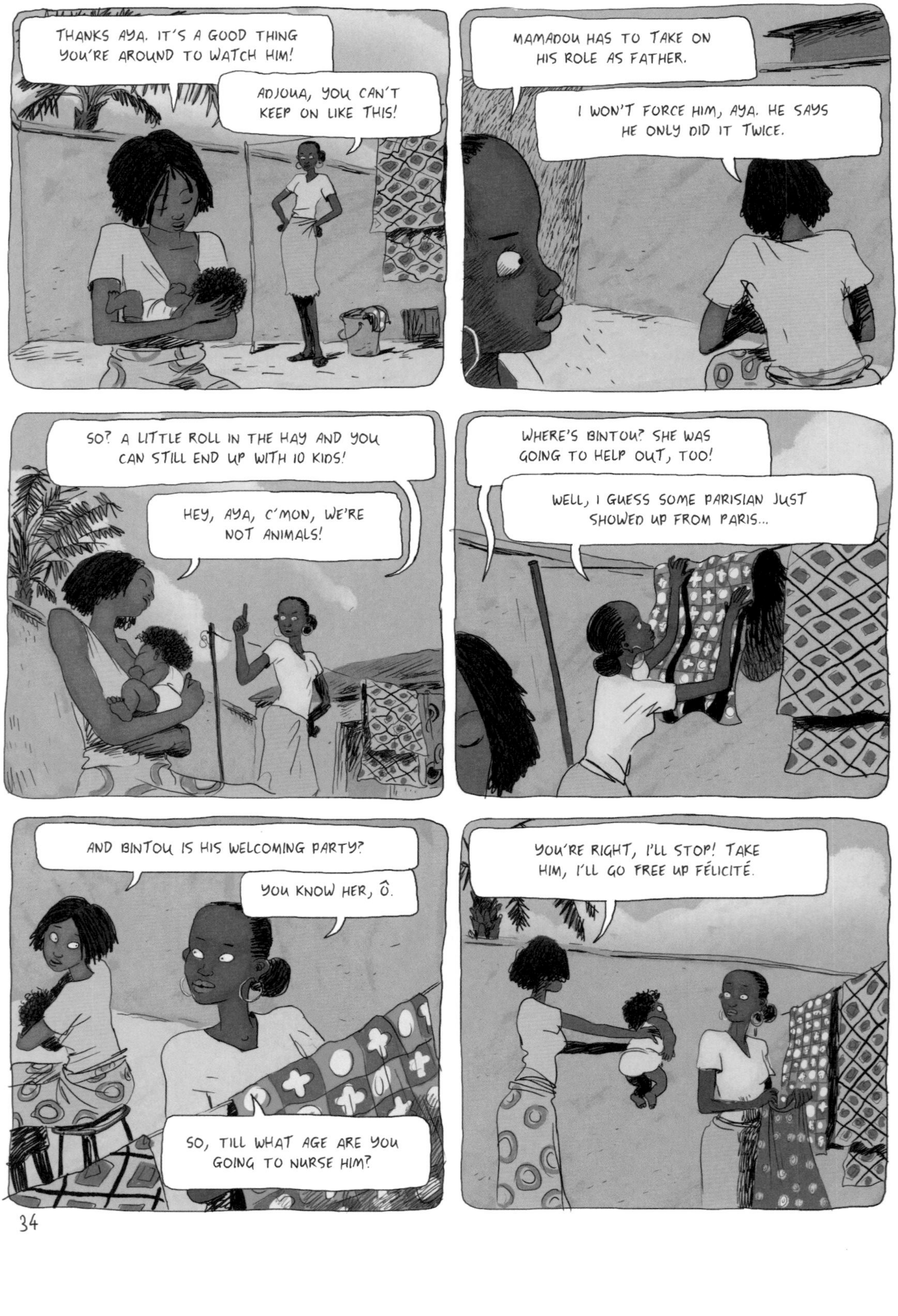
THANKS AYA. IT'S A GOOD THING YOU'RE AROUND TO WATCH HIM!
ADJOUA, YOU CAN'T KEEP ON LIKE THIS!
MAMADOU HAS TO TAKE ON HIS ROLE AS FATHER.
I WON'T FORCE HIM, AYA. HE SAYS HE ONLY DID IT TWICE.
SO? A LITTLE ROLL IN THE HAY AND YOU CAN STILL END UP WITH 10 KIDS!
HEY, AYA, C'MON, WE'RE NOT ANIMALS!
WHERE'S BINTOU? SHE WAS GOING TO HELP OUT, TOO!
WELL, I GUESS SOME PARISIAN JUST SHOWED UP FROM PARIS...
AND BINTOU IS HIS WELCOMING PARTY?
YOU KNOW HER, Ô.
SO, TILL WHAT AGE ARE YOU GOING TO NURSE HIM?
YOU'RE RIGHT, I'LL STOP! TAKE HIM, I'LL GO FREE UP FÉLICITÉ.

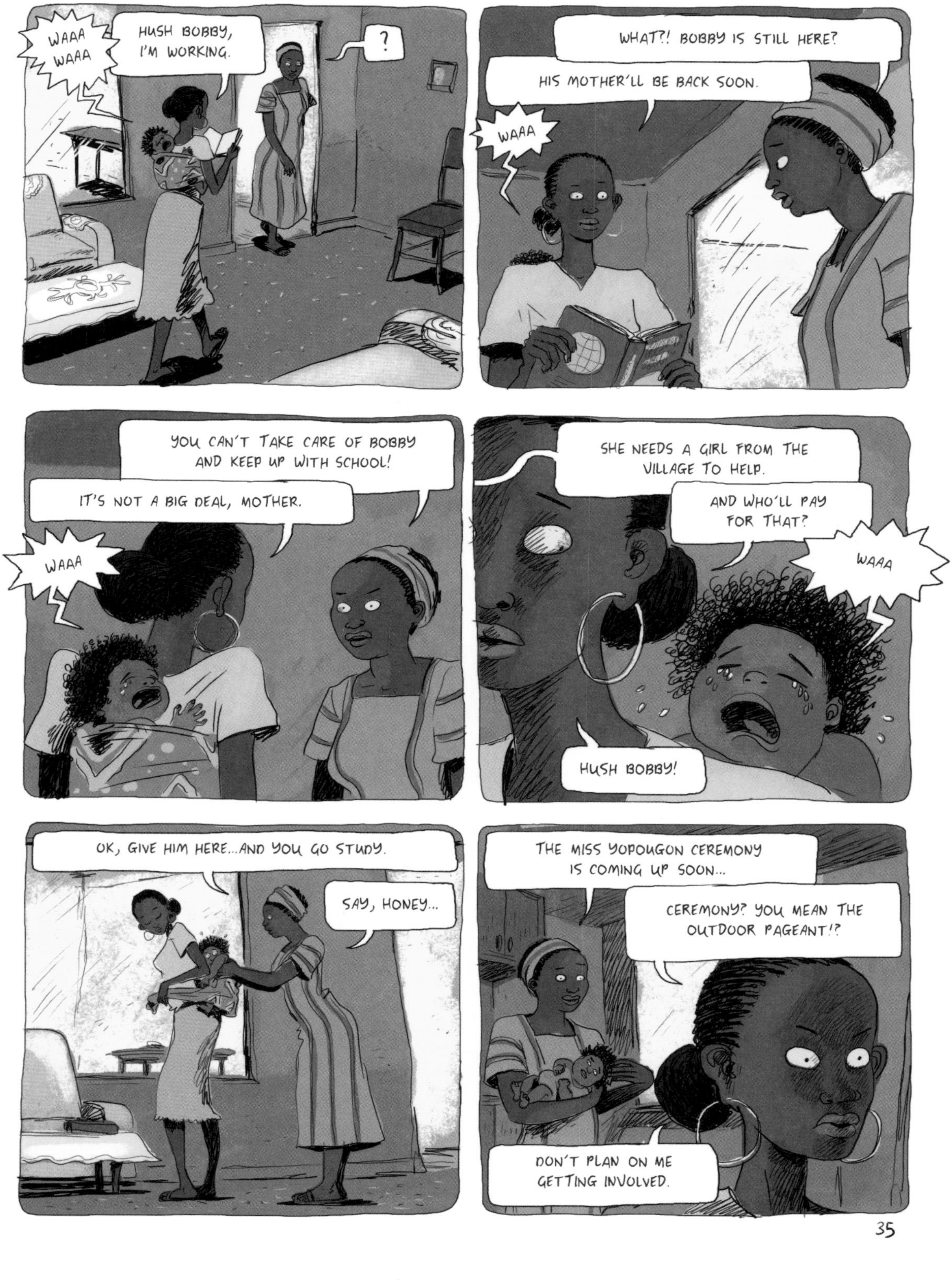
WAAA WAAA
HUSH BOBBY, I'M WORKING.
?
WHAT?! BOBBY IS STILL HERE?
HIS MOTHER'LL BE BACK SOON.
WAAA
YOU CAN'T TAKE CARE OF BOBBY AND KEEP UP WITH SCHOOL!
IT'S NOT A BIG DEAL, MOTHER.
WAAA
SHE NEEDS A GIRL FROM THE VILLAGE TO HELP.
AND WHO'LL PAY FOR THAT?
WAAA
HUSH BOBBY!
OK, GIVE HIM HERE...AND YOU GO STUDY.
SAY, HONEY...
THE MISS YOPOUGON CEREMONY IS COMING UP SOON...
CEREMONY? YOU MEAN THE OUTDOOR PAGEANT!?
DON'T PLAN ON ME GETTING INVOLVED.

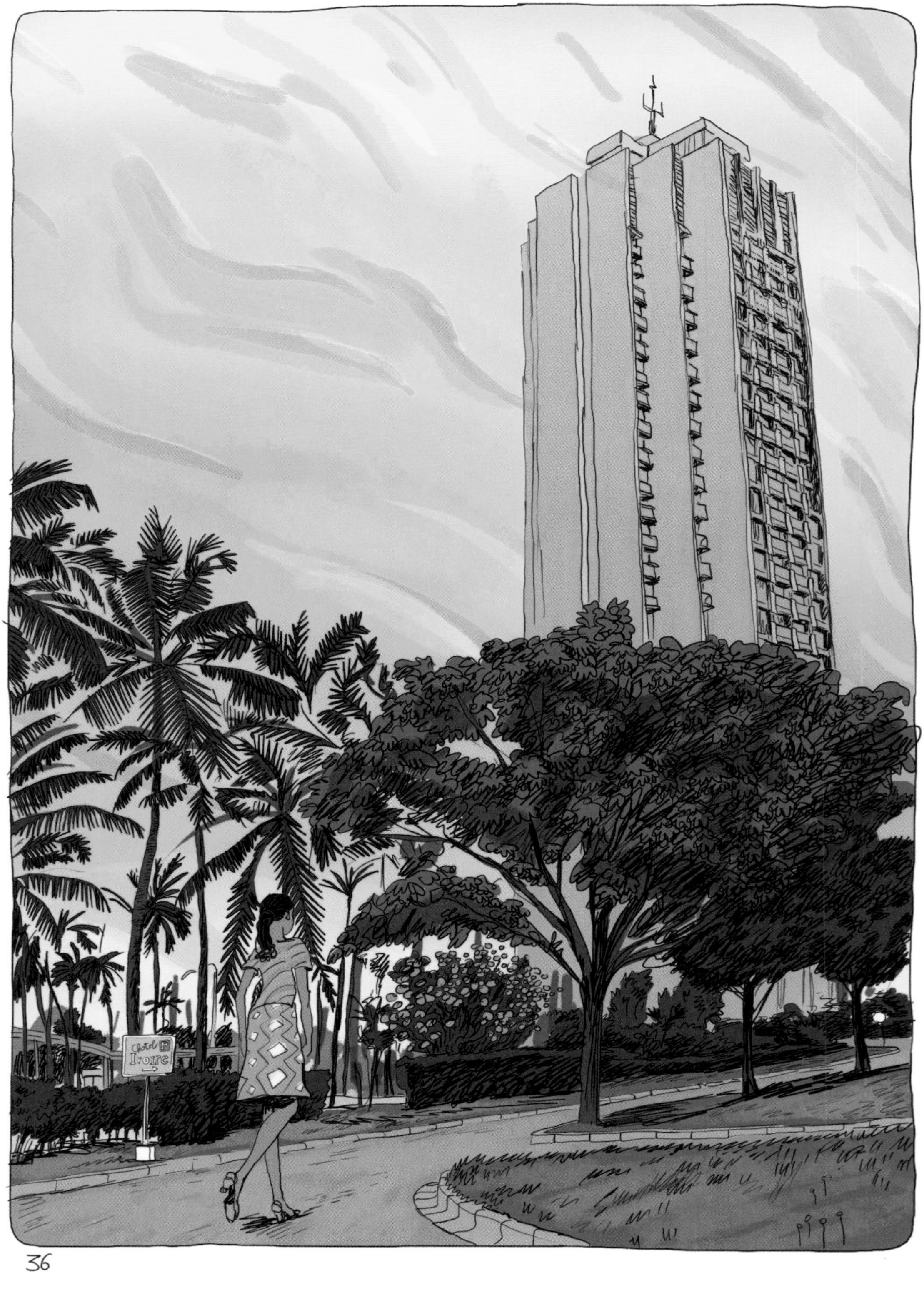
Hotel P
Ivoire

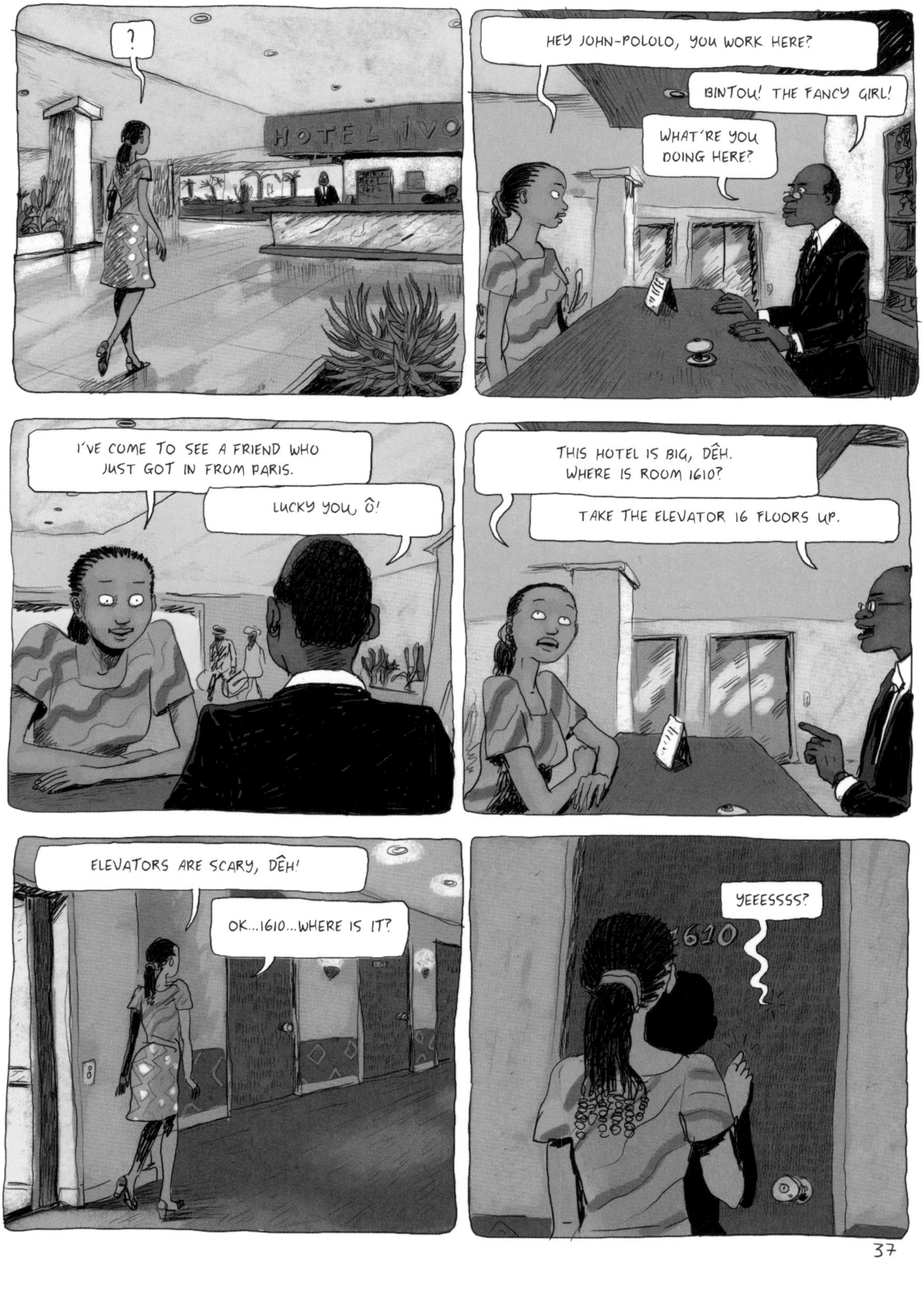
?
HOTEL IVO
HEY JOHN-POLOLO, YOU WORK HERE?
BINTOU! THE FANCY GIRL!
WHAT'RE YOU DOING HERE?
I'VE COME TO SEE A FRIEND WHO JUST GOT IN FROM PARIS.
LUCKY YOU, Ô!
THIS HOTEL IS BIG, DÊH. WHERE IS ROOM 1610?
TAKE THE ELEVATOR 16 FLOORS UP.
ELEVATORS ARE SCARY, DÊH!
OK...1610...WHERE IS IT?
1610
YEEESSSS?

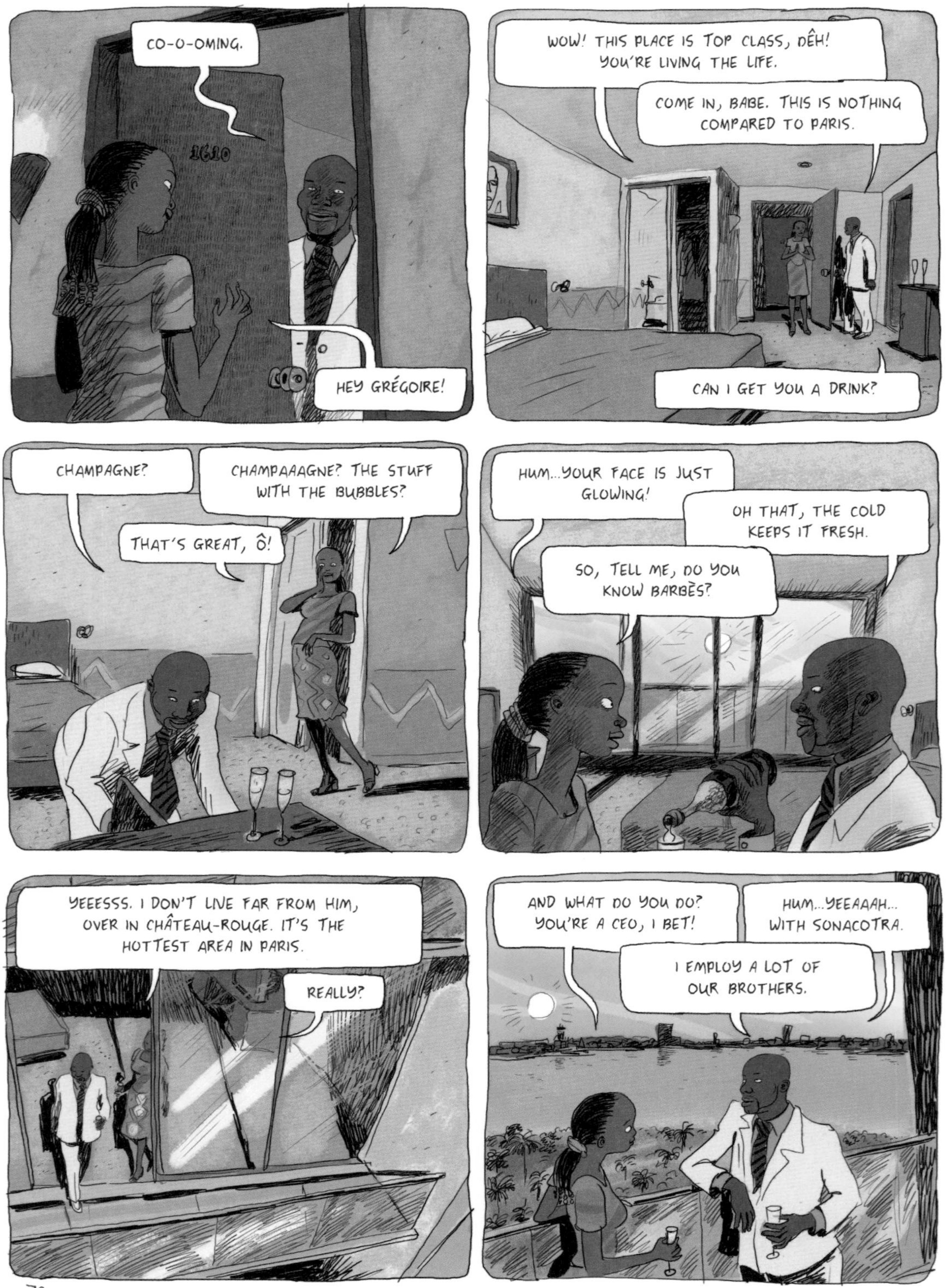
CO-O-OMING.
HEY GRÉGOIRE!
WOW! THIS PLACE IS TOP CLASS, DÊH! YOU'RE LIVING THE LIFE.
COME IN, BABE. THIS IS NOTHING COMPARED TO PARIS.
CAN I GET YOU A DRINK?
CHAMPAGNE?
CHAMPAAAGNE? THE STUFF WITH THE BUBBLES?
THAT'S GREAT, Ô!
HUM...YOUR FACE IS JUST GLOWING!
OH THAT, THE COLD KEEPS IT FRESH.
SO, TELL ME, DO YOU KNOW BARBÈS?
YEEESSS. I DON'T LIVE FAR FROM HIM, OVER IN CHÂTEAU-ROUGE. IT'S THE HOTTEST AREA IN PARIS.
REALLY?
AND WHAT DO YOU DO? YOU'RE A CEO, I BET!
HUM...YEEAAAH... WITH SONACOTRA.
I EMPLOY A LOT OF OUR BROTHERS.

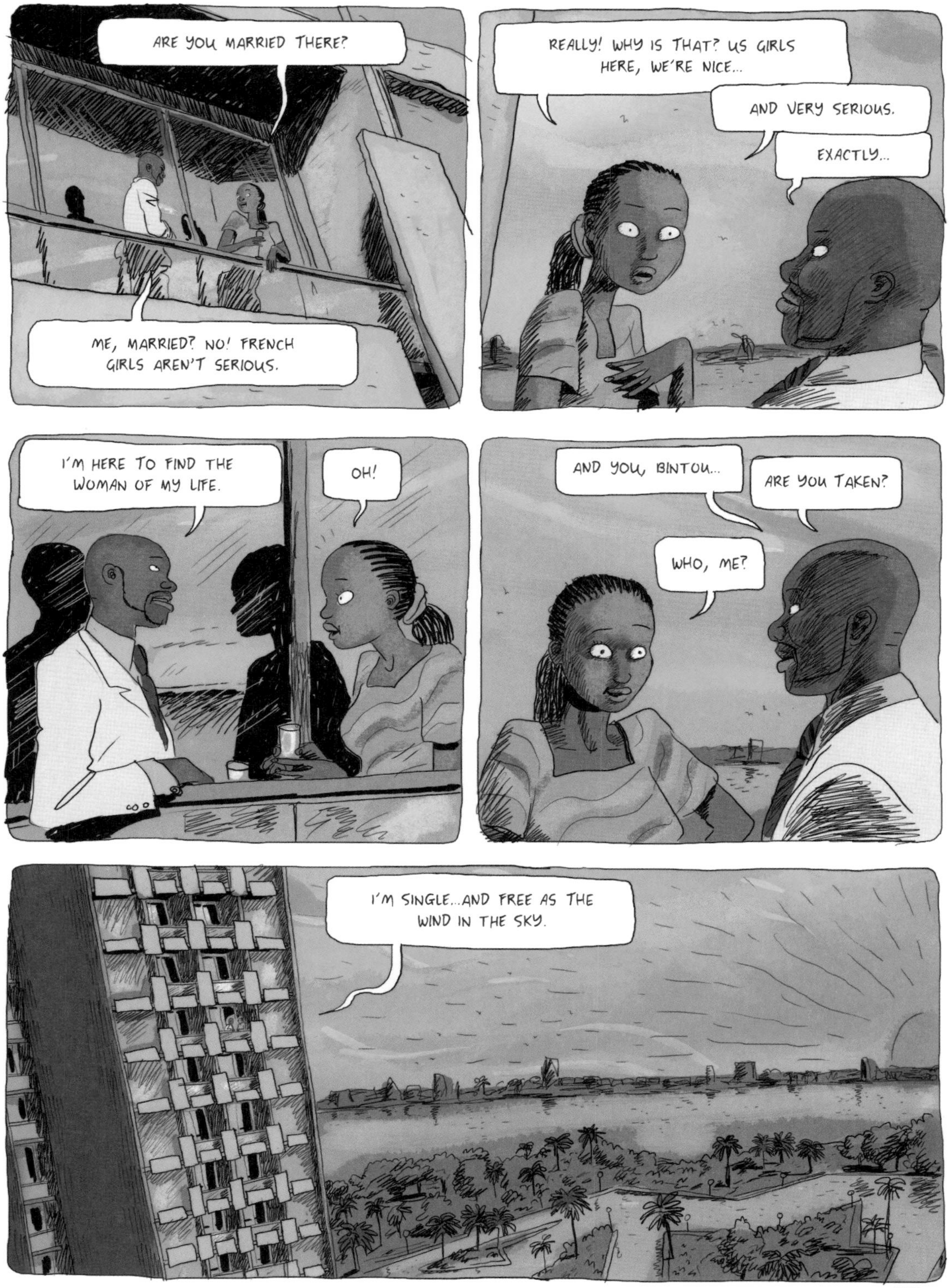
ARE YOU MARRIED THERE?
ME, MARRIED? NO! FRENCH GIRLS AREN'T SERIOUS.
REALLY! WHY IS THAT? US GIRLS HERE, WE'RE NICE...
AND VERY SERIOUS.
EXACTLY...
I'M HERE TO FIND THE WOMAN OF MY LIFE.
OH!
AND YOU, BINTOU...
ARE YOU TAKEN?
WHO, ME?
I'M SINGLE...AND FREE AS THE WIND IN THE SKY.

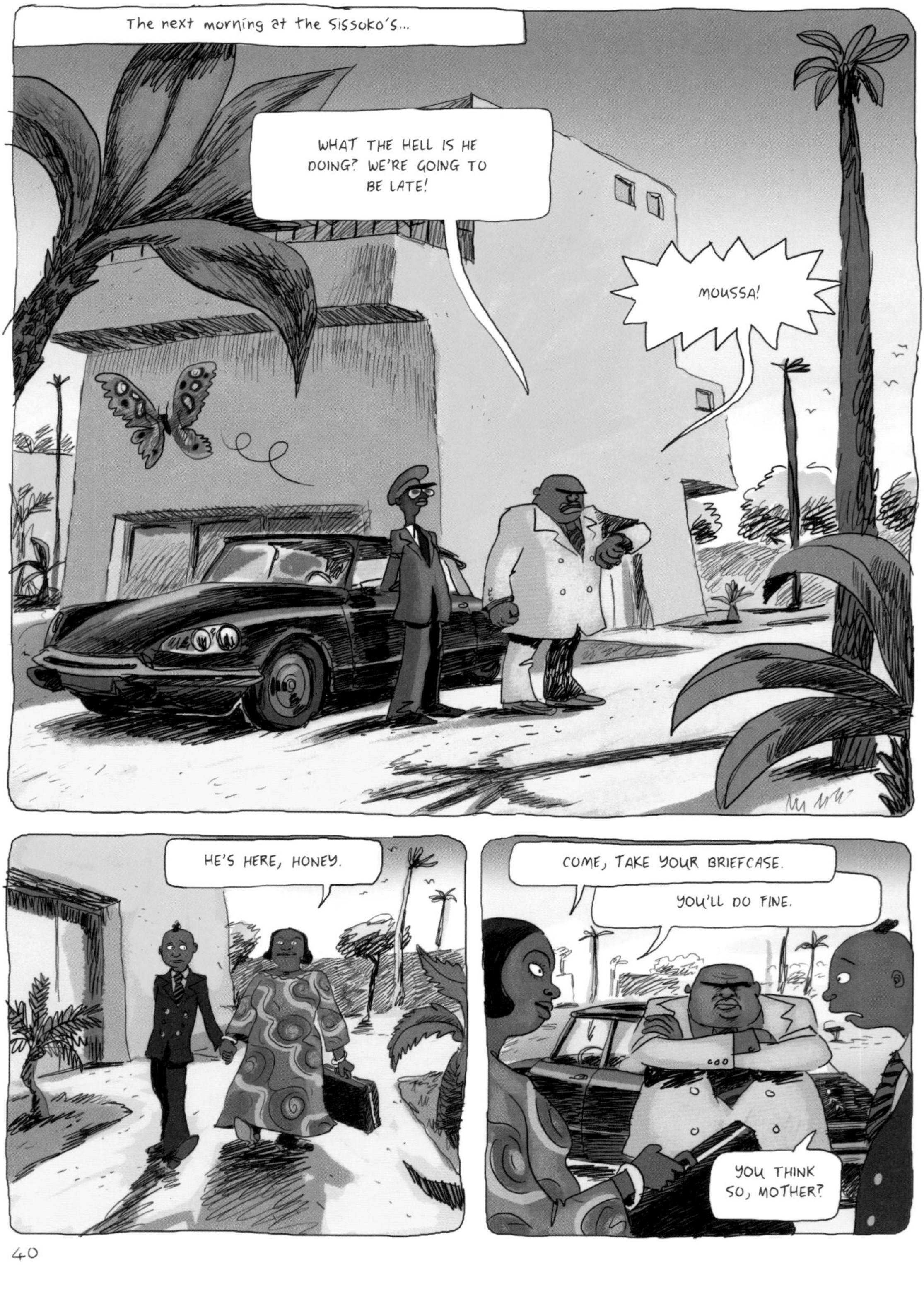
The next morning at the Sissoko's...
WHAT THE HELL IS HE DOING? WE'RE GOING TO BE LATE!
MOUSSA!
HE'S HERE, HONEY.
COME, TAKE YOUR BRIEFCASE.
YOU'LL DO FINE.
YOU THINK SO, MOTHER?

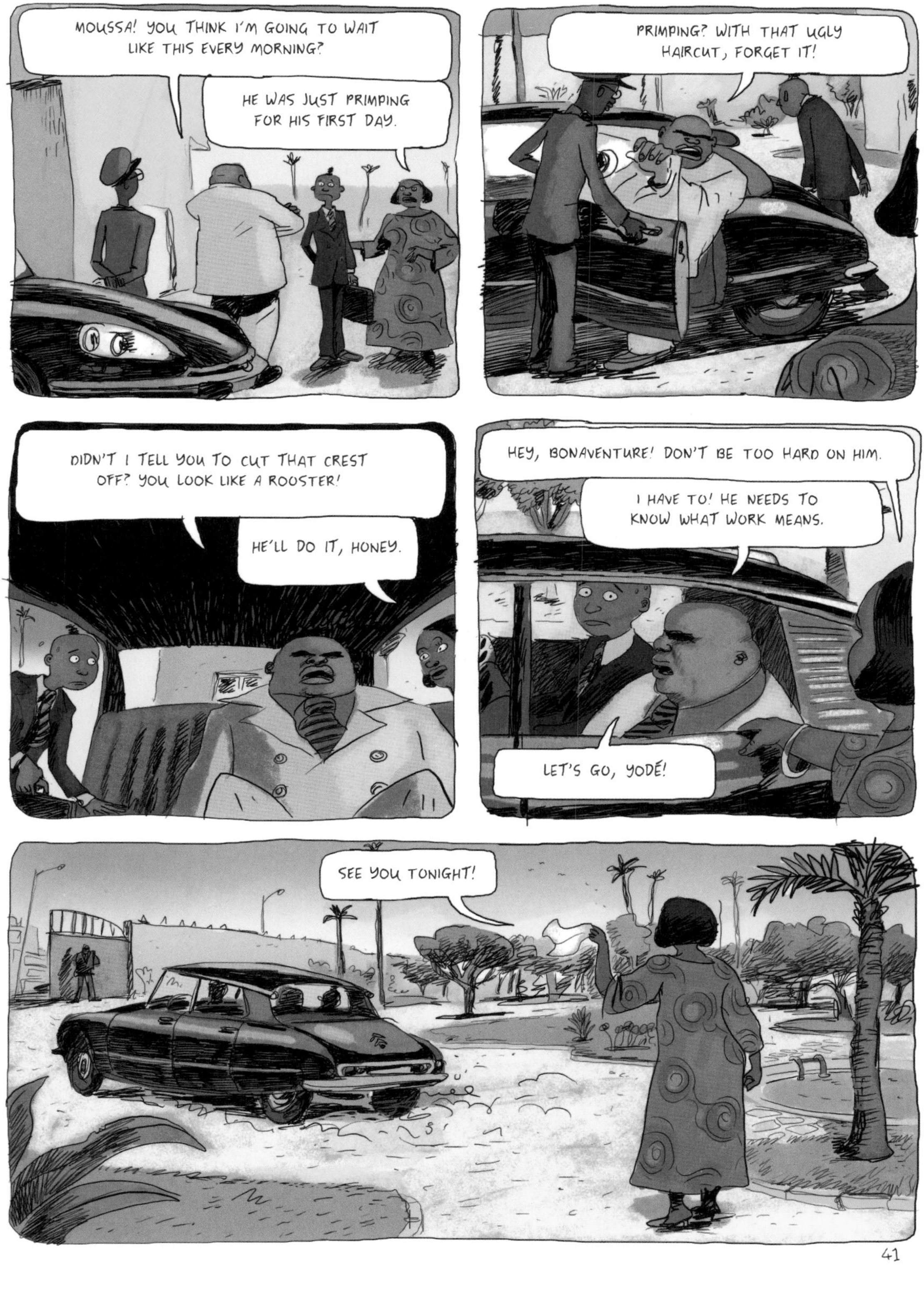

MOUSSA! YOU THINK I'M GOING TO WAIT LIKE THIS EVERY MORNING?
HE WAS JUST PRIMPING FOR HIS FIRST DAY.
PRIMPING? WITH THAT UGLY HAIRCUT, FORGET IT!
DIDN'T I TELL YOU TO CUT THAT CREST OFF? YOU LOOK LIKE A ROOSTER!
HE'LL DO IT, HONEY.
HEY, BONAVENTURE! DON'T BE TOO HARD ON HIM.
I HAVE TO! HE NEEDS TO KNOW WHAT WORK MEANS.
LET'S GO, YODÉ!
SEE YOU TONIGHT!

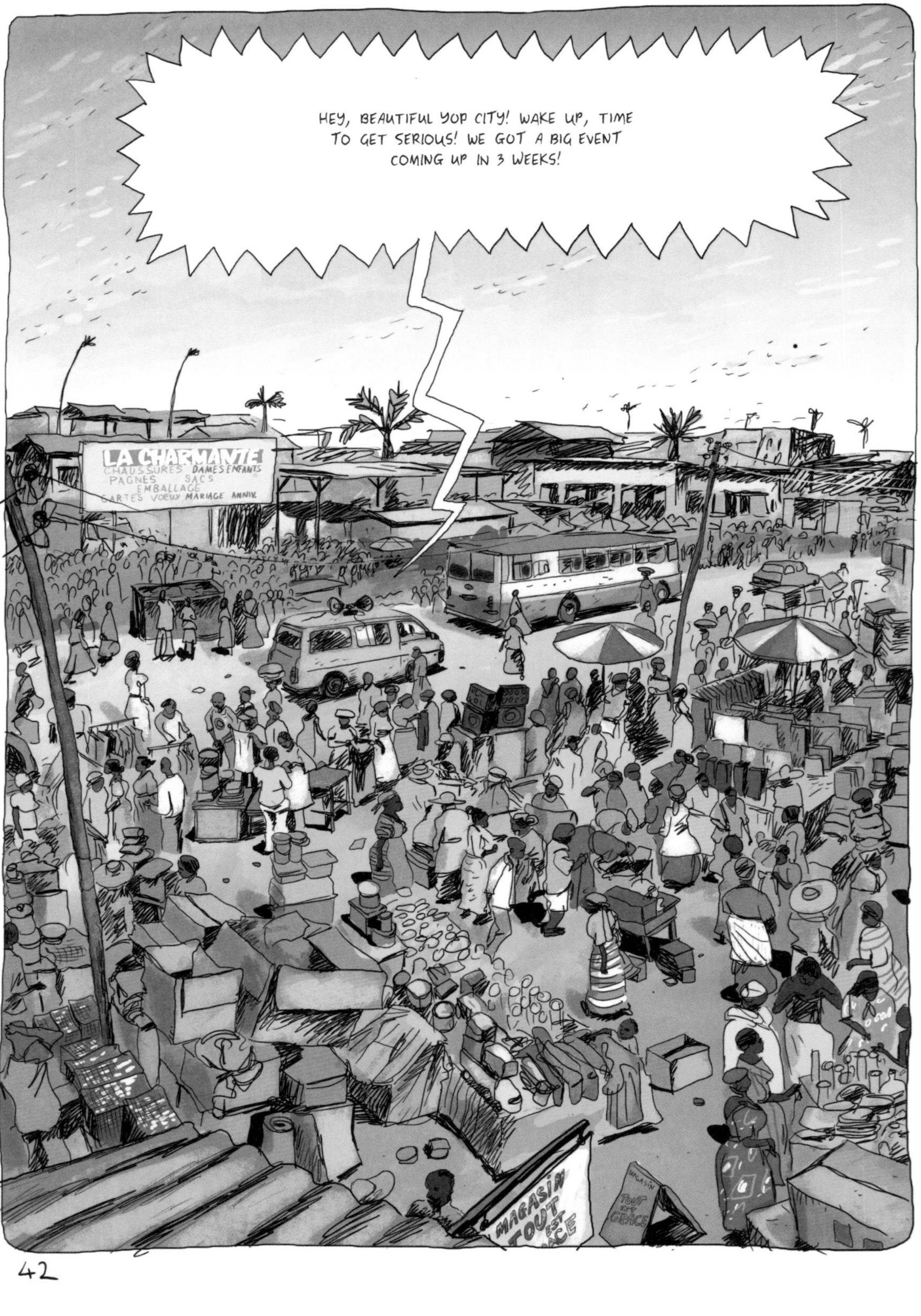
HEY, BEAUTIFUL YOP CITY! WAKE UP, TIME TO GET SERIOUS! WE GOT A BIG EVENT COMING UP IN 3 WEEKS!
LA CHARMANTE
CHAUSSURES DAMES ENFANTS
PAGNES SACS
EMBALLAGE
CARTES VOEUX MARIAGE ANNIV.

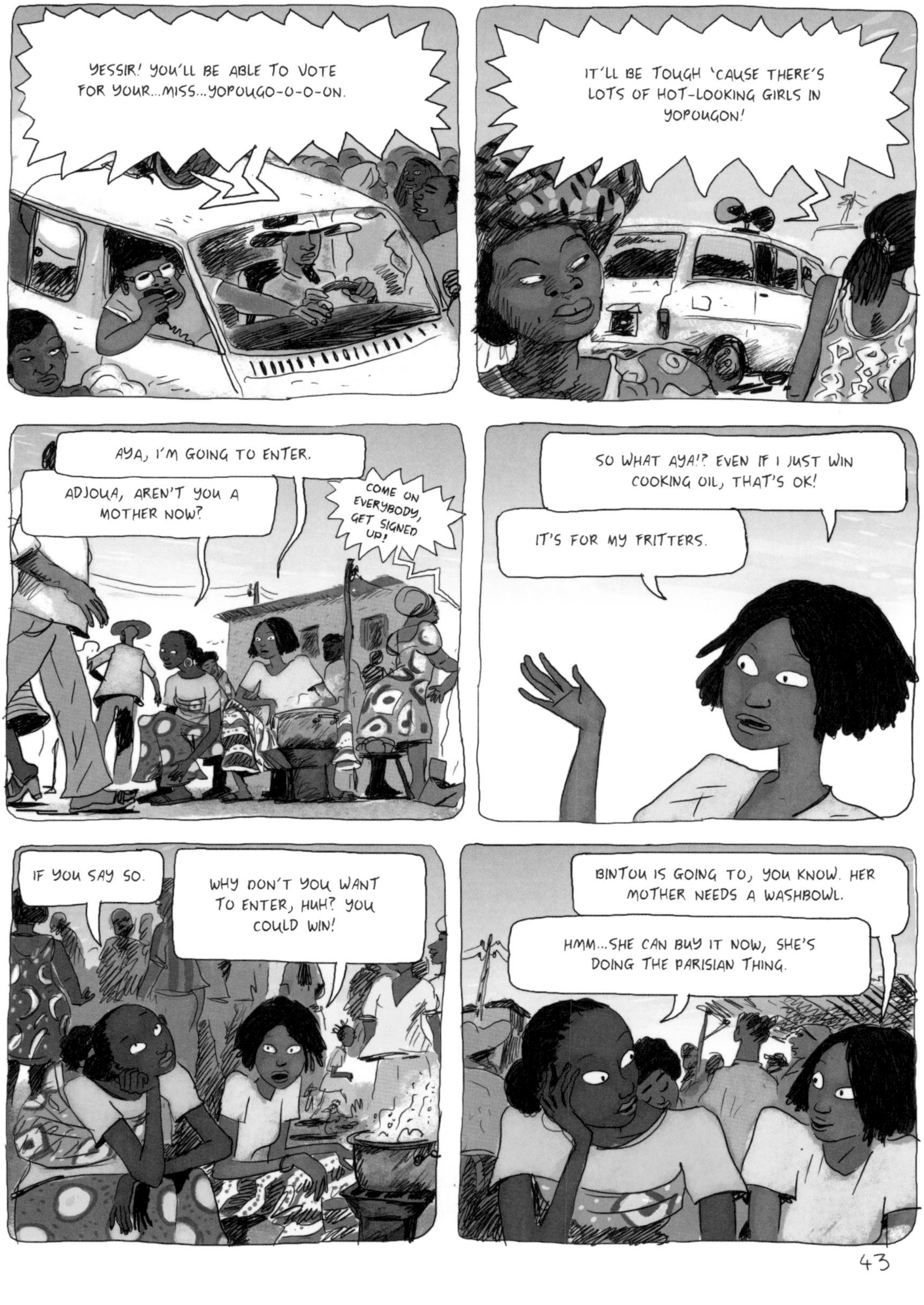
YESSIR! YOU'LL BE ABLE TO VOTE FOR YOUR...MISS...YOPOUGO-O-O-ON.
IT'LL BE TOUGH 'CAUSE THERE'S LOTS OF HOT-LOOKING GIRLS IN YOPOUGON!
AYA, I'M GOING TO ENTER.
ADJOUA, AREN'T YOU A MOTHER NOW?
COME ON EVERYBODY, GET SIGNED UP!
SO WHAT AYA!? EVEN IF I JUST WIN COOKING OIL, THAT'S OK!
IT'S FOR MY FRITTERS.
IF YOU SAY SO.
WHY DON'T YOU WANT TO ENTER, HUH? YOU COULD WIN!
BINTOU IS GOING TO, YOU KNOW. HER MOTHER NEEDS A WASHBOWL.
HMM...SHE CAN BUY IT NOW, SHE'S DOING THE PARISIAN THING.

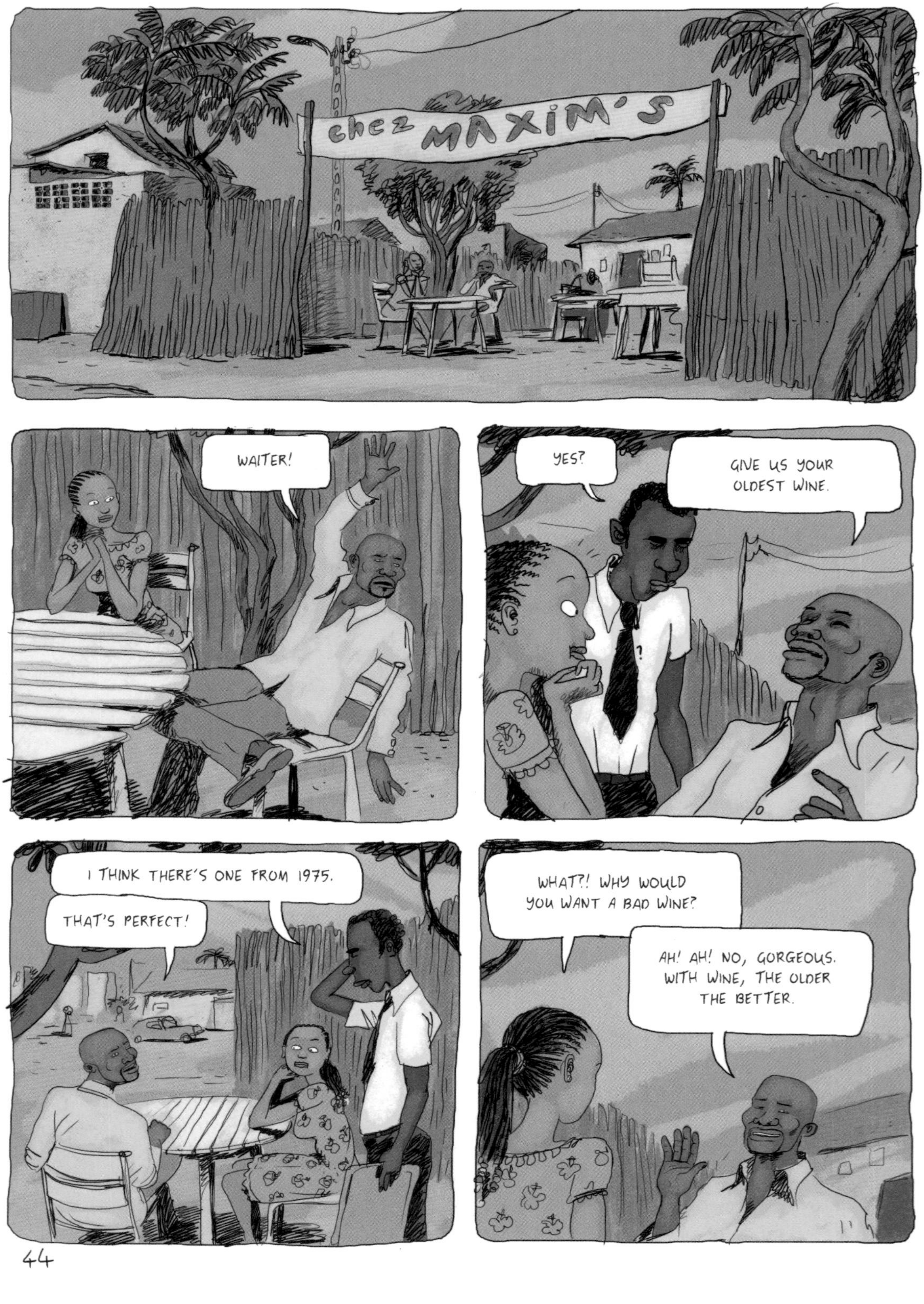
chez MAXIM'S
WAITER!
YES?
GIVE US YOUR OLDEST WINE.
I THINK THERE'S ONE FROM 1975.
THAT'S PERFECT!
WHAT?! WHY WOULD YOU WANT A BAD WINE?
AH! AH! NO, GORGEOUS. WITH WINE, THE OLDER THE BETTER.

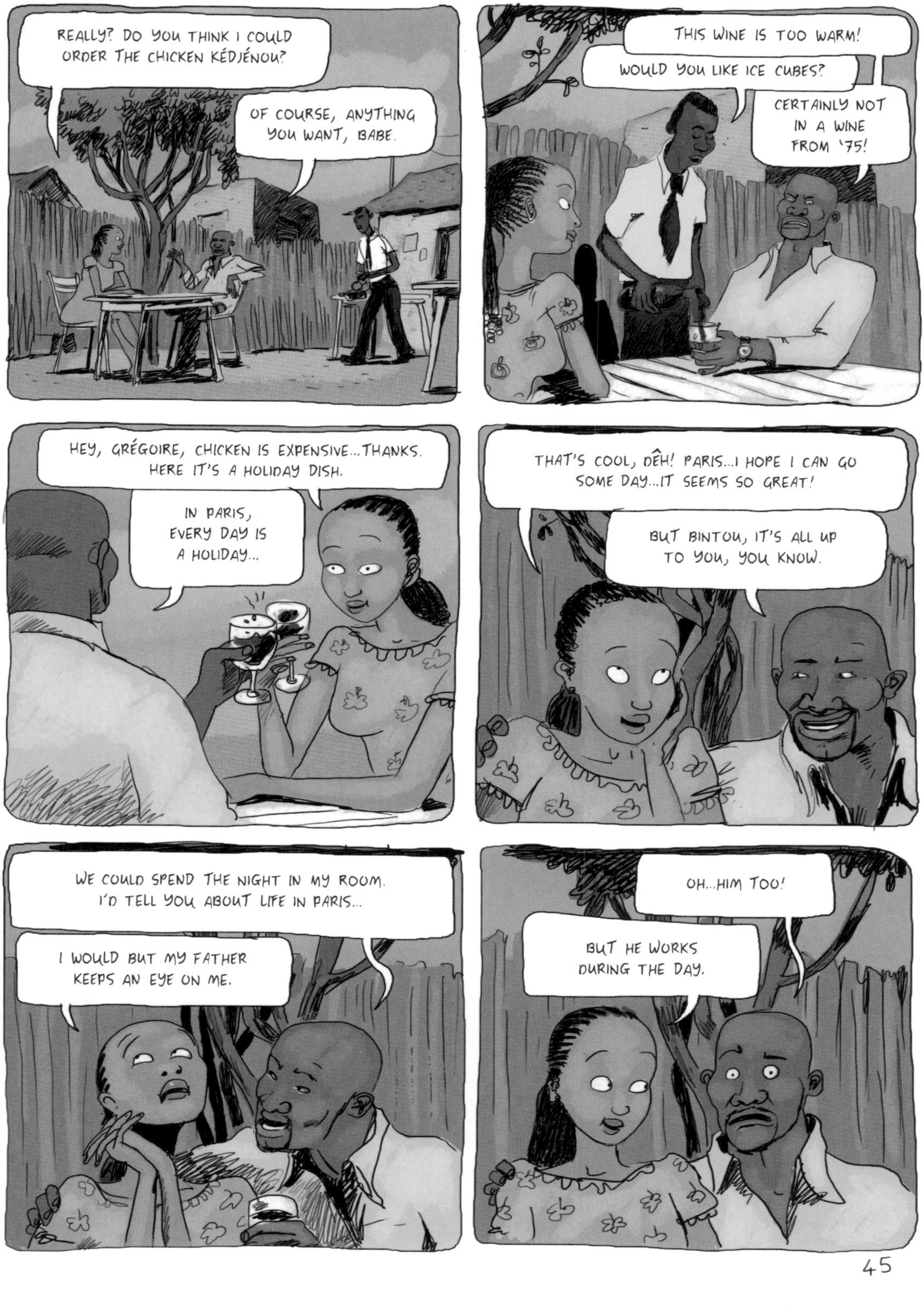
REALLY? DO YOU THINK I COULD ORDER THE CHICKEN KÉDJÉNOU?
OF COURSE, ANYTHING YOU WANT, BABE.
THIS WINE IS TOO WARM!
WOULD YOU LIKE ICE CUBES?
CERTAINLY NOT IN A WINE FROM '75!
HEY, GRÉGOIRE, CHICKEN IS EXPENSIVE...THANKS. HERE IT'S A HOLIDAY DISH.
IN PARIS, EVERY DAY IS A HOLIDAY...
THAT'S COOL, DÊH! PARIS...I HOPE I CAN GO SOME DAY...IT SEEMS SO GREAT!
BUT BINTOU, IT'S ALL UP TO YOU, YOU KNOW.
WE COULD SPEND THE NIGHT IN MY ROOM. I'D TELL YOU ABOUT LIFE IN PARIS...
I WOULD BUT MY FATHER KEEPS AN EYE ON ME.
OH...HIM TOO!
BUT HE WORKS DURING THE DAY.

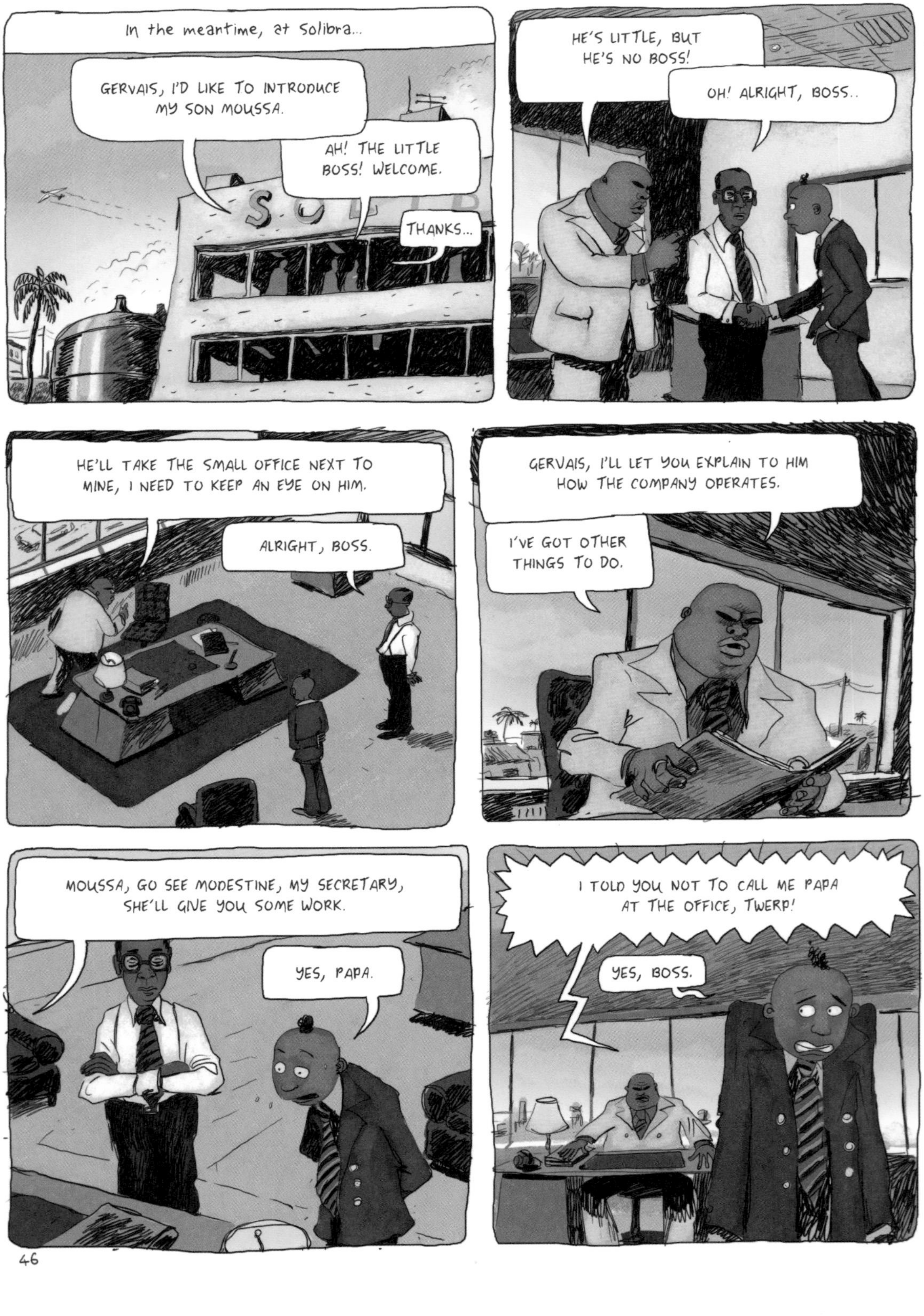
In the meantime, at Solibra...
GERVAIS, I'D LIKE TO INTRODUCE MY SON MOUSSA.
AH! THE LITTLE BOSS! WELCOME.
THANKS...
HE'S LITTLE, BUT HE'S NO BOSS!
OH! ALRIGHT, BOSS..
HE'LL TAKE THE SMALL OFFICE NEXT TO MINE, I NEED TO KEEP AN EYE ON HIM.
ALRIGHT, BOSS.
GERVAIS, I'LL LET YOU EXPLAIN TO HIM HOW THE COMPANY OPERATES.
I'VE GOT OTHER THINGS TO DO.
MOUSSA, GO SEE MODESTINE, MY SECRETARY, SHE'LL GIVE YOU SOME WORK.
YES, PAPA.
I TOLD YOU NOT TO CALL ME PAPA AT THE OFFICE, TWERP!
YES, BOSS.

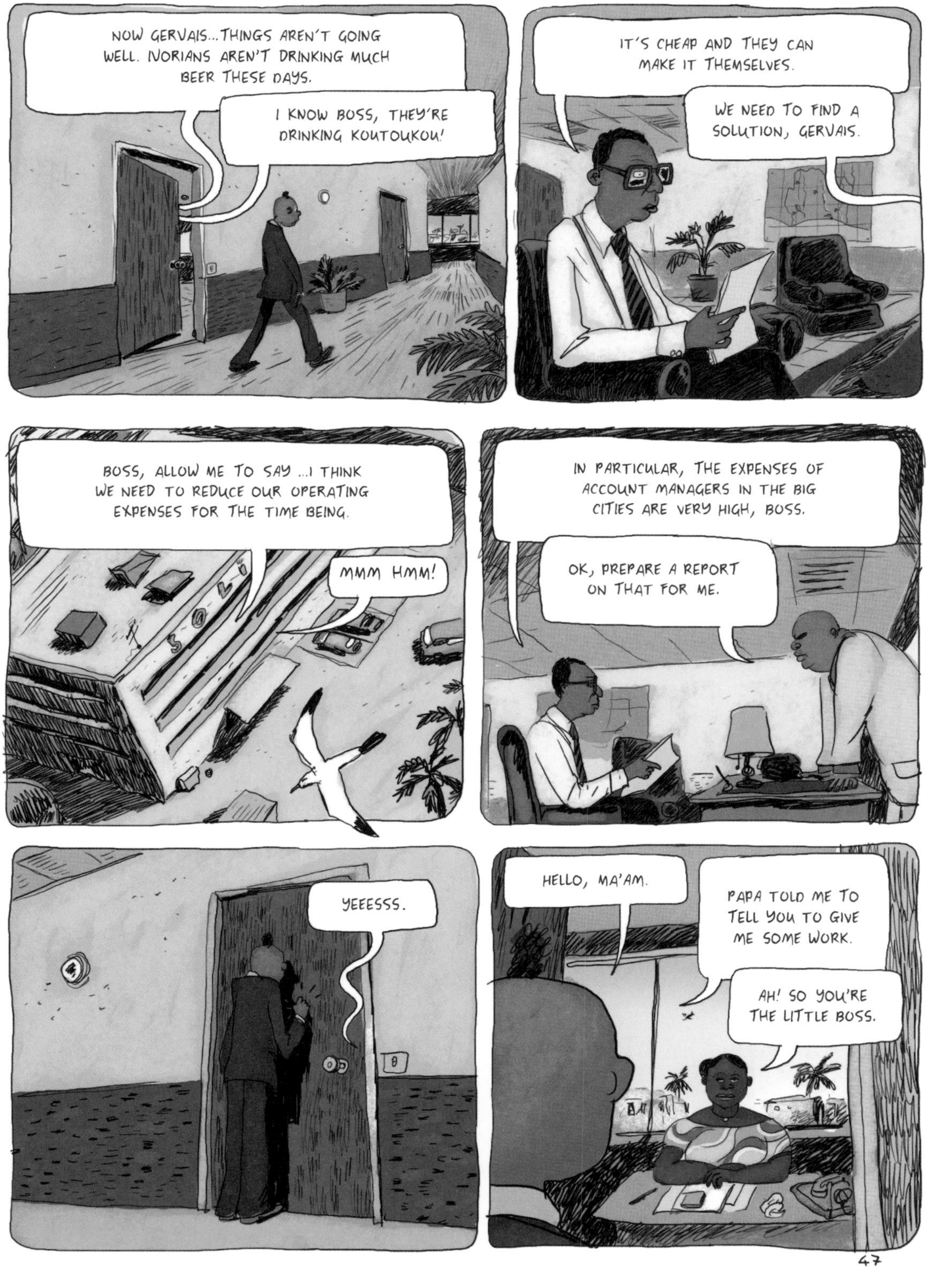
NOW GERVAIS...THINGS AREN'T GOING WELL. IVORIANS AREN'T DRINKING MUCH BEER THESE DAYS.
I KNOW BOSS, THEY'RE DRINKING KOUTOUKOU!
IT'S CHEAP AND THEY CAN MAKE IT THEMSELVES.
WE NEED TO FIND A SOLUTION, GERVAIS.
BOSS, ALLOW ME TO SAY ...I THINK WE NEED TO REDUCE OUR OPERATING EXPENSES FOR THE TIME BEING.
MMM HMM!
IN PARTICULAR, THE EXPENSES OF ACCOUNT MANAGERS IN THE BIG CITIES ARE VERY HIGH, BOSS.
OK, PREPARE A REPORT ON THAT FOR ME.
YEEESSS.
HELLO, MA'AM.
PAPA TOLD ME TO TELL YOU TO GIVE ME SOME WORK.
AH! SO YOU'RE THE LITTLE BOSS.

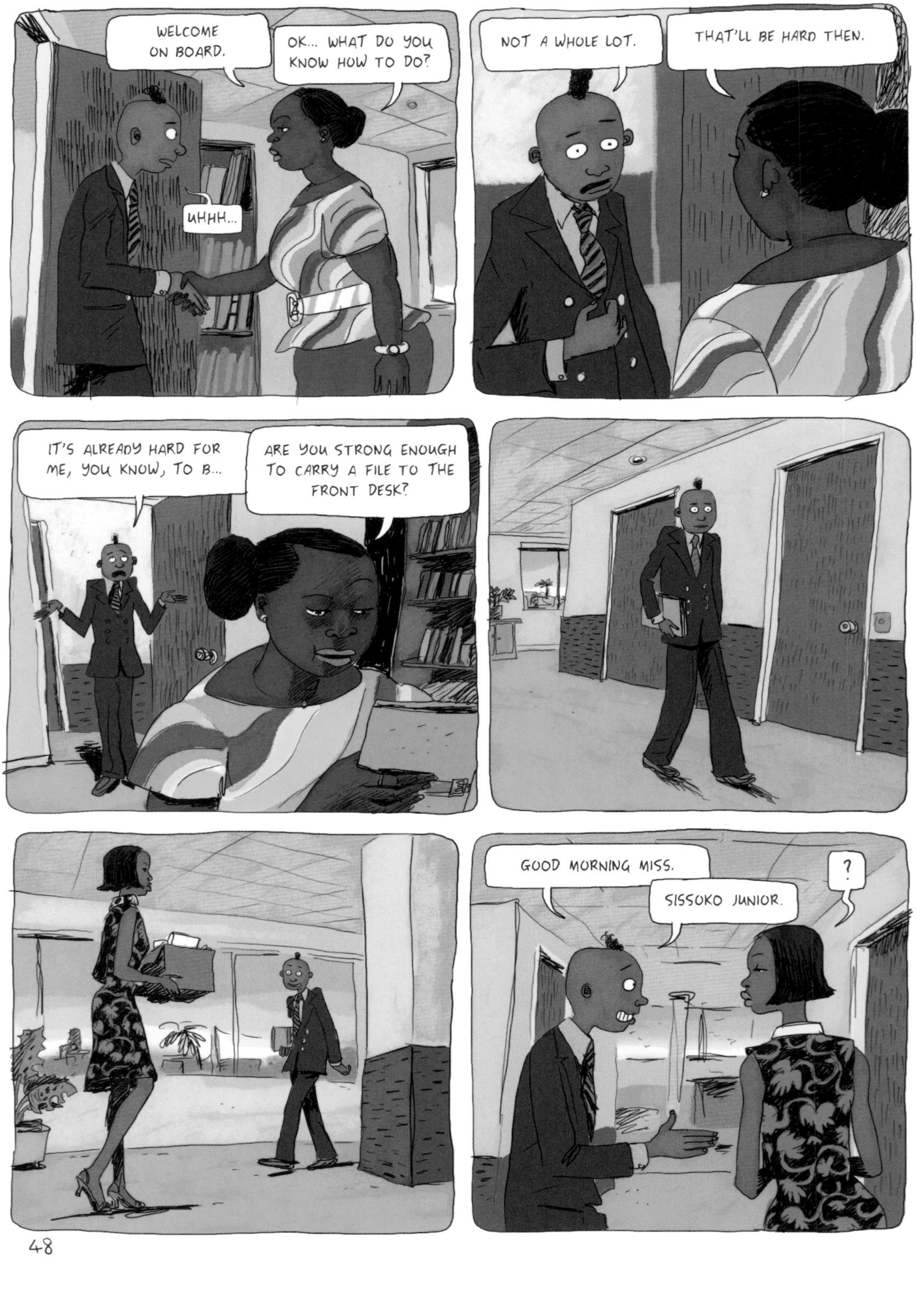
WELCOME ON BOARD.
OK... WHAT DO YOU KNOW HOW TO DO?
UHHH...
NOT A WHOLE LOT.
THAT'LL BE HARD THEN.
IT'S ALREADY HARD FOR ME, YOU KNOW, TO B...
ARE YOU STRONG ENOUGH TO CARRY A FILE TO THE FRONT DESK?
GOOD MORNING MISS.
SISSOKO JUNIOR.
?

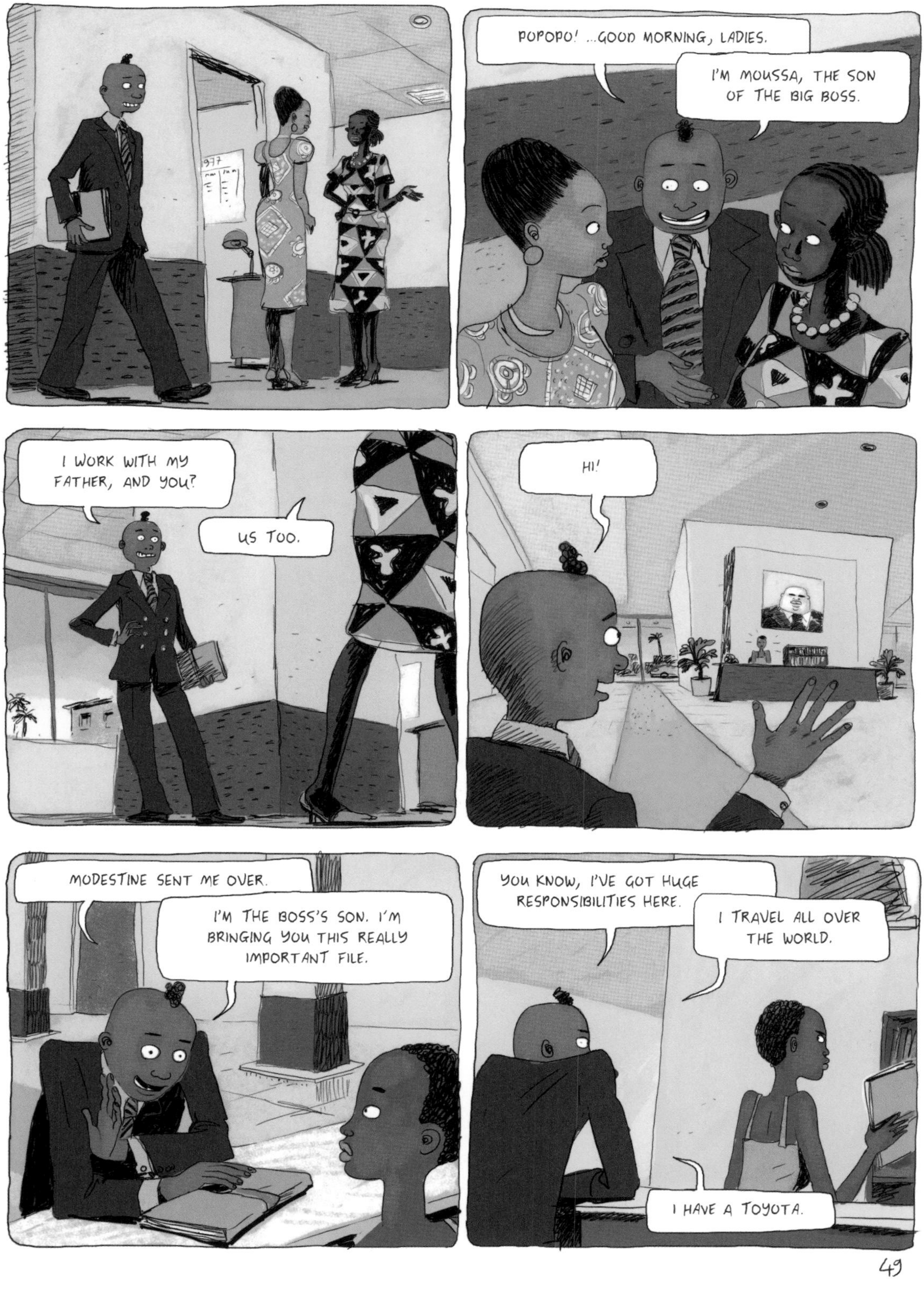
POPOPO! ...GOOD MORNING, LADIES.
I'M MOUSSA, THE SON OF THE BIG BOSS.
I WORK WITH MY FATHER, AND YOU?
US TOO.
HI!
MODESTINE SENT ME OVER.
I'M THE BOSS'S SON. I'M BRINGING YOU THIS REALLY IMPORTANT FILE.
YOU KNOW, I'VE GOT HUGE RESPONSIBILITIES HERE.
I TRAVEL ALL OVER THE WORLD.
I HAVE A TOYOTA.

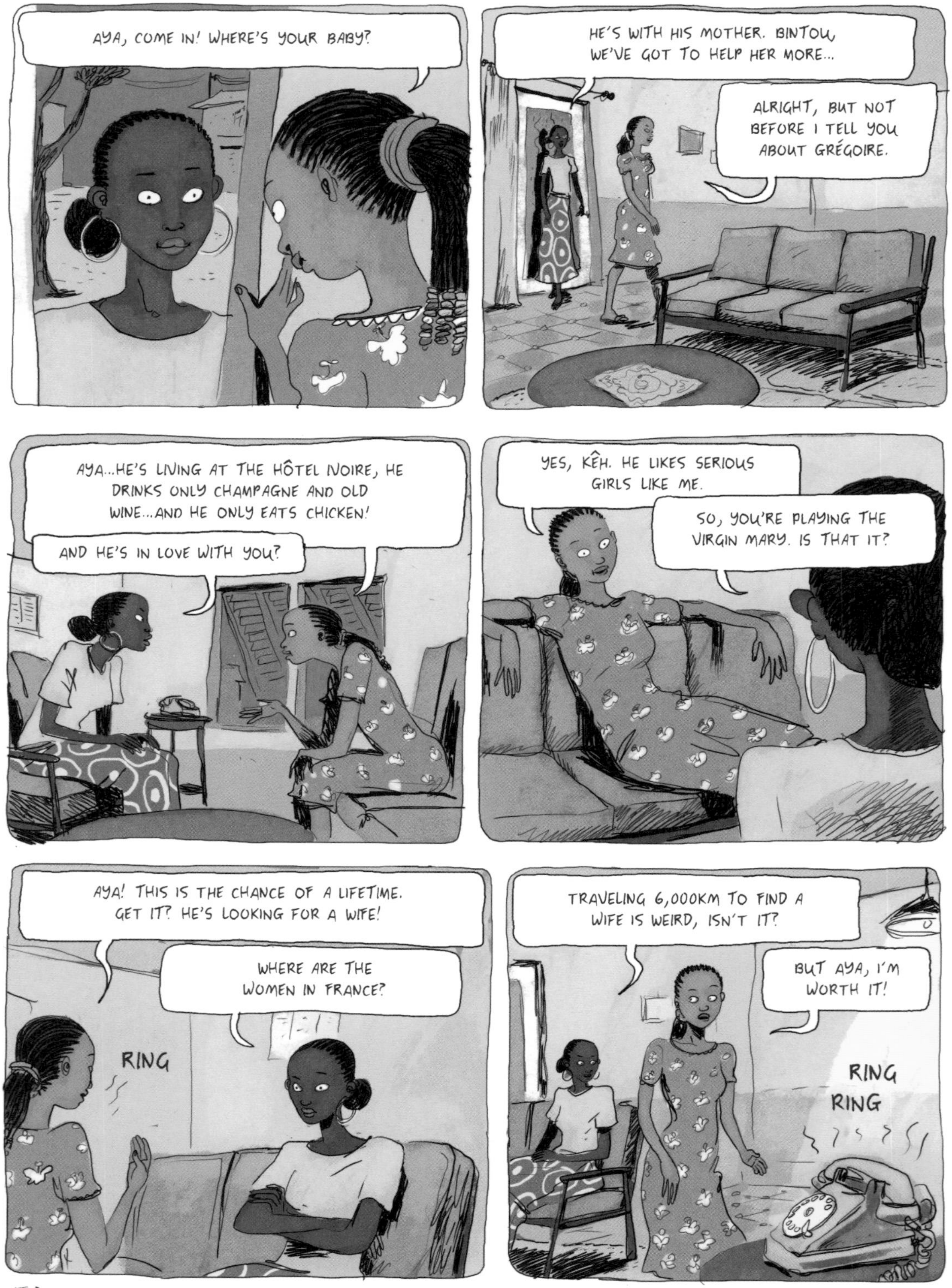
AYA, COME IN! WHERE'S YOUR BABY?
HE'S WITH HIS MOTHER. BINTOU, WE'VE GOT TO HELP HER MORE...
ALRIGHT, BUT NOT BEFORE I TELL YOU ABOUT GRÉGOIRE.
AYA...HE'S LIVING AT THE HÔTEL NOIRE, HE DRINKS ONLY CHAMPAGNE AND OLD WINE...AND HE ONLY EATS CHICKEN!
AND HE'S IN LOVE WITH YOU?
YES, KÊH. HE LIKES SERIOUS GIRLS LIKE ME.
SO, YOU'RE PLAYING THE VIRGIN MARY. IS THAT IT?
AYA! THIS IS THE CHANCE OF A LIFETIME. GET IT? HE'S LOOKING FOR A WIFE!
WHERE ARE THE WOMEN IN FRANCE?
RING
TRAVELING 6,000KM TO FIND A WIFE IS WEIRD, ISN'T IT?
BUT AYA, I'M WORTH IT!
RING
RING

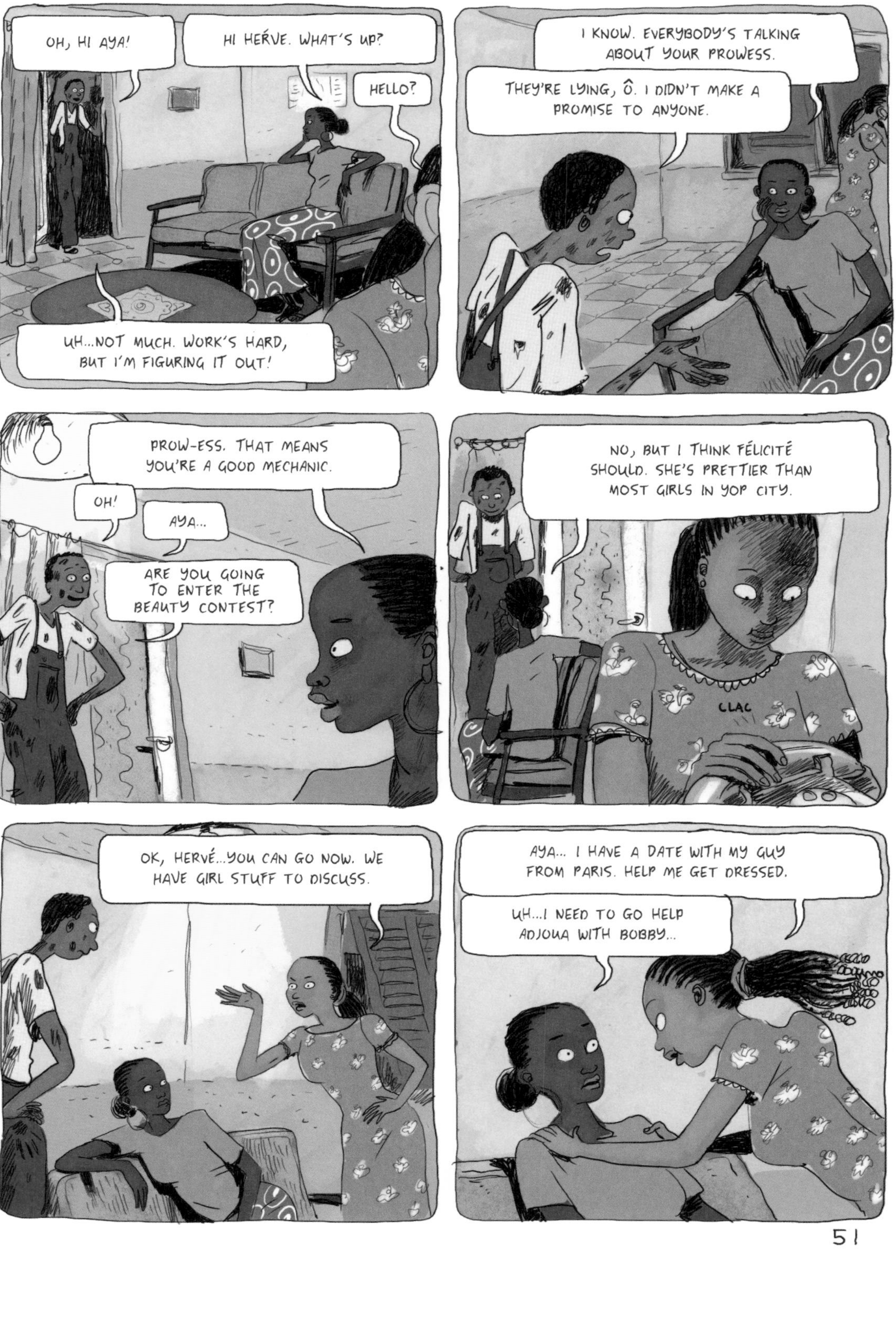
OH, HI AYA!
HI HERVE. WHAT'S UP?
HELLO?
UH...NOT MUCH. WORK'S HARD, BUT I'M FIGURING IT OUT!
I KNOW. EVERYBODY'S TALKING ABOUT YOUR PROWESS.
THEY'RE LYING, Ô. I DIDN'T MAKE A PROMISE TO ANYONE.
PROW-ESS. THAT MEANS YOU'RE A GOOD MECHANIC.
OH!
AYA...
ARE YOU GOING TO ENTER THE BEAUTY CONTEST?
NO, BUT I THINK FÉLICITÉ SHOULD. SHE'S PRETTIER THAN MOST GIRLS IN YOP CITY.
CLAC
OK, HERVÉ...YOU CAN GO NOW. WE HAVE GIRL STUFF TO DISCUSS.
AYA... I HAVE A DATE WITH MY GUY FROM PARIS. HELP ME GET DRESSED.
UH...I NEED TO GO HELP ADJOUA WITH BOBBY...

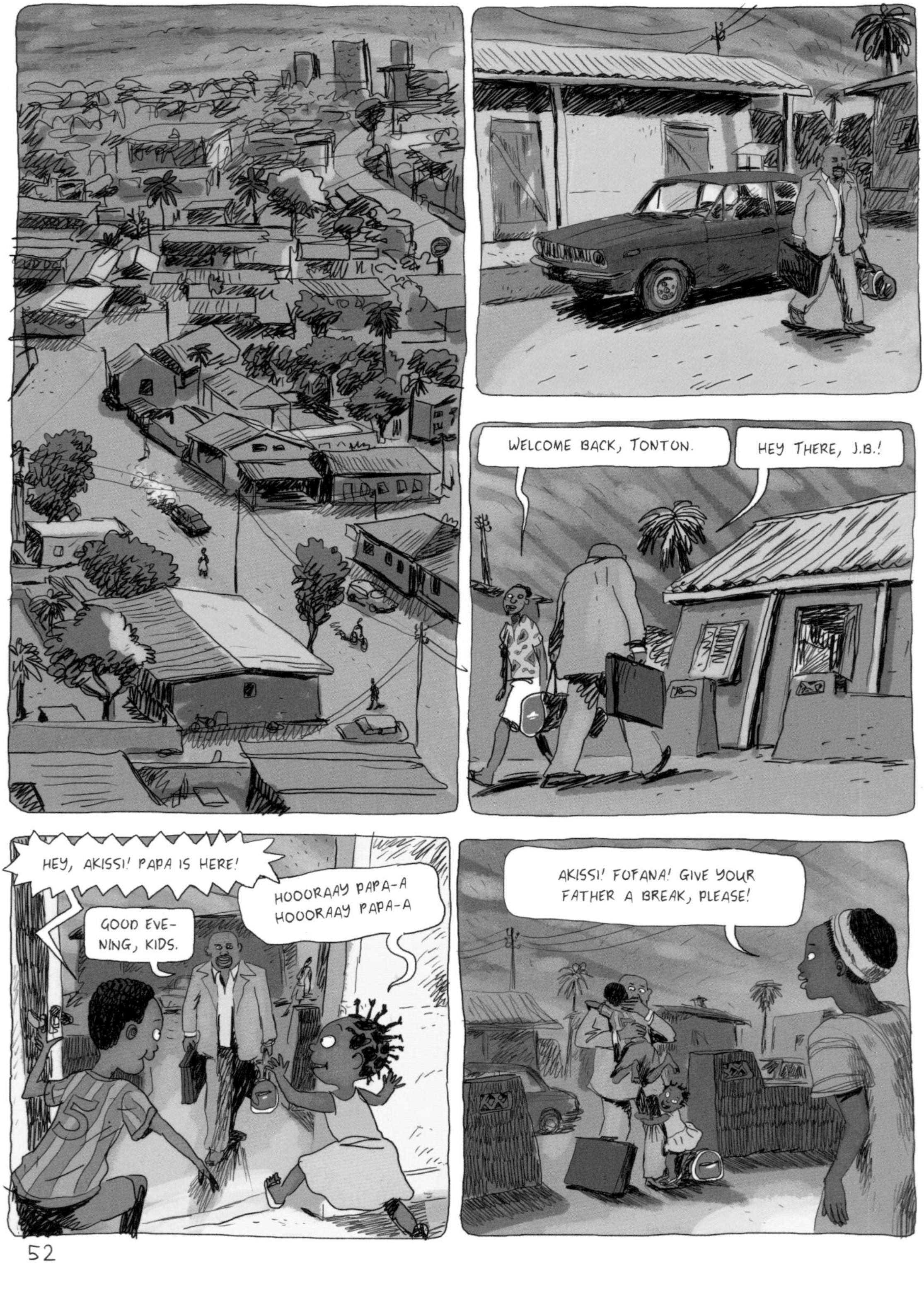
WELCOME BACK, TONTON.
HEY THERE, J.B.!
HEY, AKISSI! PAPA IS HERE!
GOOD EVENING, KIDS.
HOOORAAY PAPA-A HOOORAAY PAPA-A
AKISSI! FOFANA! GIVE YOUR FATHER A BREAK, PLEASE!

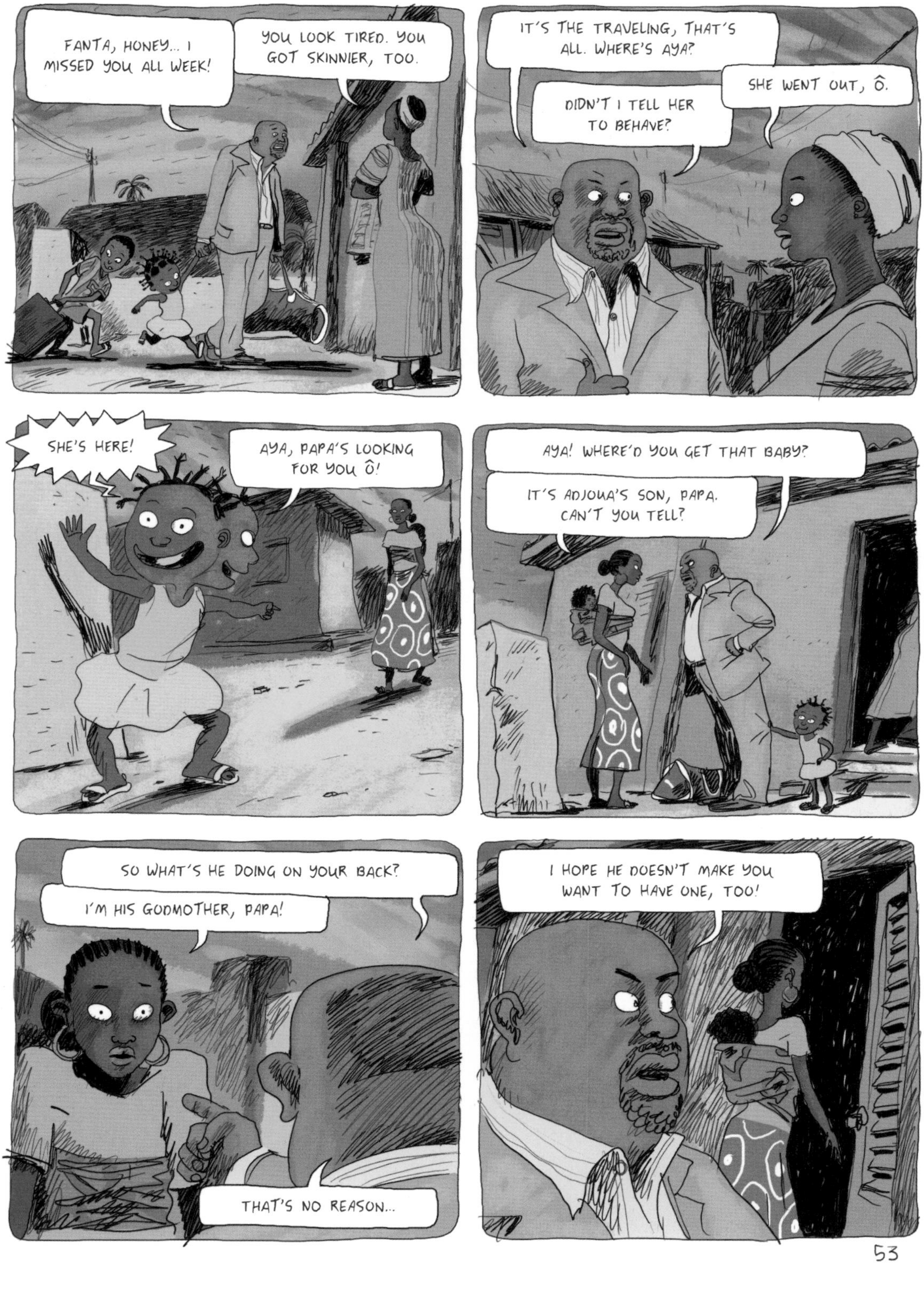
FANTA, HONEY... I MISSED YOU ALL WEEK!
YOU LOOK TIRED. YOU GOT SKINNIER, TOO.
IT'S THE TRAVELING, THAT'S ALL. WHERE'S AYA?
SHE WENT OUT, Ô.
DIDN'T I TELL HER TO BEHAVE?
SHE'S HERE!
AYA, PAPA'S LOOKING FOR YOU Ô!
AYA! WHERE'D YOU GET THAT BABY?
IT'S ADJOUA'S SON, PAPA. CAN'T YOU TELL?
SO WHAT'S HE DOING ON YOUR BACK?
I'M HIS GODMOTHER, PAPA!
THAT'S NO REASON...
I HOPE HE DOESN'T MAKE YOU WANT TO HAVE ONE, TOO!

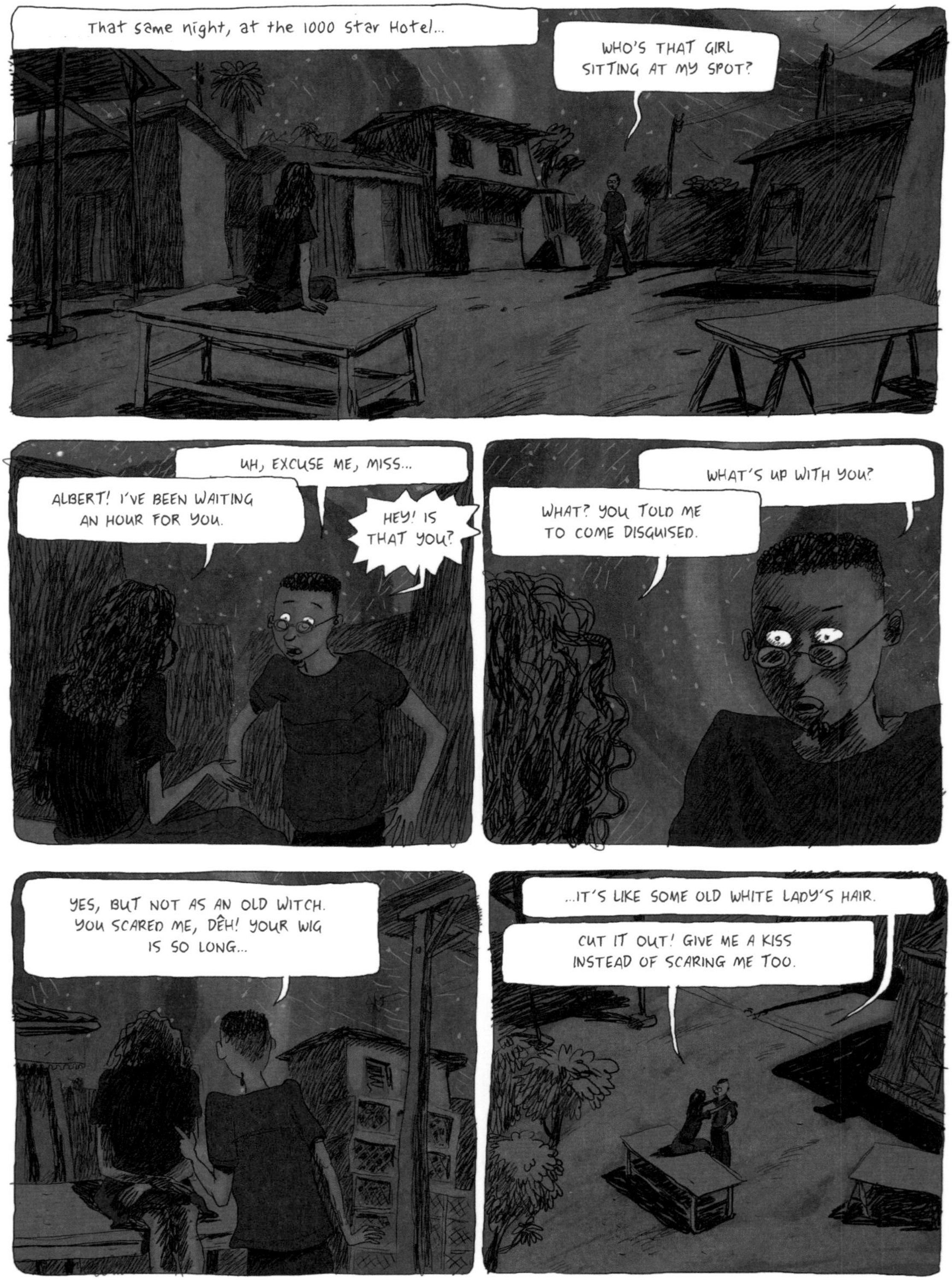
That same night, at the 1000 Star Hotel...
WHO'S THAT GIRL SITTING AT MY SPOT?
UH, EXCUSE ME, MISS...
ALBERT! I'VE BEEN WAITING AN HOUR FOR YOU.
HEY! IS THAT YOU?
WHAT'S UP WITH YOU?
WHAT? YOU TOLD ME TO COME DISGUISED.
YES, BUT NOT AS AN OLD WITCH. YOU SCARED ME, DÊH! YOUR WIG IS SO LONG...
...IT'S LIKE SOME OLD WHITE LADY'S HAIR.
CUT IT OUT! GIVE ME A KISS INSTEAD OF SCARING ME TOO.

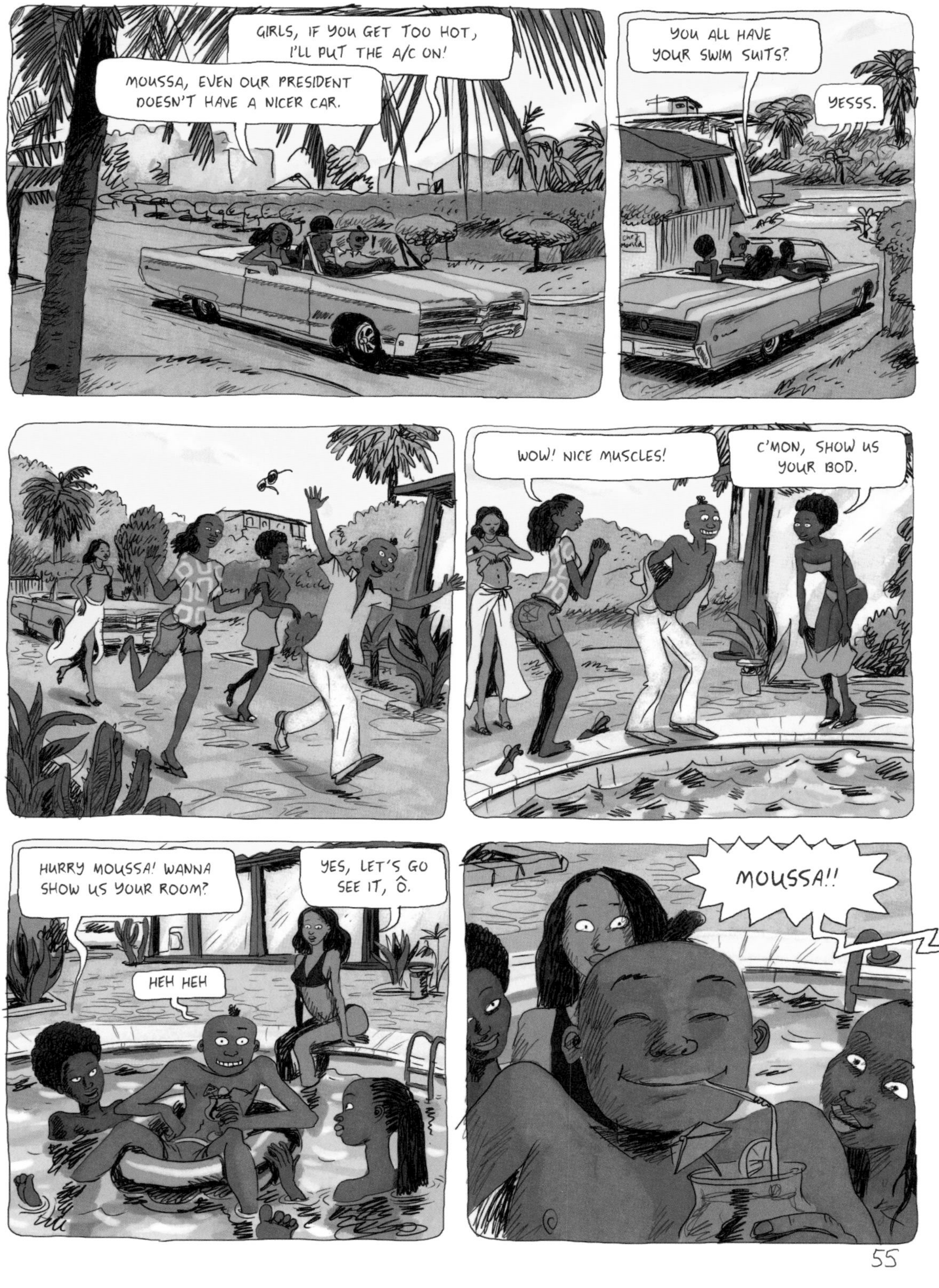
GIRLS, IF YOU GET TOO HOT, I'LL PUT THE A/C ON!
MOUSSA, EVEN OUR PRESIDENT DOESN'T HAVE A NICER CAR.
YOU ALL HAVE YOUR SWIM SUITS?
YESSS.
WOW! NICE MUSCLES!
C'MON, SHOW US YOUR BOD.
HURRY MOUSSA! WANNA SHOW US YOUR ROOM?
YES, LET'S GO SEE IT, Ô.
HEH HEH
MOUSSA!!

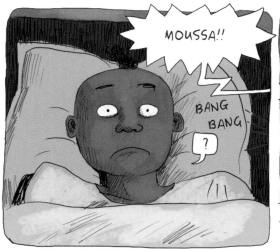

MOUSSA!!

BANG BANG

?

ARE YOU STILL SLEEPING!?!

YOUR FATHER'S WAITING!

YOU'RE NOT EVEN READY!!

SORRY, MOTHER. I'VE GOT PALU...I'M SICK...

AND YOU JUST REALIZED THAT NOW?

SO WHAT AM I GOING TO TELL YOUR FATHER, HUH?

UH...THAT I'M DEAD?

MOUSSA! DON'T SAY THAT, THE WITCH DOCTORS MIGHT HEAR YOU!

PLEASE...I'D JUST LIKE TO STAY IN BED FOR ONCE...

FOR ONCE? THIS IS ONLY YOUR SECOND DAY AT WORK!

OK.

I'LL GO TALK TO YOUR FATHER.

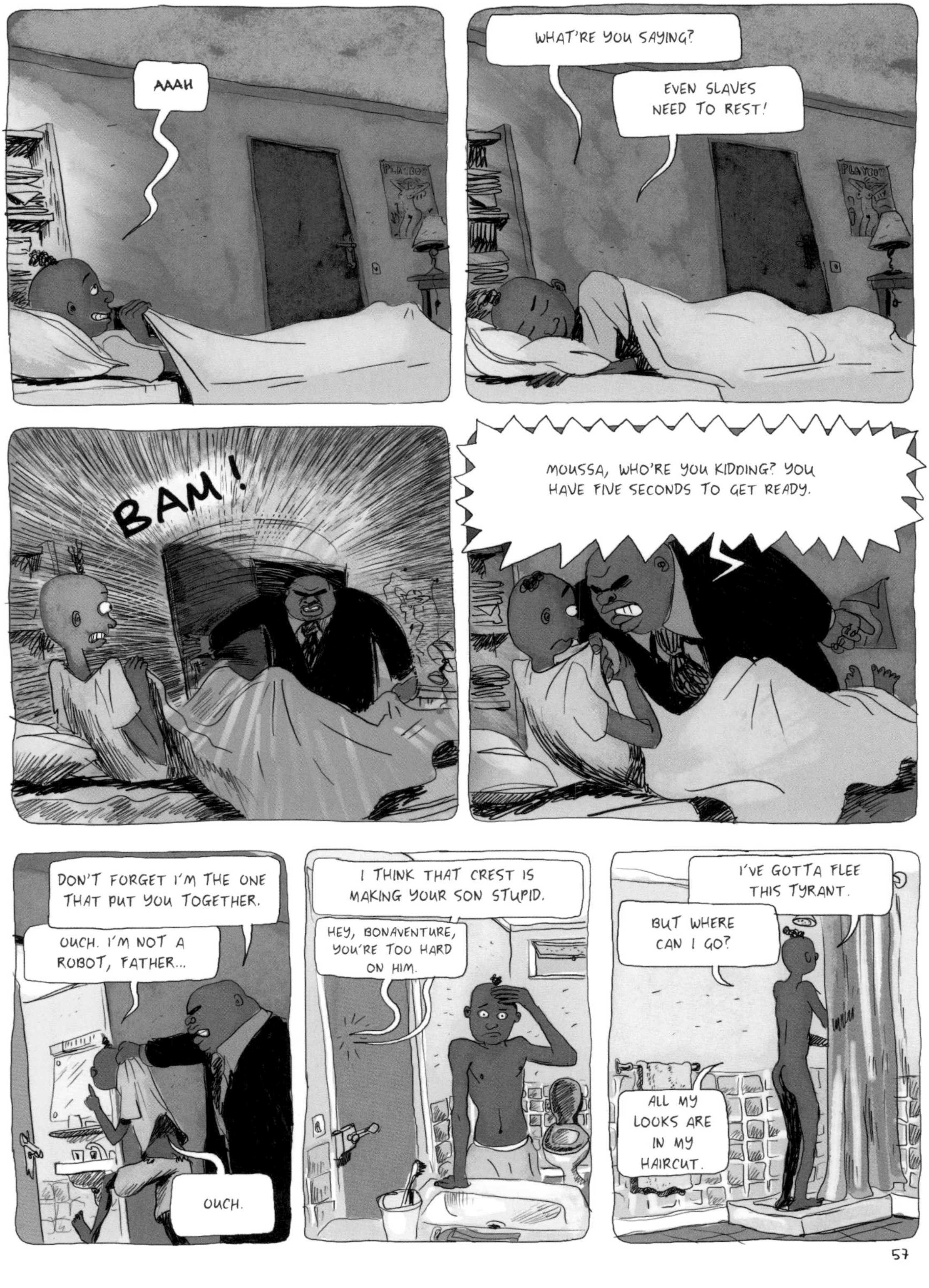
AAAH
WHAT'RE YOU SAYING?
EVEN SLAVES NEED TO REST!
BAM!
MOUSSA, WHO'RE YOU KIDDING? YOU HAVE FIVE SECONDS TO GET READY.
DON'T FORGET I'M THE ONE THAT PUT YOU TOGETHER.
OUCH. I'M NOT A ROBOT, FATHER...
OUCH.
I THINK THAT CREST IS MAKING YOUR SON STUPID.
HEY, BONAVENTURE, YOU'RE TOO HARD ON HIM.
I'VE GOTTA FLEE THIS TYRANT.
BUT WHERE CAN I GO?
ALL MY LOOKS ARE IN MY HAIRCUT.

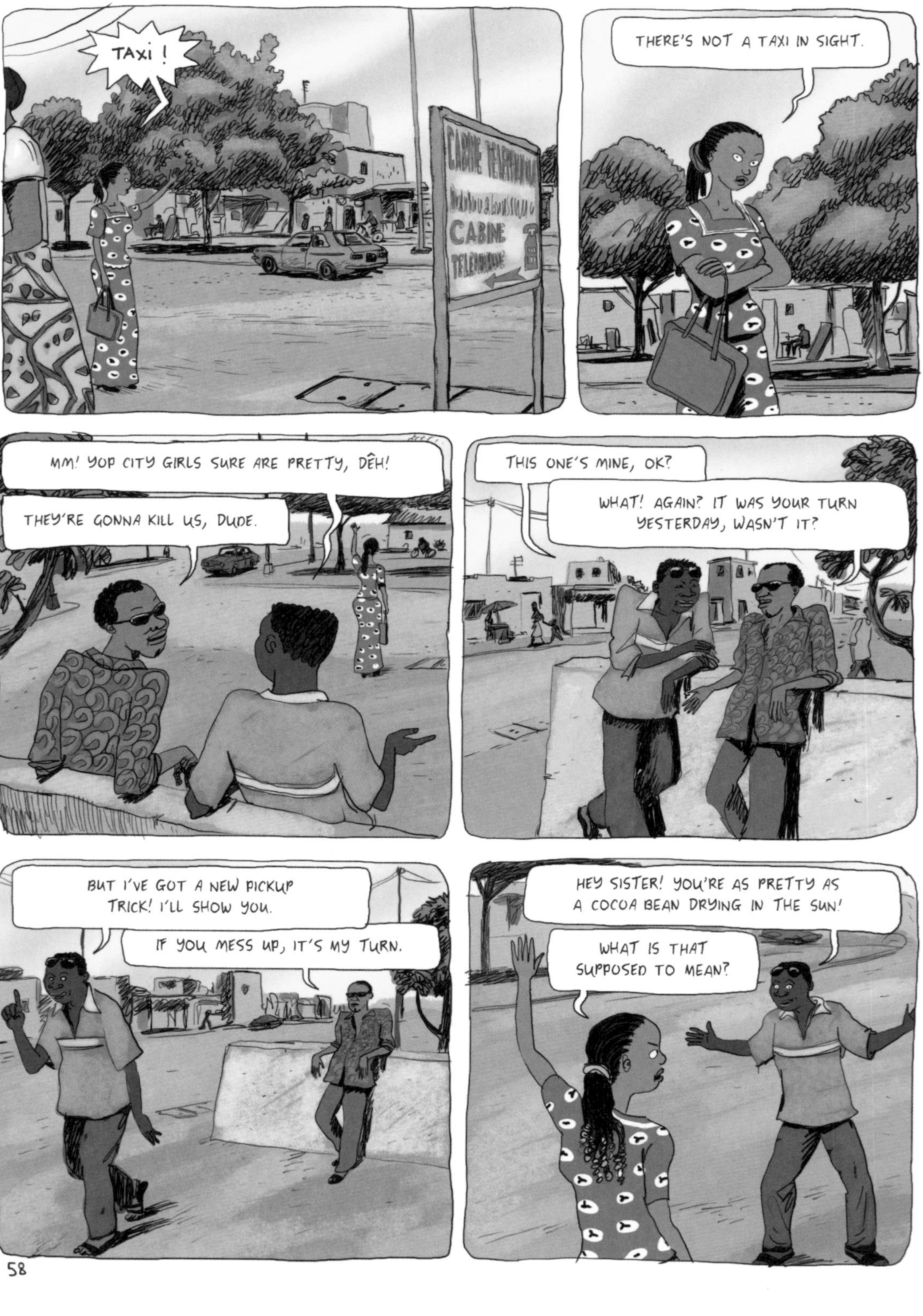
TAXi !
THERE'S NOT A TAXI IN SIGHT.
CABINE TELEPHONIQUE
MM! YOP CITY GIRLS SURE ARE PRETTY, DÊH!
THEY'RE GONNA KILL US, DUDE.
THIS ONE'S MINE, OK?
WHAT! AGAIN? IT WAS YOUR TURN YESTERDAY, WASN'T IT?
BUT I'VE GOT A NEW PICKUP TRICK! I'LL SHOW YOU.
IF YOU MESS UP, IT'S MY TURN.
HEY SISTER! YOU'RE AS PRETTY AS A COCOA BEAN DRYING IN THE SUN!
WHAT IS THAT SUPPOSED TO MEAN?

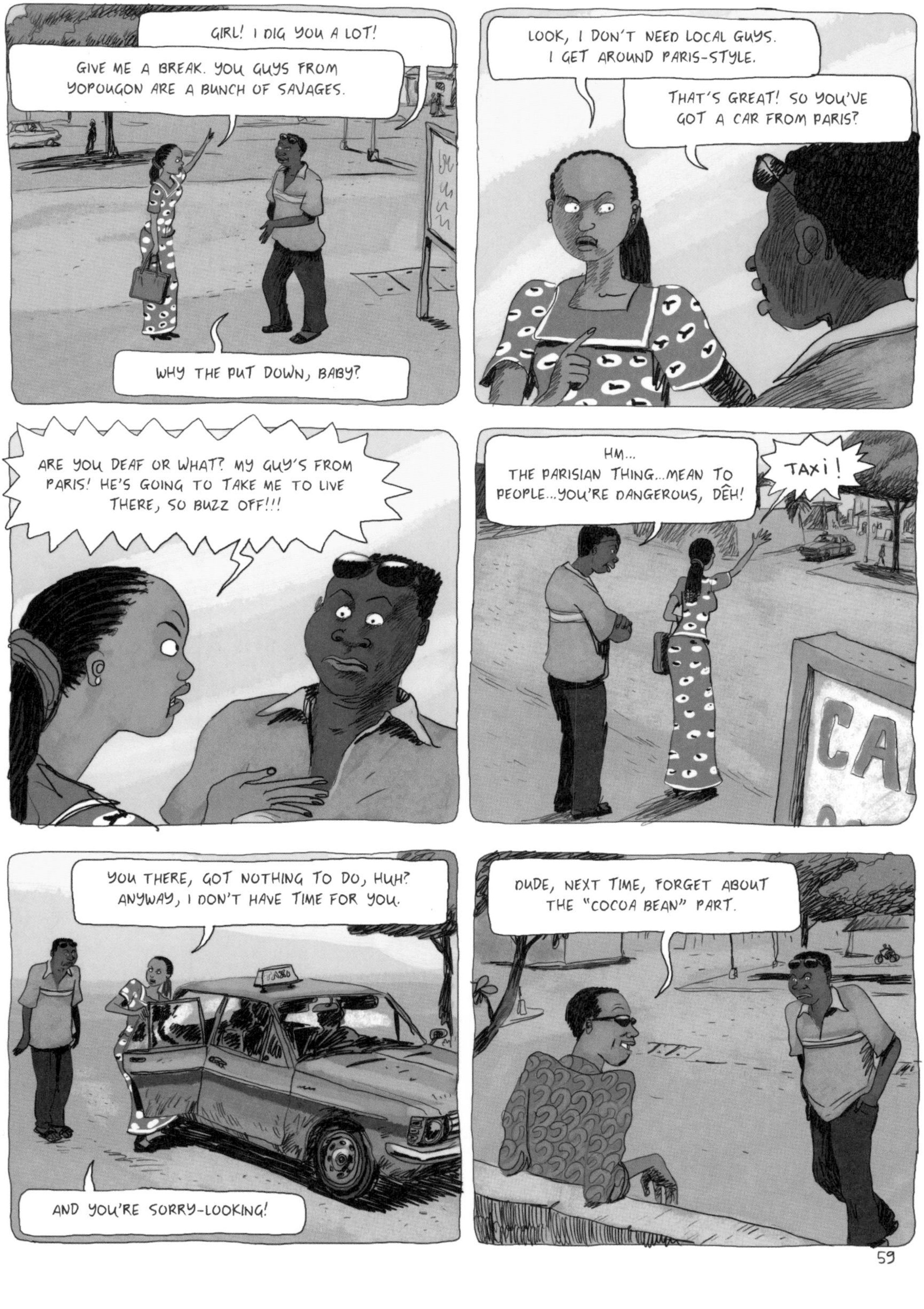
GIRL! I DIG YOU A LOT!
GIVE ME A BREAK. YOU GUYS FROM YOPOUGON ARE A BUNCH OF SAVAGES.
WHY THE PUT DOWN, BABY?
LOOK, I DON'T NEED LOCAL GUYS. I GET AROUND PARIS-STYLE.
THAT'S GREAT! SO YOU'VE GOT A CAR FROM PARIS?
ARE YOU DEAF OR WHAT? MY GUY'S FROM PARIS! HE'S GOING TO TAKE ME TO LIVE THERE, SO BUZZ OFF!!!
HM... THE PARISIAN THING...MEAN TO PEOPLE...YOU'RE DANGEROUS, DÊH!
TAXi!
YOU THERE, GOT NOTHING TO DO, HUH? ANYWAY, I DON'T HAVE TIME FOR YOU.
AND YOU'RE SORRY-LOOKING!
DUDE, NEXT TIME, FORGET ABOUT THE "COCOA BEAN" PART.

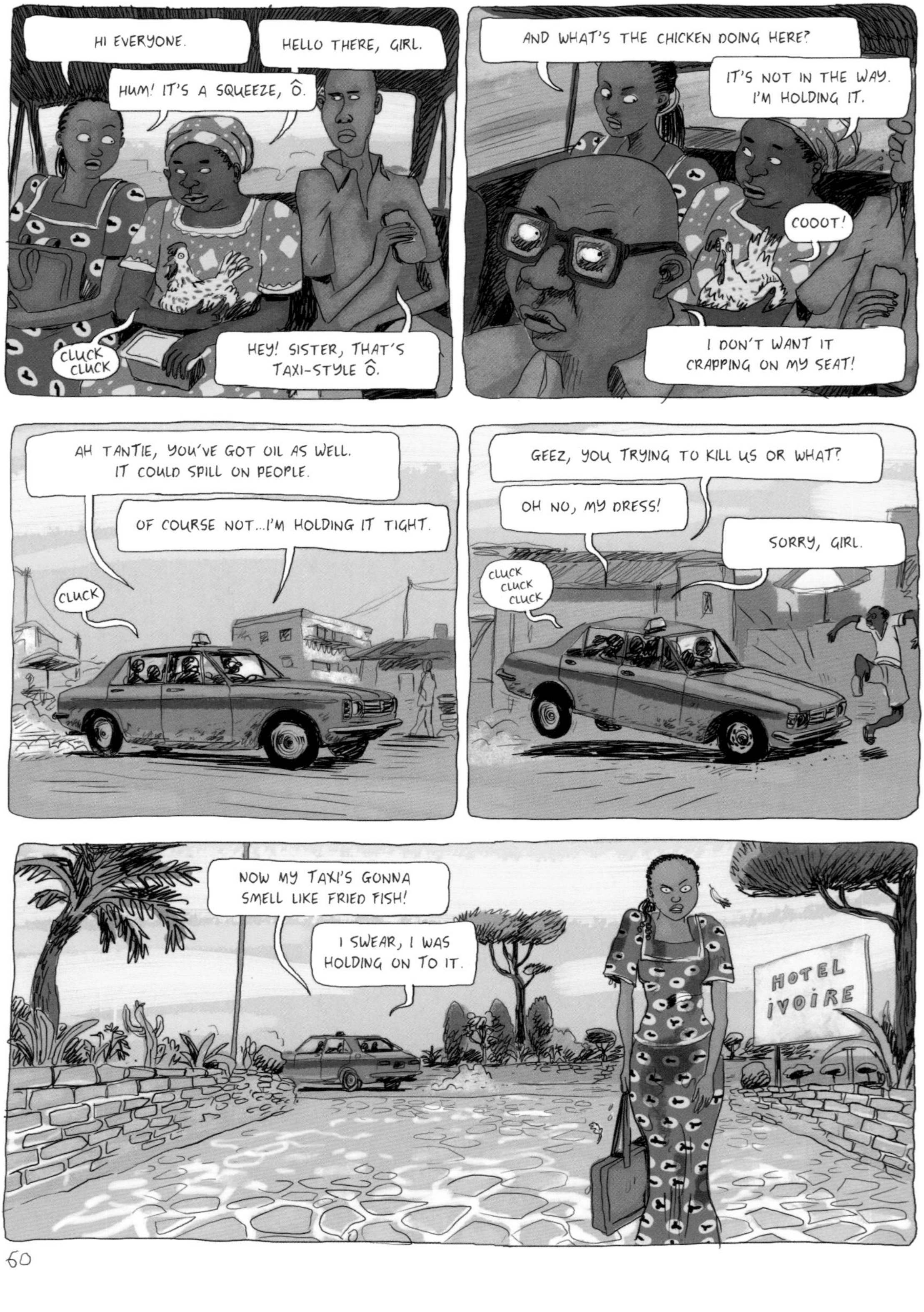
HI EVERYONE.
HELLO THERE, GIRL.
HUM! IT'S A SQUEEZE, Ô.
CLUCK CLUCK
HEY! SISTER, THAT'S TAXI-STYLE Ô.
AND WHAT'S THE CHICKEN DOING HERE?
IT'S NOT IN THE WAY. I'M HOLDING IT.
COOOT!
I DON'T WANT IT CRAPPING ON MY SEAT!
AH TANTIE, YOU'VE GOT OIL AS WELL. IT COULD SPILL ON PEOPLE.
OF COURSE NOT...I'M HOLDING IT TIGHT.
CLUCK
GEEZ, YOU TRYING TO KILL US OR WHAT?
OH NO, MY DRESS!
SORRY, GIRL.
CLUCK CLUCK CLUCK
NOW MY TAXI'S GONNA SMELL LIKE FRIED FISH!
I SWEAR, I WAS HOLDING ON TO IT.
HOTEL IVOIRE

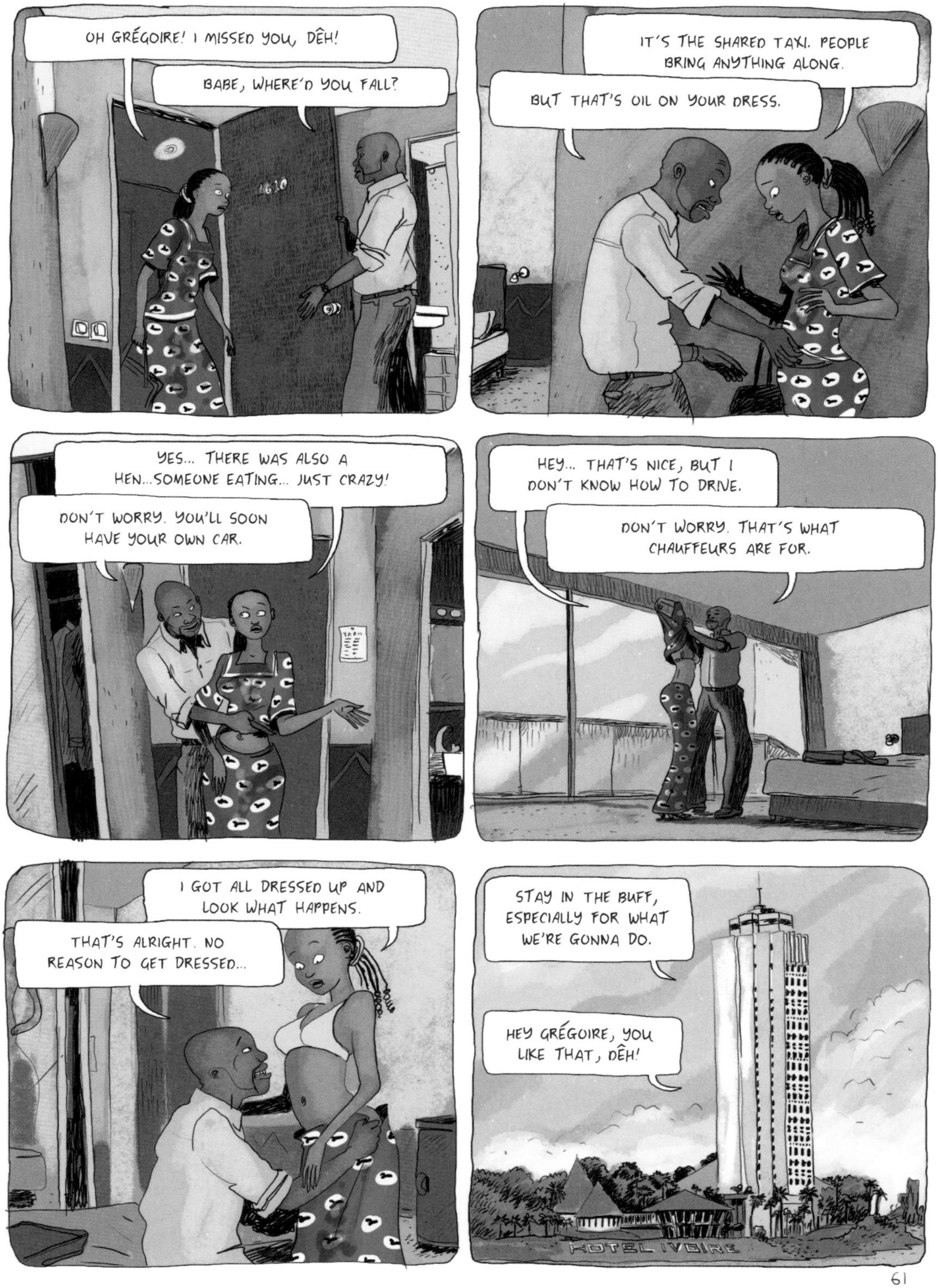
OH GRÉGOIRE! I MISSED YOU, DÊH!
BABE, WHERE'D YOU FALL?
IT'S THE SHARED TAXI. PEOPLE BRING ANYTHING ALONG.
BUT THAT'S OIL ON YOUR DRESS.
YES... THERE WAS ALSO A HEN...SOMEONE EATING... JUST CRAZY!
DON'T WORRY. YOU'LL SOON HAVE YOUR OWN CAR.
HEY... THAT'S NICE, BUT I DON'T KNOW HOW TO DRIVE.
DON'T WORRY. THAT'S WHAT CHAUFFEURS ARE FOR.
I GOT ALL DRESSED UP AND LOOK WHAT HAPPENS.
THAT'S ALRIGHT. NO REASON TO GET DRESSED...
STAY IN THE BUFF, ESPECIALLY FOR WHAT WE'RE GONNA DO.
HEY GRÉGOIRE, YOU LIKE THAT, DÊH!
HOTEL IVOIRE

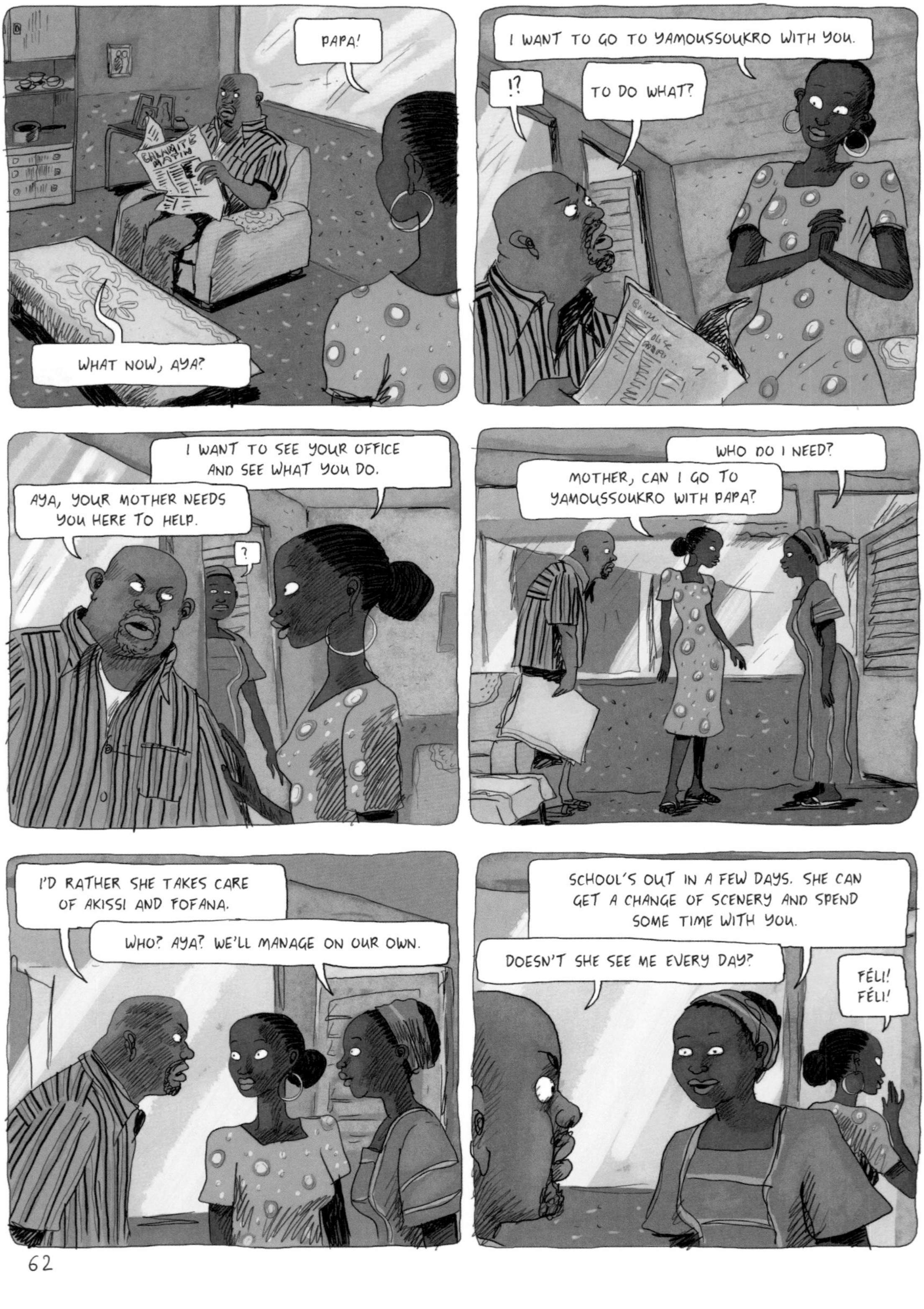
PAPA!
WHAT NOW, AYA?
I WANT TO GO TO YAMOUSSOUKRO WITH YOU.
!?
TO DO WHAT?
I WANT TO SEE YOUR OFFICE AND SEE WHAT YOU DO.
AYA, YOUR MOTHER NEEDS YOU HERE TO HELP.
?
MOTHER, CAN I GO TO YAMOUSSOUKRO WITH PAPA?
WHO DO I NEED?
I'D RATHER SHE TAKES CARE OF AKISSI AND FOFANA.
WHO? AYA? WE'LL MANAGE ON OUR OWN.
SCHOOL'S OUT IN A FEW DAYS. SHE CAN GET A CHANGE OF SCENERY AND SPEND SOME TIME WITH YOU.
DOESN'T SHE SEE ME EVERY DAY?
FÉLI! FÉLI!

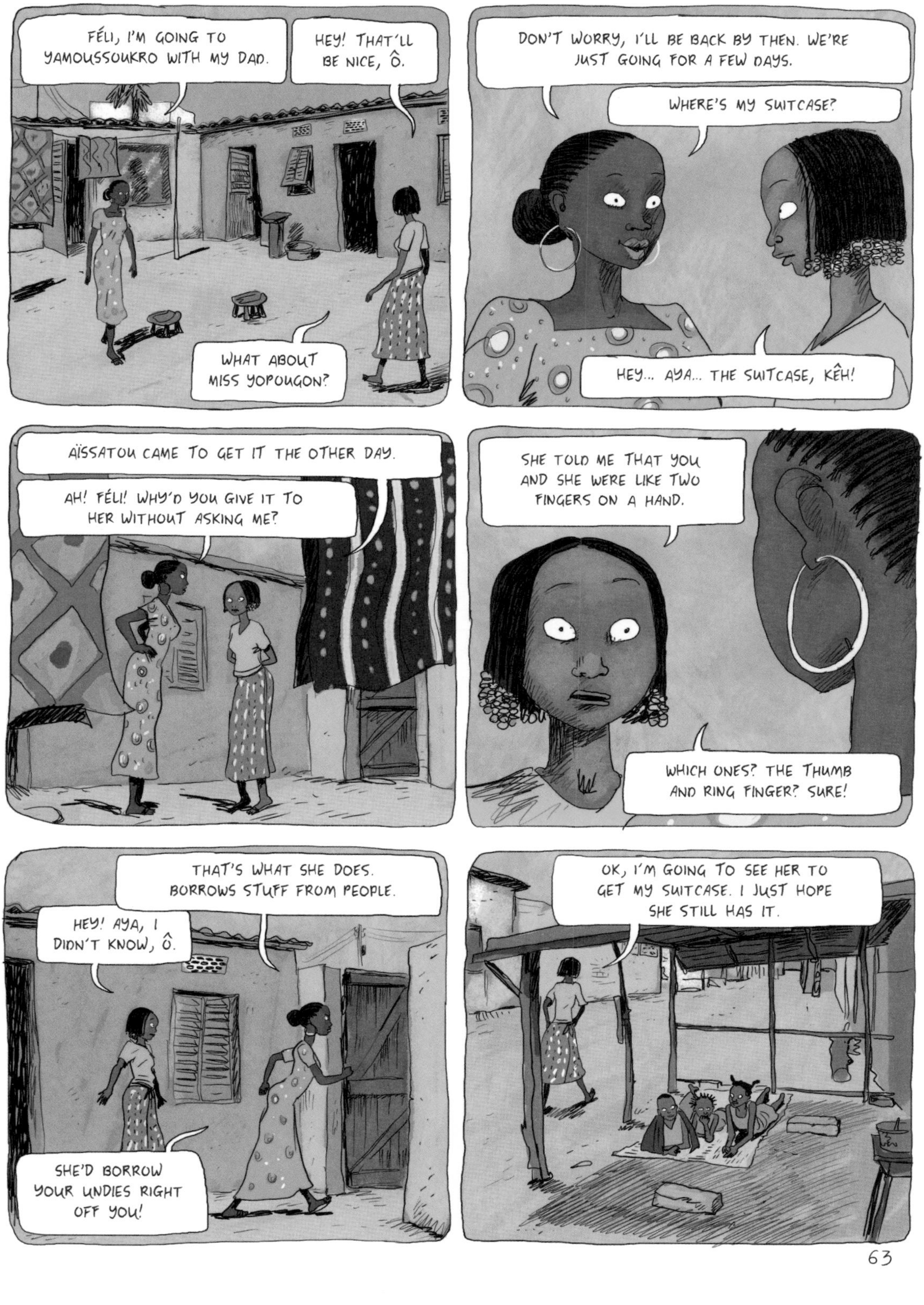
FÉLI, I'M GOING TO YAMOUSSOUKRO WITH MY DAD.
HEY! THAT'LL BE NICE, Ô.
WHAT ABOUT MISS YOPOUGON?
DON'T WORRY, I'LL BE BACK BY THEN. WE'RE JUST GOING FOR A FEW DAYS.
WHERE'S MY SUITCASE?
HEY... AYA... THE SUITCASE, KÊH!
AÏSSATOU CAME TO GET IT THE OTHER DAY.
AH! FÉLI! WHY'D YOU GIVE IT TO HER WITHOUT ASKING ME?
SHE TOLD ME THAT YOU AND SHE WERE LIKE TWO FINGERS ON A HAND.
WHICH ONES? THE THUMB AND RING FINGER? SURE!
THAT'S WHAT SHE DOES. BORROWS STUFF FROM PEOPLE.
HEY! AYA, I DIDN'T KNOW, Ô.
SHE'D BORROW YOUR UNDIES RIGHT OFF YOU!
OK, I'M GOING TO SEE HER TO GET MY SUITCASE. I JUST HOPE SHE STILL HAS IT.

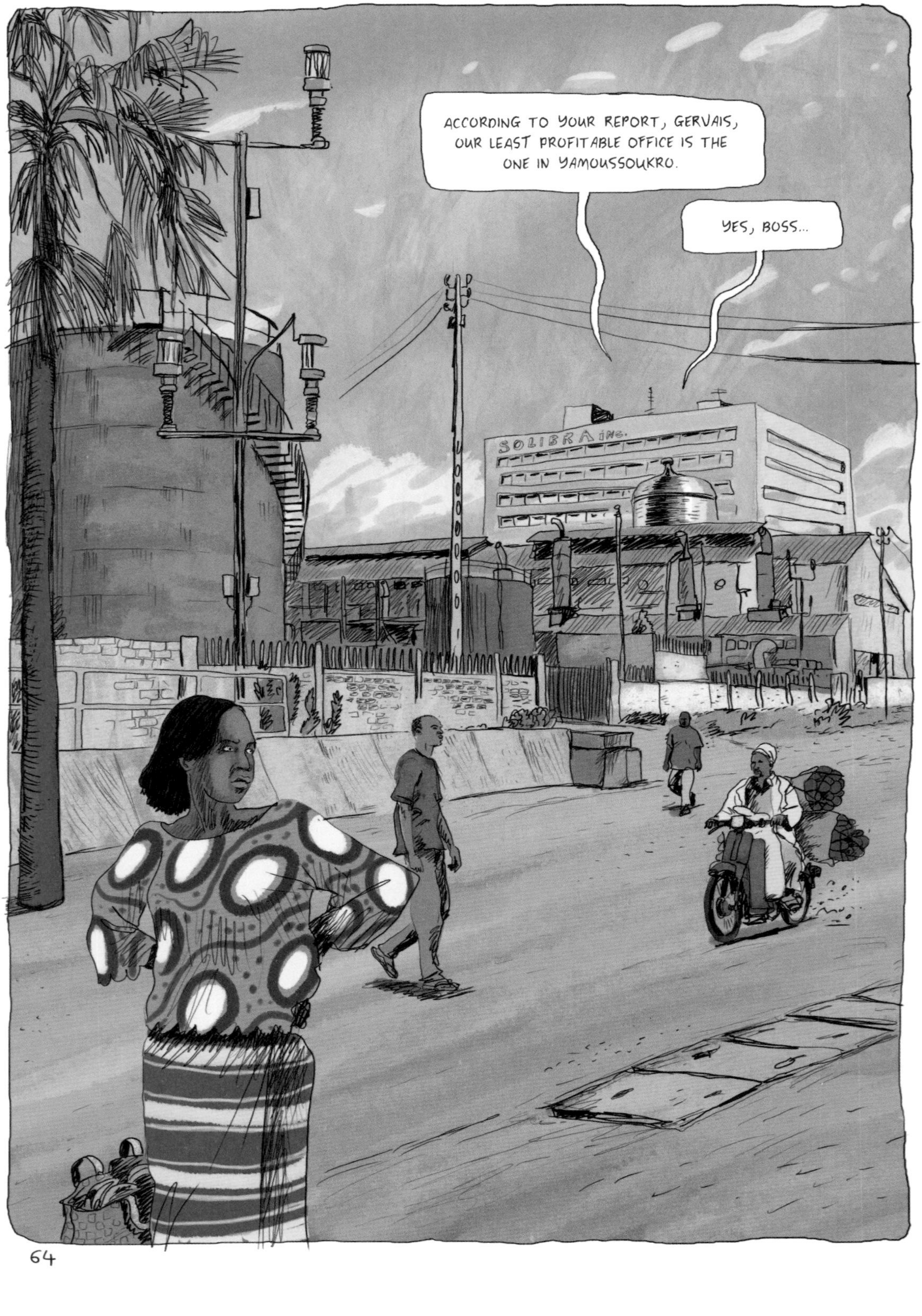
ACCORDING TO YOUR REPORT, GERVAIS, OUR LEAST PROFITABLE OFFICE IS THE ONE IN YAMOUSSOUKRO.
YES, BOSS...
SOLIBRA inc.

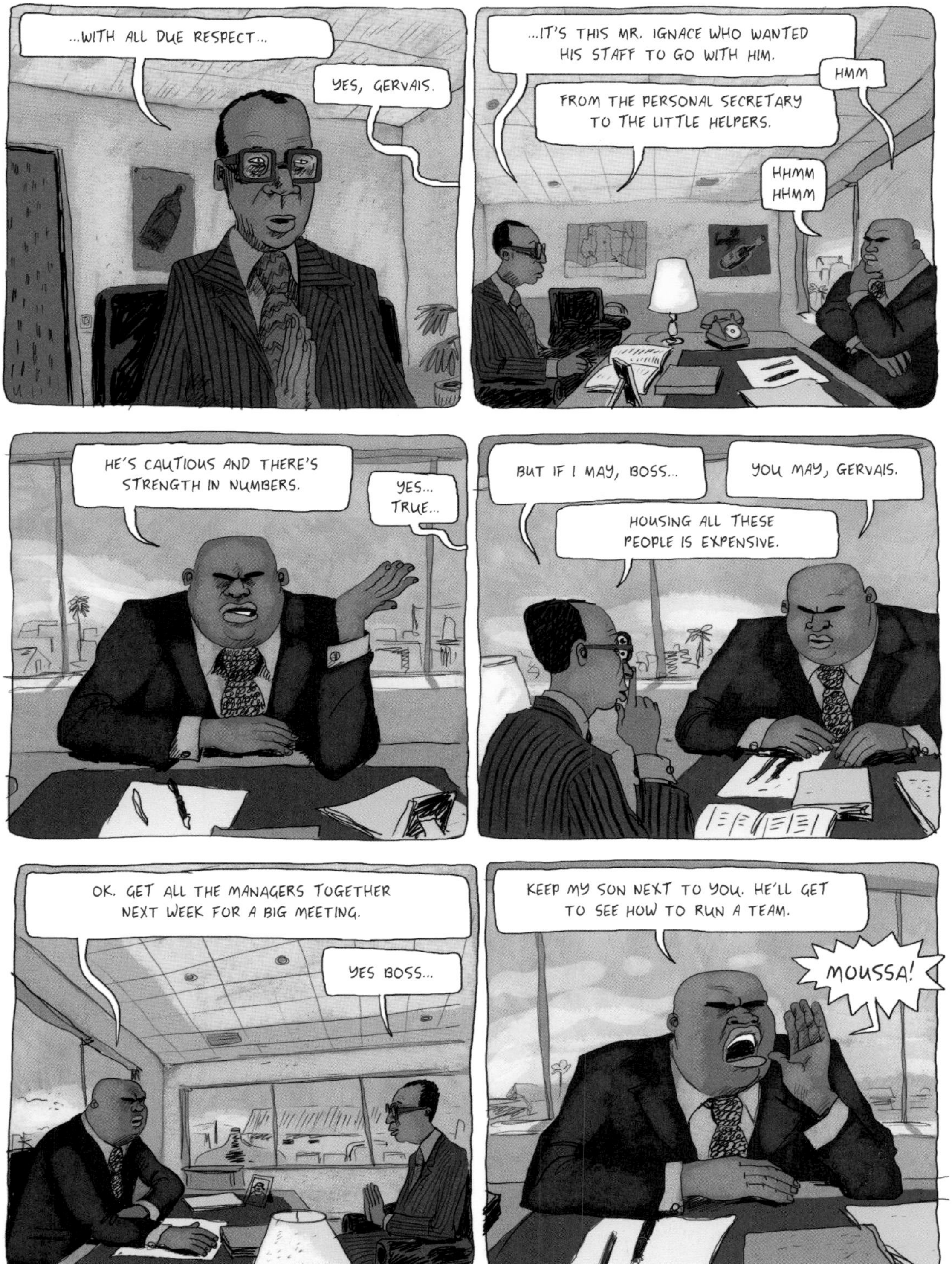
...WITH ALL DUE RESPECT...
YES, GERVAIS.
...IT'S THIS MR. IGNACE WHO WANTED HIS STAFF TO GO WITH HIM.
HMM
FROM THE PERSONAL SECRETARY TO THE LITTLE HELPERS.
HHMM HHMM
HE'S CAUTIOUS AND THERE'S STRENGTH IN NUMBERS.
YES... TRUE...
BUT IF I MAY, BOSS...
YOU MAY, GERVAIS.
HOUSING ALL THESE PEOPLE IS EXPENSIVE.
OK. GET ALL THE MANAGERS TOGETHER NEXT WEEK FOR A BIG MEETING.
YES BOSS...
KEEP MY SON NEXT TO YOU. HE'LL GET TO SEE HOW TO RUN A TEAM.
MOUSSA!

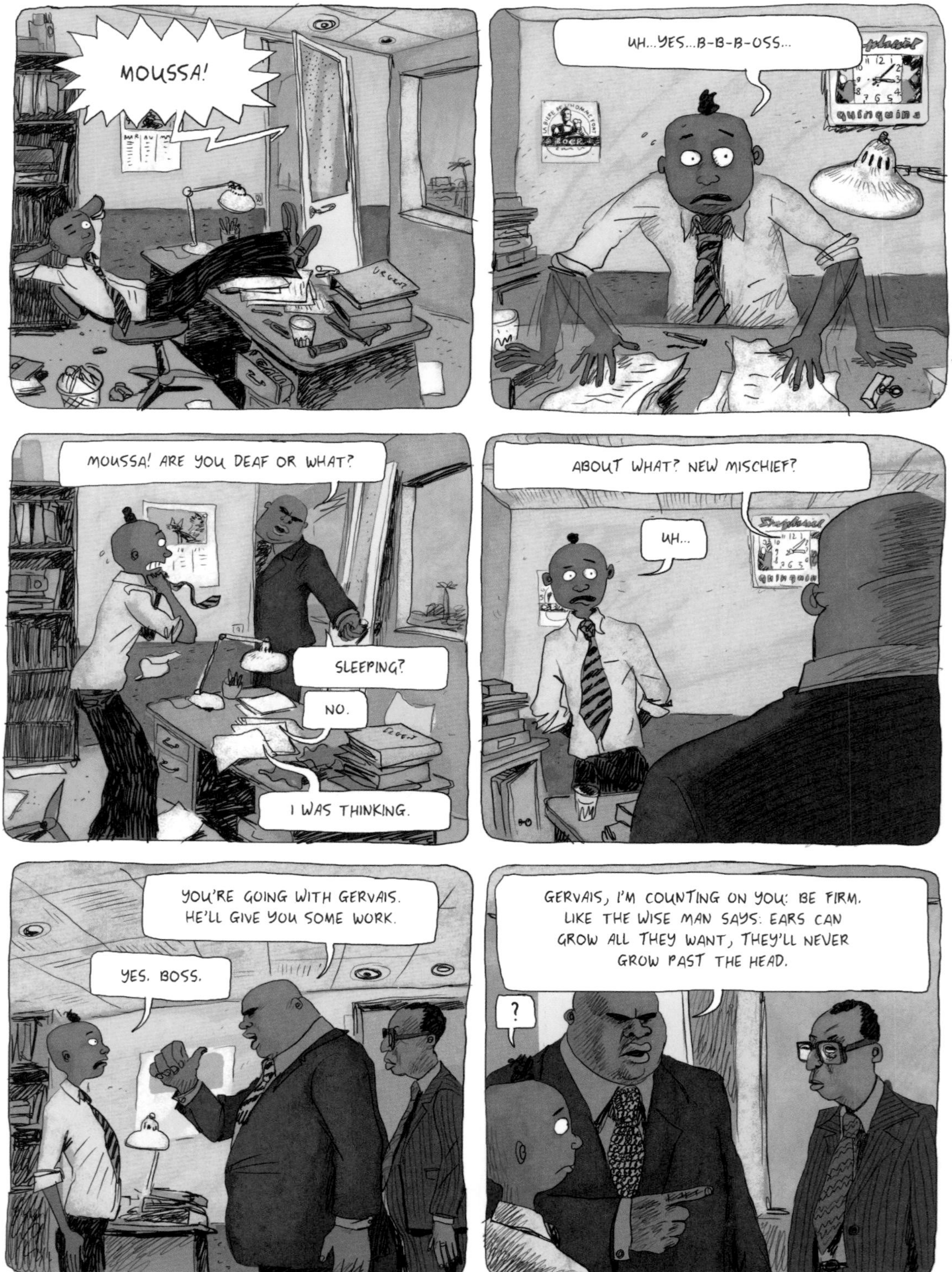
MOUSSA!
UH...YES...B-B-B-OSS...
MOUSSA! ARE YOU DEAF OR WHAT?
SLEEPING?
NO.
I WAS THINKING.
ABOUT WHAT? NEW MISCHIEF?
UH...
YOU'RE GOING WITH GERVAIS. HE'LL GIVE YOU SOME WORK.
YES. BOSS.
GERVAIS, I'M COUNTING ON YOU: BE FIRM. LIKE THE WISE MAN SAYS: EARS CAN GROW ALL THEY WANT, THEY'LL NEVER GROW PAST THE HEAD.
?

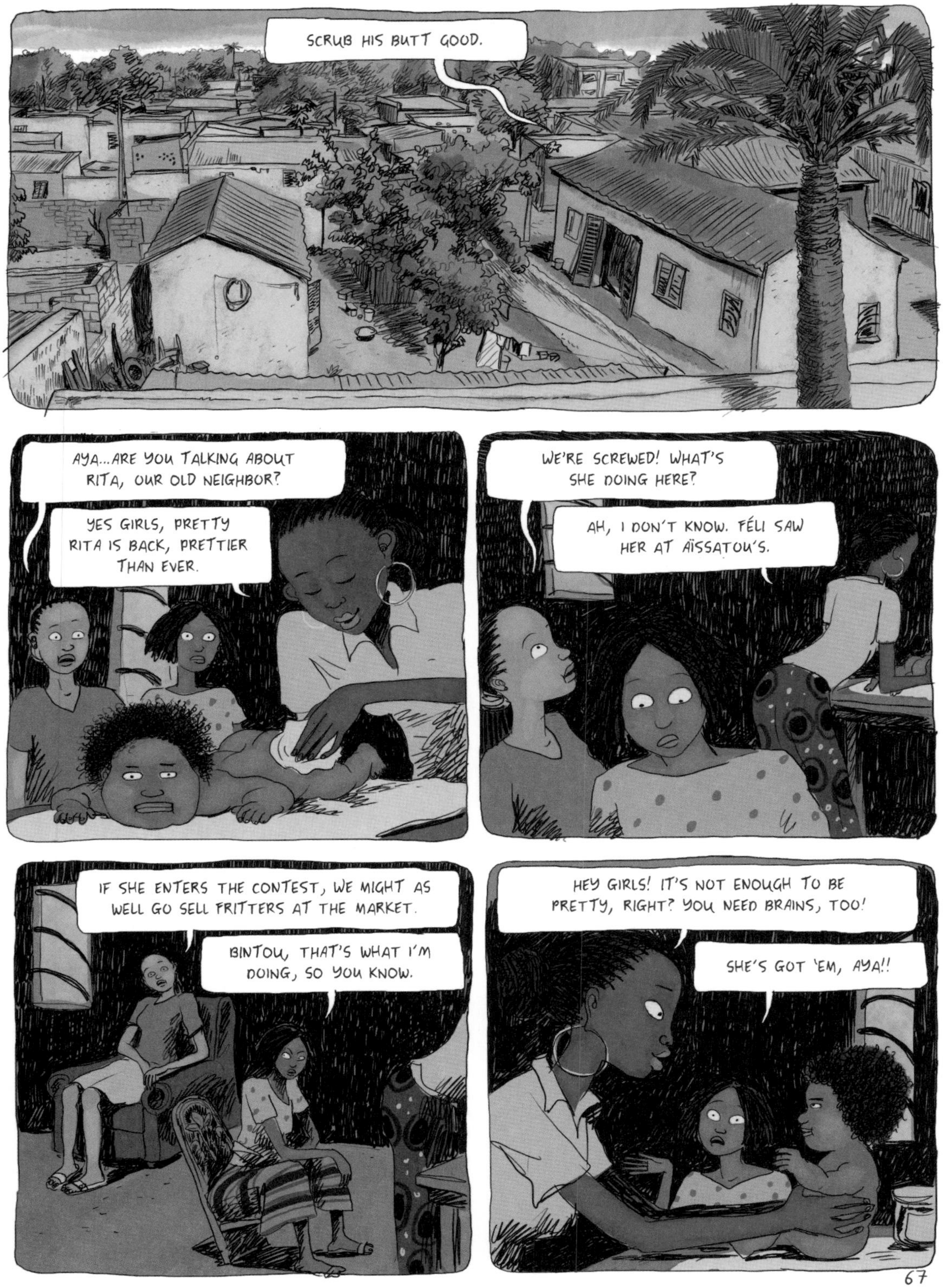
SCRUB HIS BUTT GOOD.
AYA...ARE YOU TALKING ABOUT RITA, OUR OLD NEIGHBOR?
YES GIRLS, PRETTY RITA IS BACK, PRETTIER THAN EVER.
WE'RE SCREWED! WHAT'S SHE DOING HERE?
AH, I DON'T KNOW. FÉLI SAW HER AT AÏSSATOU'S.
IF SHE ENTERS THE CONTEST, WE MIGHT AS WELL GO SELL FRITTERS AT THE MARKET.
BINTOU, THAT'S WHAT I'M DOING, SO YOU KNOW.
HEY GIRLS! IT'S NOT ENOUGH TO BE PRETTY, RIGHT? YOU NEED BRAINS, TOO!
SHE'S GOT 'EM, AYA!!

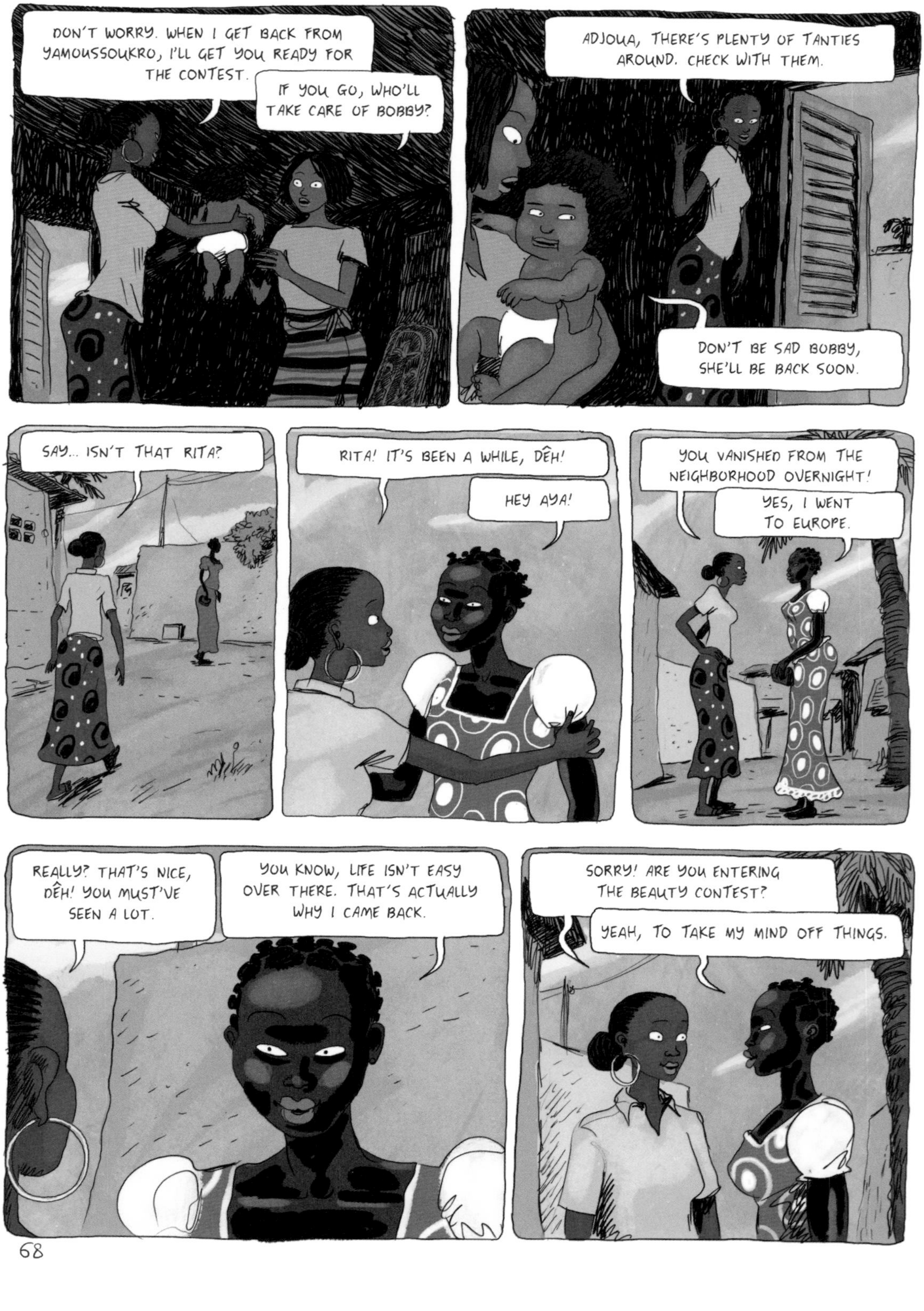

DON'T WORRY. WHEN I GET BACK FROM YAMOUSSOUKRO, I'LL GET YOU READY FOR THE CONTEST.
IF YOU GO, WHO'LL TAKE CARE OF BOBBY?
ADJOUA, THERE'S PLENTY OF TANTIES AROUND. CHECK WITH THEM.
DON'T BE SAD BOBBY, SHE'LL BE BACK SOON.
SAY... ISN'T THAT RITA?
RITA! IT'S BEEN A WHILE, DÊH!
HEY AYA!
YOU VANISHED FROM THE NEIGHBORHOOD OVERNIGHT!
YES, I WENT TO EUROPE.
REALLY? THAT'S NICE, DÊH! YOU MUST'VE SEEN A LOT.
YOU KNOW, LIFE ISN'T EASY OVER THERE. THAT'S ACTUALLY WHY I CAME BACK.
SORRY! ARE YOU ENTERING THE BEAUTY CONTEST?
YEAH, TO TAKE MY MIND OFF THINGS.

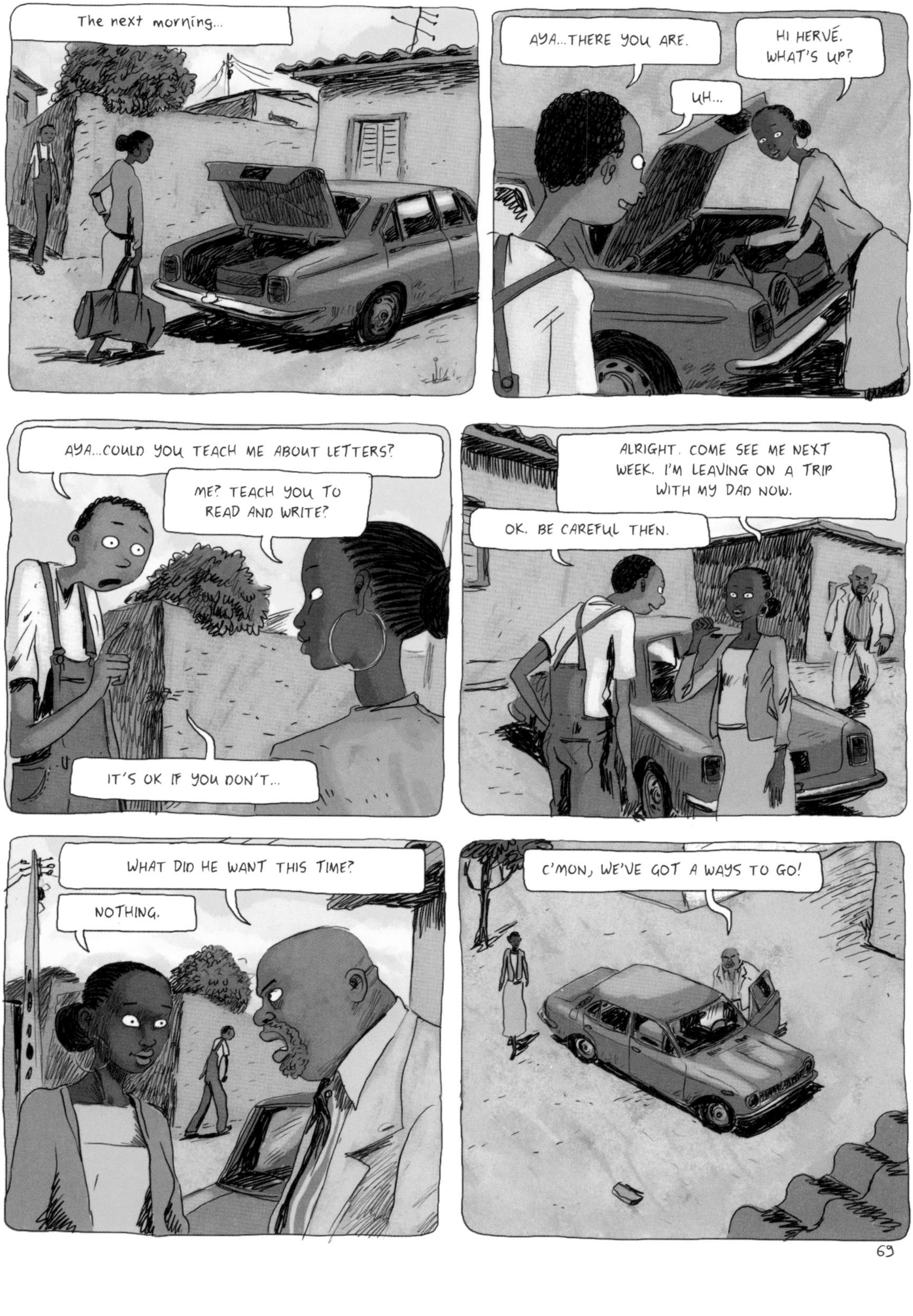
The next morning...
AYA...THERE YOU ARE.
UH...
HI HERVÉ. WHAT'S UP?
AYA...COULD YOU TEACH ME ABOUT LETTERS?
ME? TEACH YOU TO READ AND WRITE?
IT'S OK IF YOU DON'T...
ALRIGHT. COME SEE ME NEXT WEEK. I'M LEAVING ON A TRIP WITH MY DAD NOW.
OK. BE CAREFUL THEN.
WHAT DID HE WANT THIS TIME?
NOTHING.
C'MON, WE'VE GOT A WAYS TO GO!

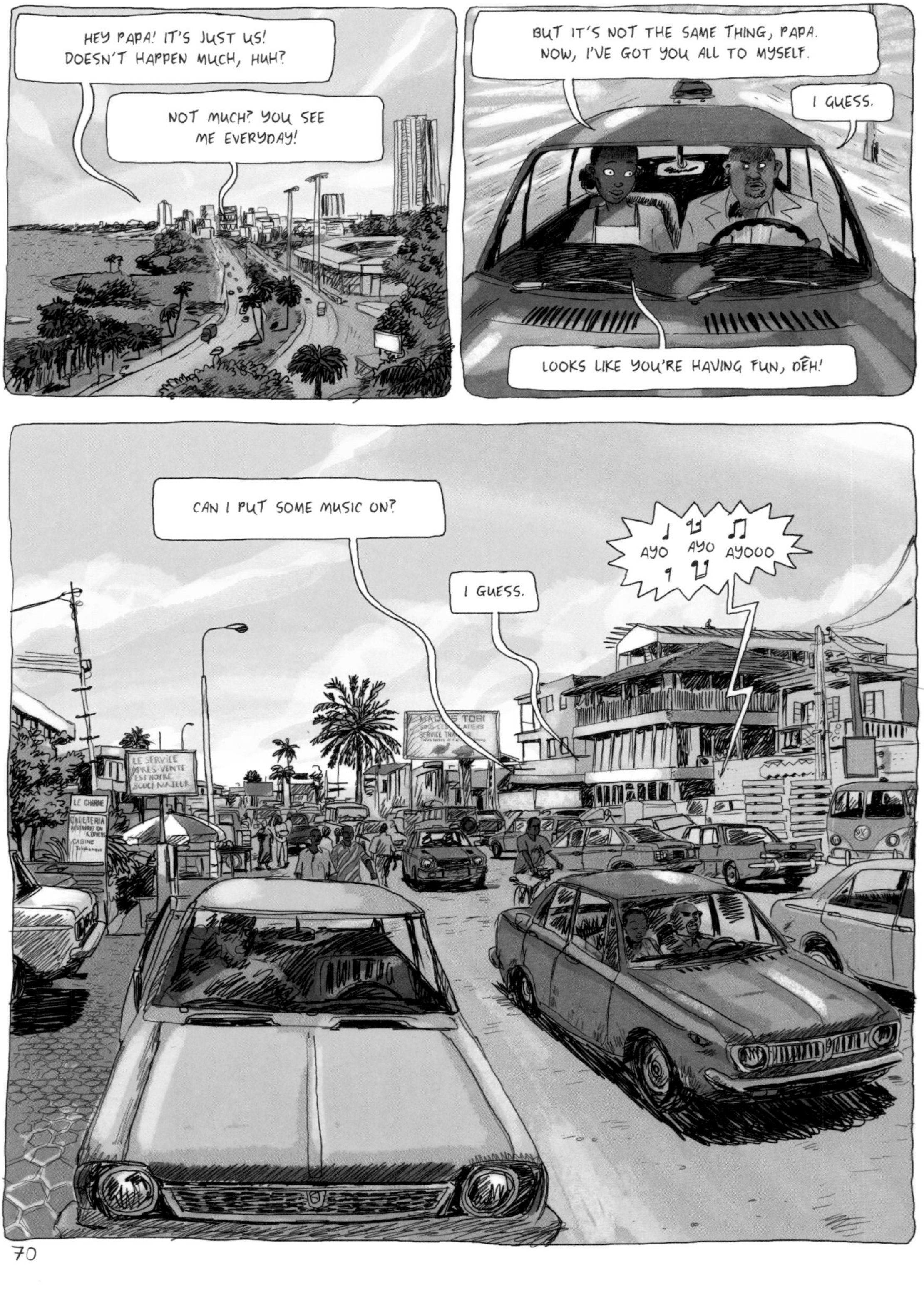
HEY PAPA! IT'S JUST US! DOESN'T HAPPEN MUCH, HUH?
NOT MUCH? YOU SEE ME EVERYDAY!
BUT IT'S NOT THE SAME THING, PAPA. NOW, I'VE GOT YOU ALL TO MYSELF.
I GUESS.
LOOKS LIKE YOU'RE HAVING FUN, DÊH!
CAN I PUT SOME MUSIC ON?
I GUESS.
AYO AYO AYOOO
LE SERVICE APRES-VENTE EST NOTRE SOUCI MAJEUR

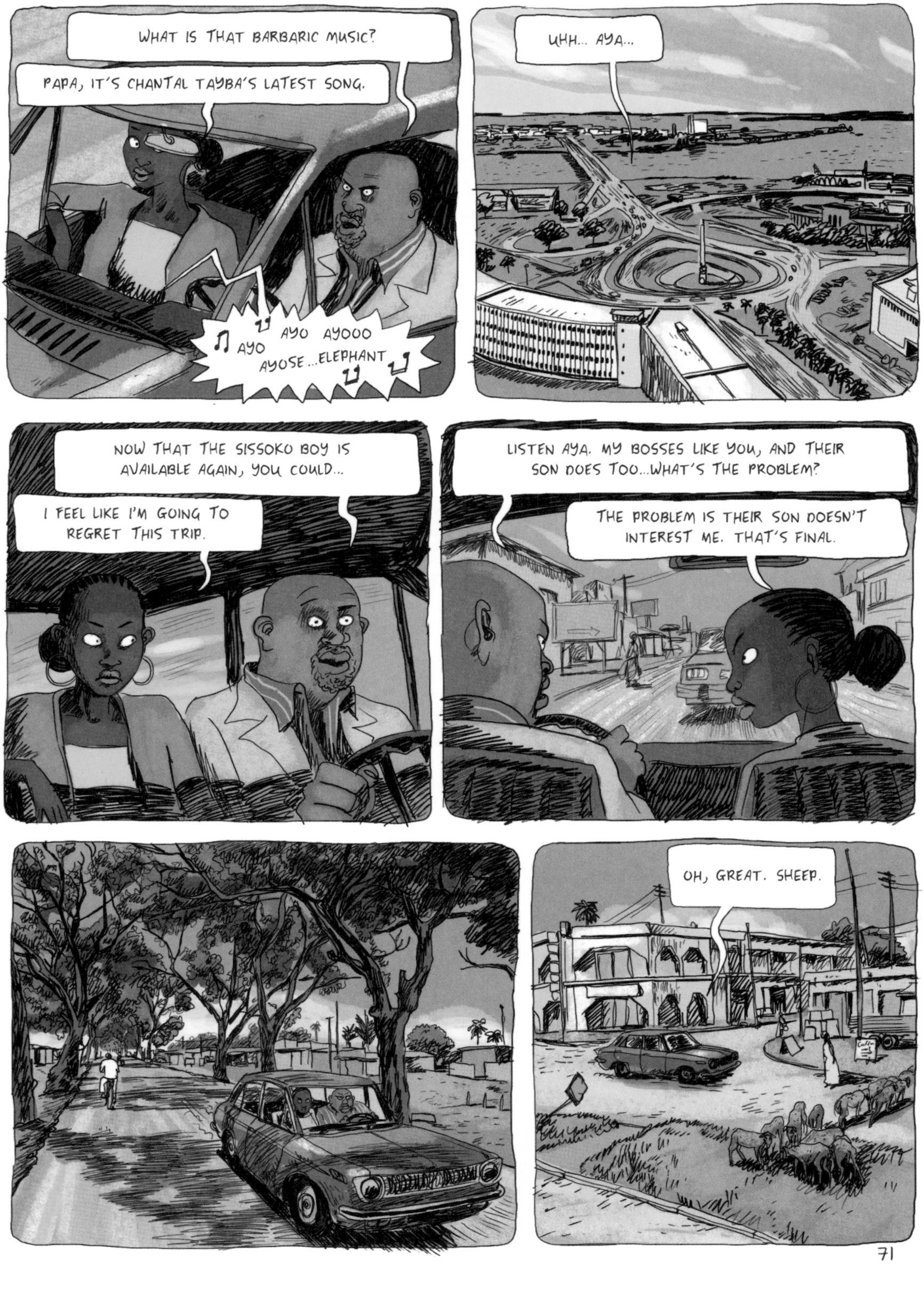

WHAT IS THAT BARBARIC MUSIC?
PAPA, IT'S CHANTAL TAYBA'S LATEST SONG.
AYO AYO AYOOO AYOSE...ELEPHANT
UHH... AYA...
NOW THAT THE SISSOKO BOY IS AVAILABLE AGAIN, YOU COULD...
I FEEL LIKE I'M GOING TO REGRET THIS TRIP.
LISTEN AYA. MY BOSSES LIKE YOU, AND THEIR SON DOES TOO...WHAT'S THE PROBLEM?
THE PROBLEM IS THEIR SON DOESN'T INTEREST ME. THAT'S FINAL.
OH, GREAT. SHEEP.

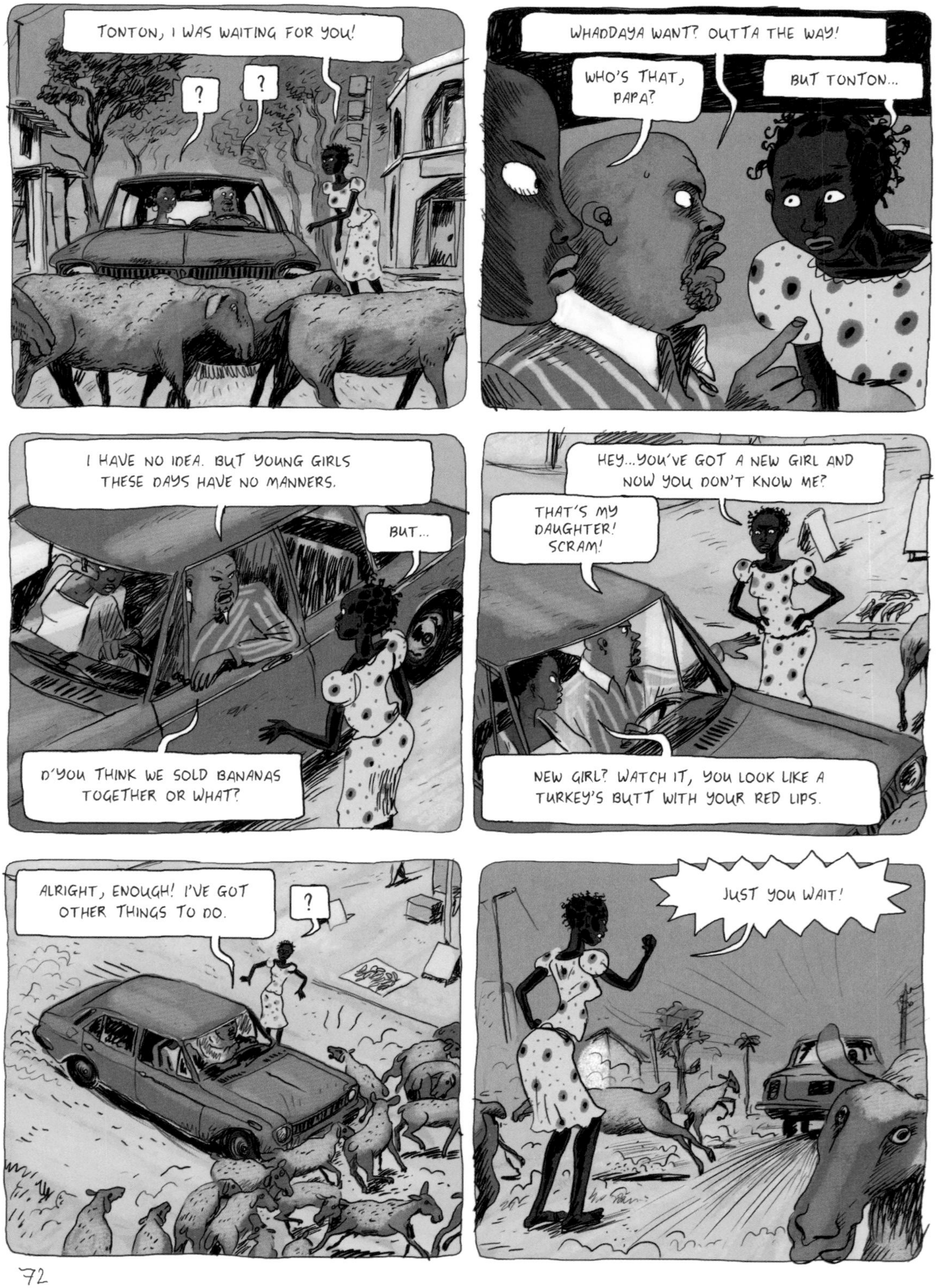
TONTON, I WAS WAITING FOR YOU!
?
?
WHADDAYA WANT? OUTTA THE WAY!
WHO'S THAT, PAPA?
BUT TONTON...
I HAVE NO IDEA. BUT YOUNG GIRLS THESE DAYS HAVE NO MANNERS.
BUT...
D'YOU THINK WE SOLD BANANAS TOGETHER OR WHAT?
HEY...YOU'VE GOT A NEW GIRL AND NOW YOU DON'T KNOW ME?
THAT'S MY DAUGHTER! SCRAM!
NEW GIRL? WATCH IT, YOU LOOK LIKE A TURKEY'S BUTT WITH YOUR RED LIPS.
ALRIGHT, ENOUGH! I'VE GOT OTHER THINGS TO DO.
?
JUST YOU WAIT!

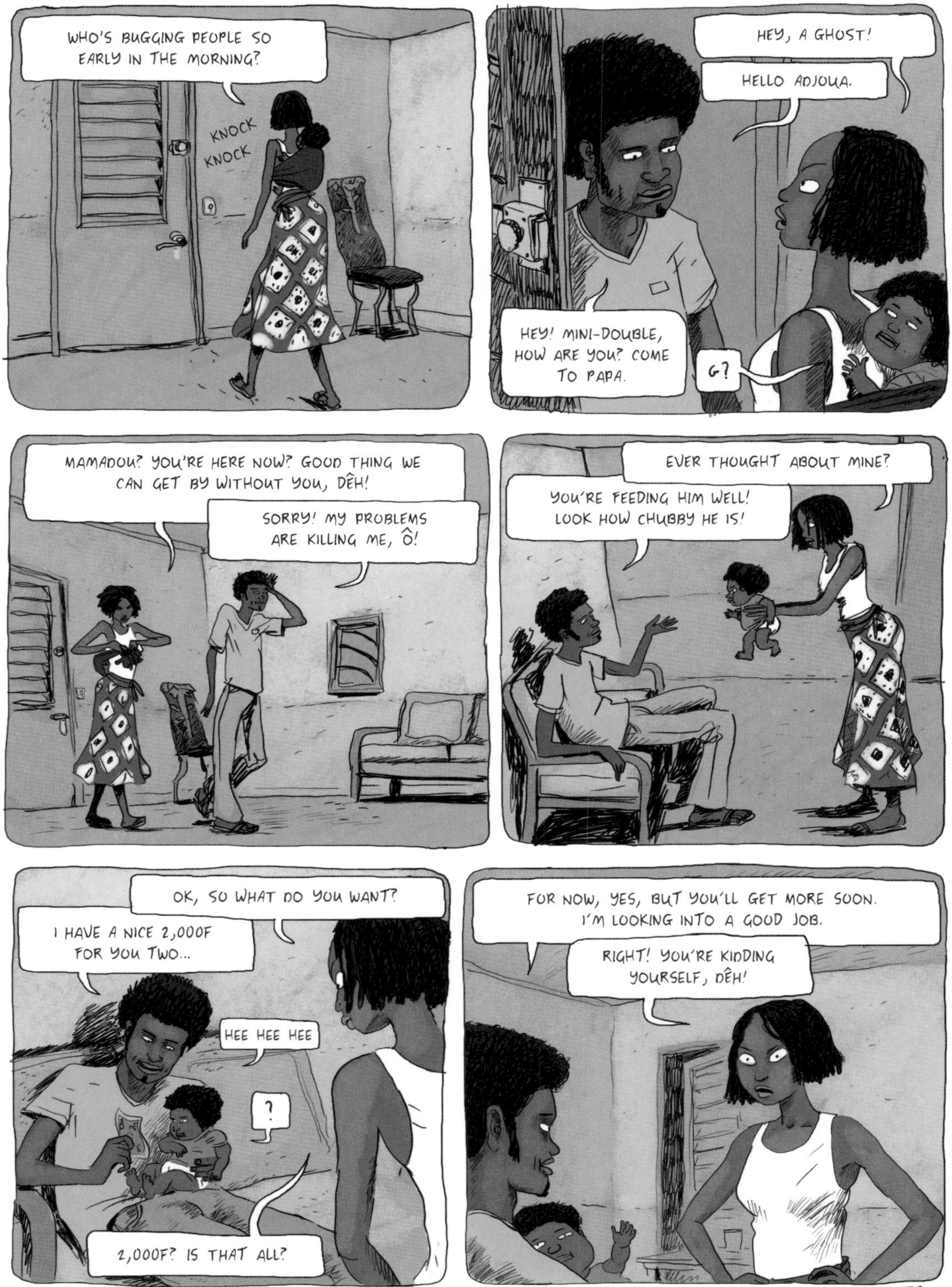

WHO'S BUGGING PEOPLE SO EARLY IN THE MORNING?
KNOCK KNOCK
HEY, A GHOST!
HELLO ADJOUA.
HEY! MINI-DOUBLE, HOW ARE YOU? COME TO PAPA.
G?
MAMADOU? YOU'RE HERE NOW? GOOD THING WE CAN GET BY WITHOUT YOU, DÊH!
SORRY! MY PROBLEMS ARE KILLING ME, Ô!
EVER THOUGHT ABOUT MINE?
YOU'RE FEEDING HIM WELL! LOOK HOW CHUBBY HE IS!
OK, SO WHAT DO YOU WANT?
I HAVE A NICE 2,000F FOR YOU TWO...
HEE HEE HEE
?
2,000F? IS THAT ALL?
FOR NOW, YES, BUT YOU'LL GET MORE SOON. I'M LOOKING INTO A GOOD JOB.
RIGHT! YOU'RE KIDDING YOURSELF, DÊH!

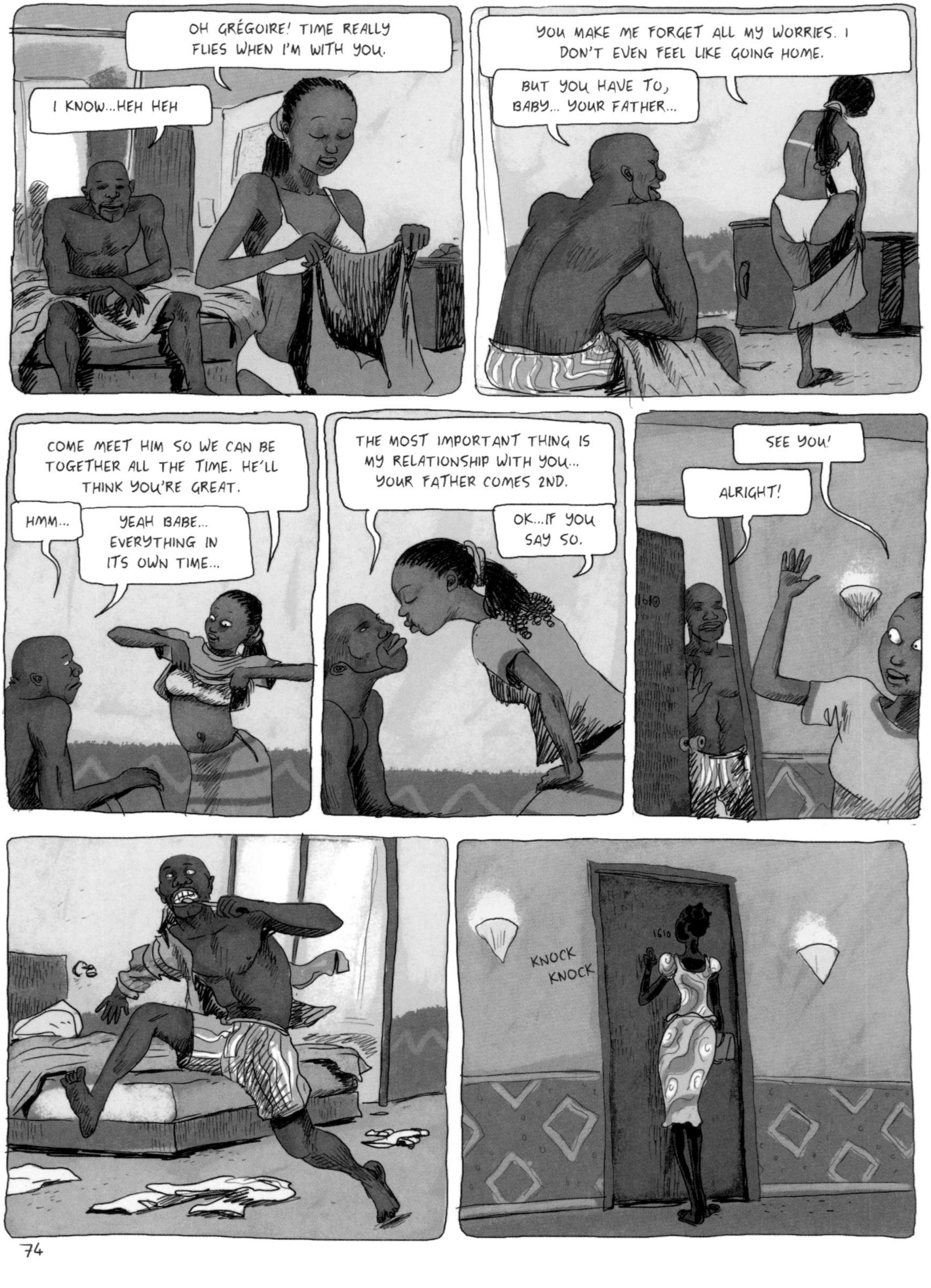
OH GRÉGOIRE! TIME REALLY FLIES WHEN I'M WITH YOU.
I KNOW...HEH HEH
YOU MAKE ME FORGET ALL MY WORRIES. I DON'T EVEN FEEL LIKE GOING HOME.
BUT YOU HAVE TO, BABY... YOUR FATHER...
COME MEET HIM SO WE CAN BE TOGETHER ALL THE TIME. HE'LL THINK YOU'RE GREAT.
HMM...
YEAH BABE... EVERYTHING IN ITS OWN TIME...
THE MOST IMPORTANT THING IS MY RELATIONSHIP WITH YOU... YOUR FATHER COMES 2ND.
OK...IF YOU SAY SO.
SEE YOU!
ALRIGHT!
1610
KNOCK KNOCK
1610

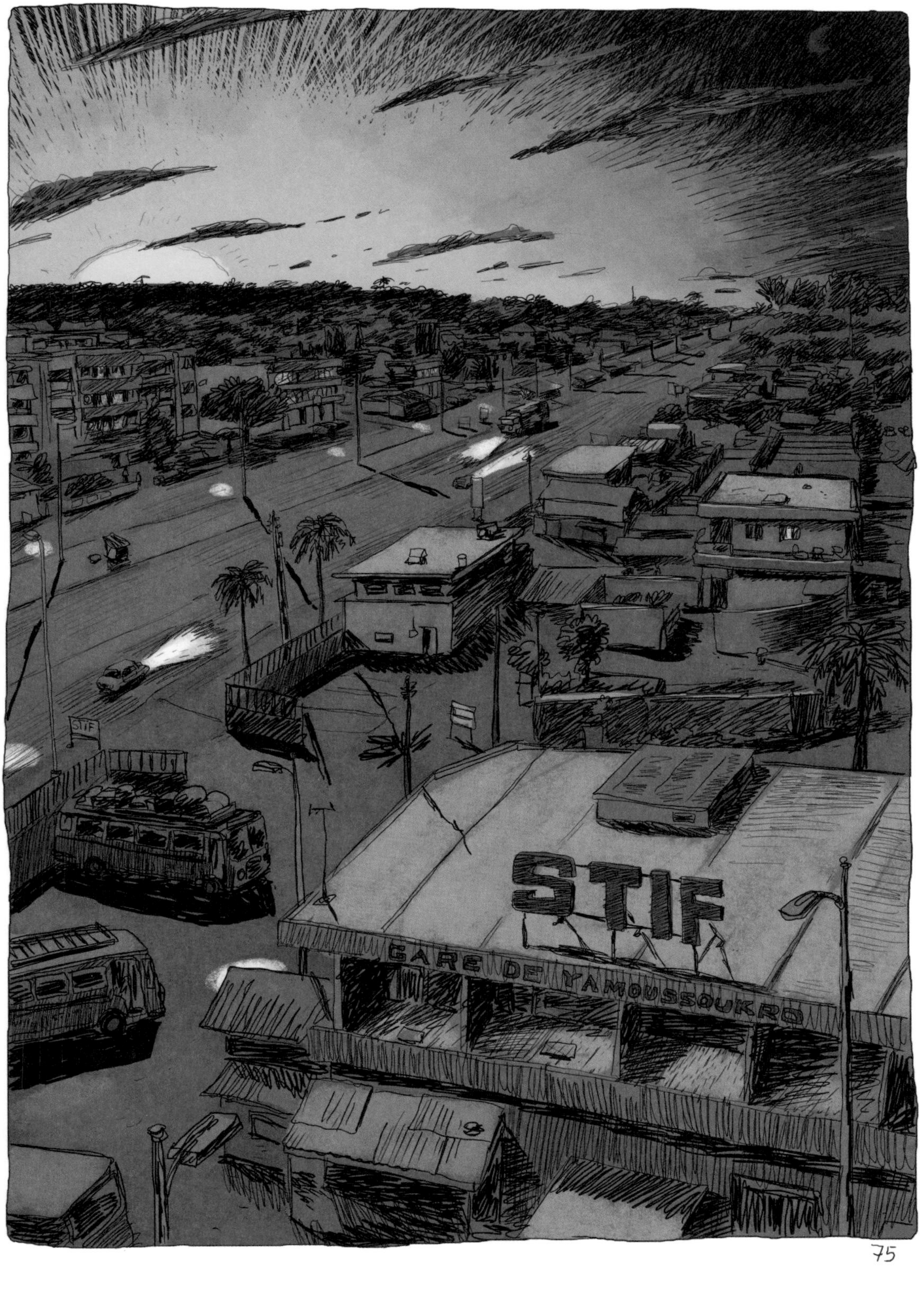
STIF
STIF
GARE DE YAMOUSSOUKRO

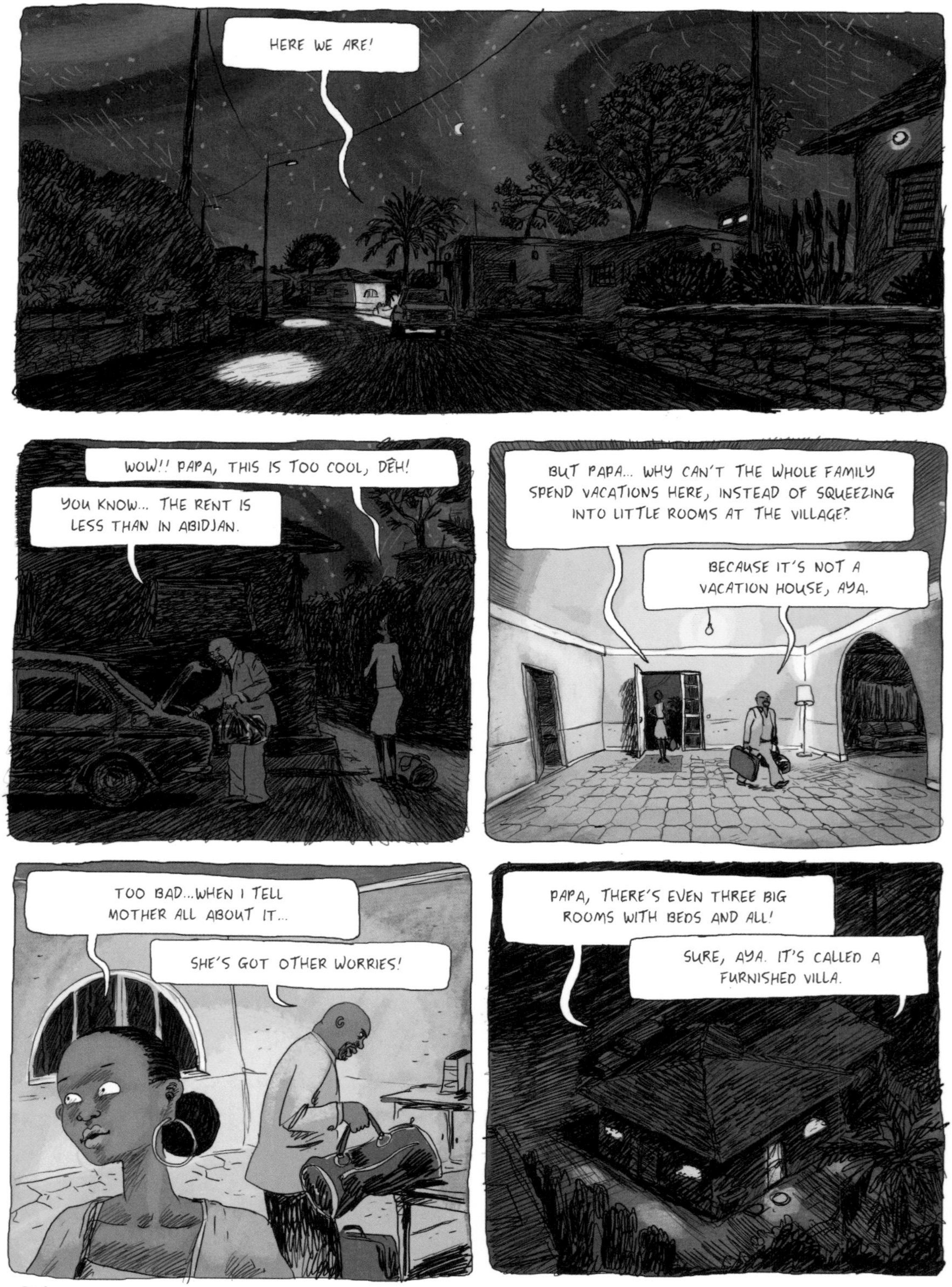
HERE WE ARE!
WOW!! PAPA, THIS IS TOO COOL, DÊH!
YOU KNOW... THE RENT IS LESS THAN IN ABIDJAN.
BUT PAPA... WHY CAN'T THE WHOLE FAMILY SPEND VACATIONS HERE, INSTEAD OF SQUEEZING INTO LITTLE ROOMS AT THE VILLAGE?
BECAUSE IT'S NOT A VACATION HOUSE, AYA.
TOO BAD...WHEN I TELL MOTHER ALL ABOUT IT...
SHE'S GOT OTHER WORRIES!
PAPA, THERE'S EVEN THREE BIG ROOMS WITH BEDS AND ALL!
SURE, AYA. IT'S CALLED A FURNISHED VILLA.

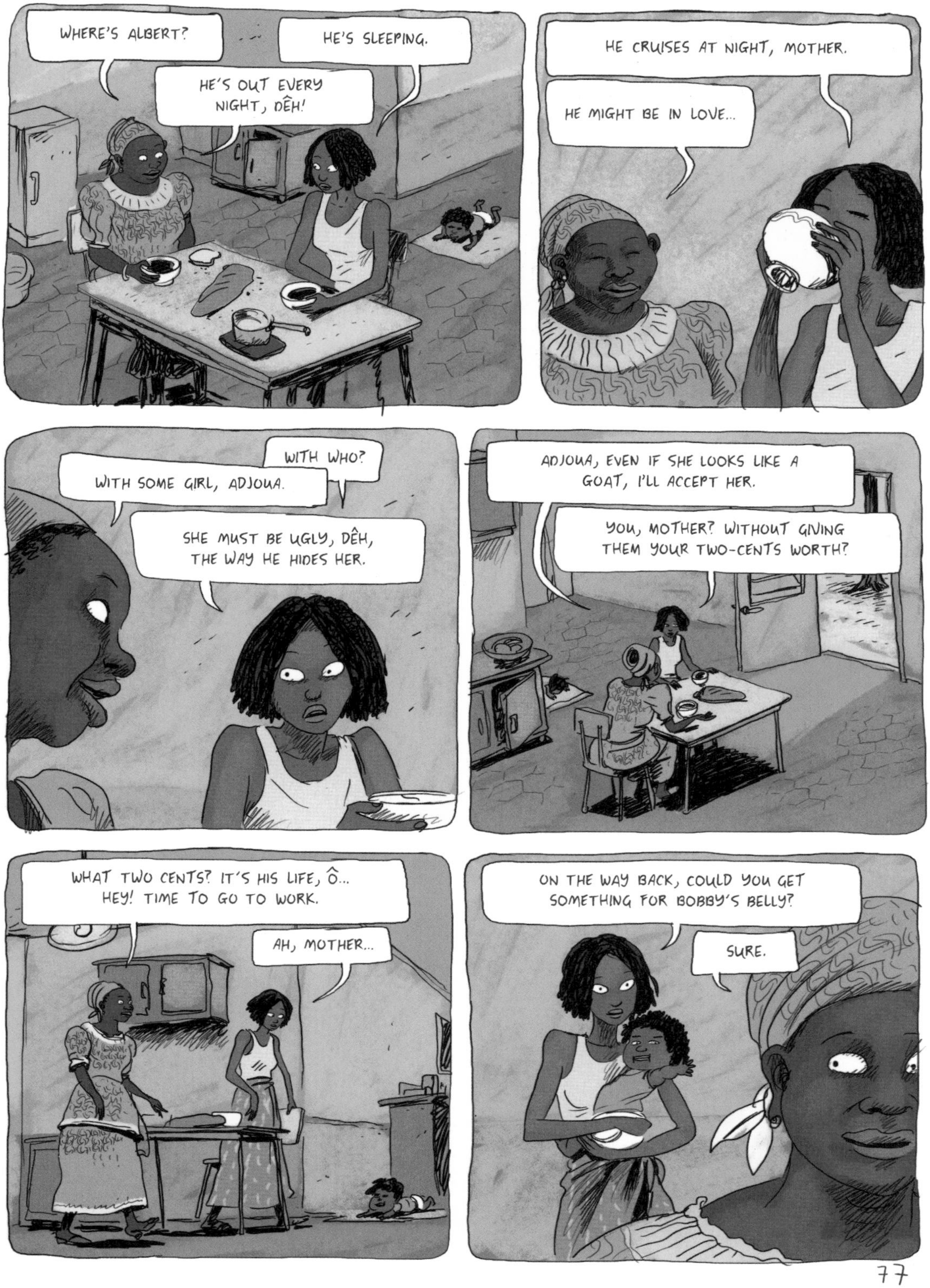
WHERE'S ALBERT?
HE'S SLEEPING.
HE'S OUT EVERY NIGHT, DÊH!
HE CRUISES AT NIGHT, MOTHER.
HE MIGHT BE IN LOVE...
WITH WHO?
WITH SOME GIRL, ADJOUA.
SHE MUST BE UGLY, DÊH, THE WAY HE HIDES HER.
ADJOUA, EVEN IF SHE LOOKS LIKE A GOAT, I'LL ACCEPT HER.
YOU, MOTHER? WITHOUT GIVING THEM YOUR TWO-CENTS WORTH?
WHAT TWO CENTS? IT'S HIS LIFE, Ô... HEY! TIME TO GO TO WORK.
AH, MOTHER...
ON THE WAY BACK, COULD YOU GET SOMETHING FOR BOBBY'S BELLY?
SURE.

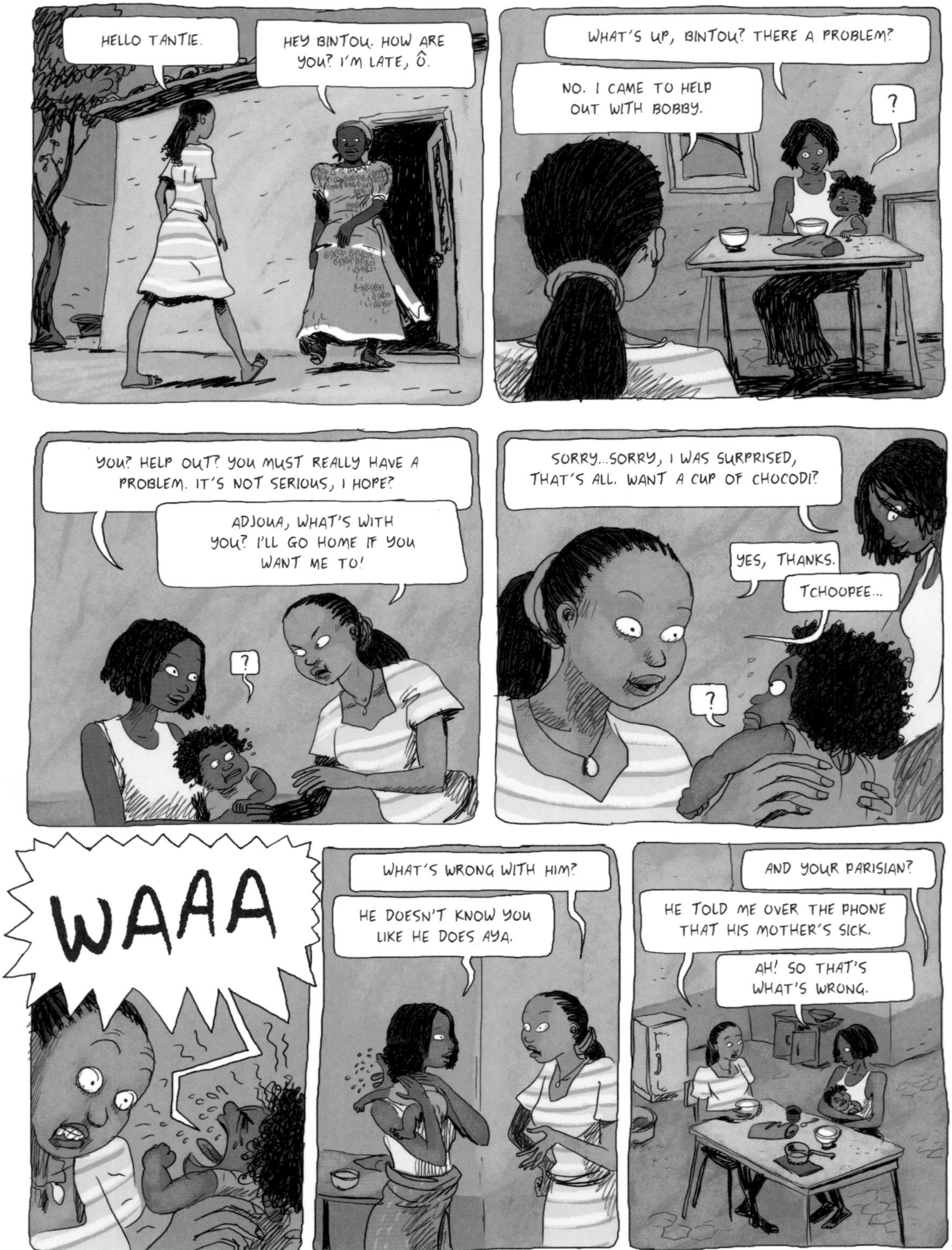
HELLO TANTIE.
HEY BINTOU. HOW ARE YOU? I'M LATE, Ô.
WHAT'S UP, BINTOU? THERE A PROBLEM?
NO. I CAME TO HELP OUT WITH BOBBY.
?
YOU? HELP OUT? YOU MUST REALLY HAVE A PROBLEM. IT'S NOT SERIOUS, I HOPE?
ADJOUA, WHAT'S WITH YOU? I'LL GO HOME IF YOU WANT ME TO!
?
SORRY...SORRY, I WAS SURPRISED, THAT'S ALL. WANT A CUP OF CHOCODI?
YES, THANKS.
TCHOOPEE...
?
WAAA
WHAT'S WRONG WITH HIM?
HE DOESN'T KNOW YOU LIKE HE DOES AYA.
AND YOUR PARISIAN?
HE TOLD ME OVER THE PHONE THAT HIS MOTHER'S SICK.
AH! SO THAT'S WHAT'S WRONG.

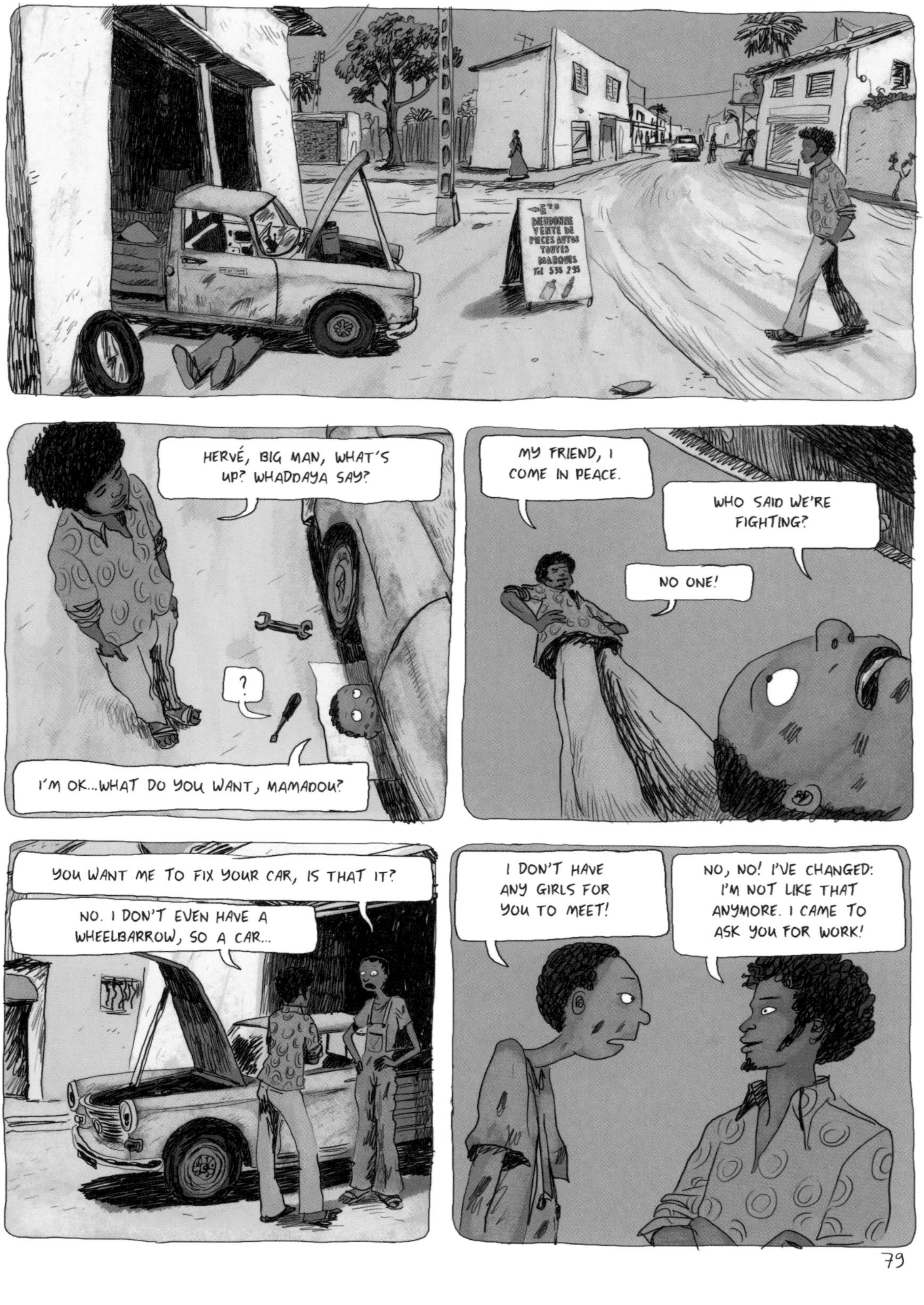

Ets
DIEUDONNE
VENTE DE
PIECES AUTOS
TOUTES
MARQUES
Tél 535 295
HERVÉ, BIG MAN, WHAT'S UP? WHADDAYA SAY?
?
I'M OK...WHAT DO YOU WANT, MAMADOU?
MY FRIEND, I COME IN PEACE.
WHO SAID WE'RE FIGHTING?
NO ONE!
YOU WANT ME TO FIX YOUR CAR, IS THAT IT?
NO. I DON'T EVEN HAVE A WHEELBARROW, SO A CAR...
I DON'T HAVE ANY GIRLS FOR YOU TO MEET!
NO, NO! I'VE CHANGED: I'M NOT LIKE THAT ANYMORE. I CAME TO ASK YOU FOR WORK!

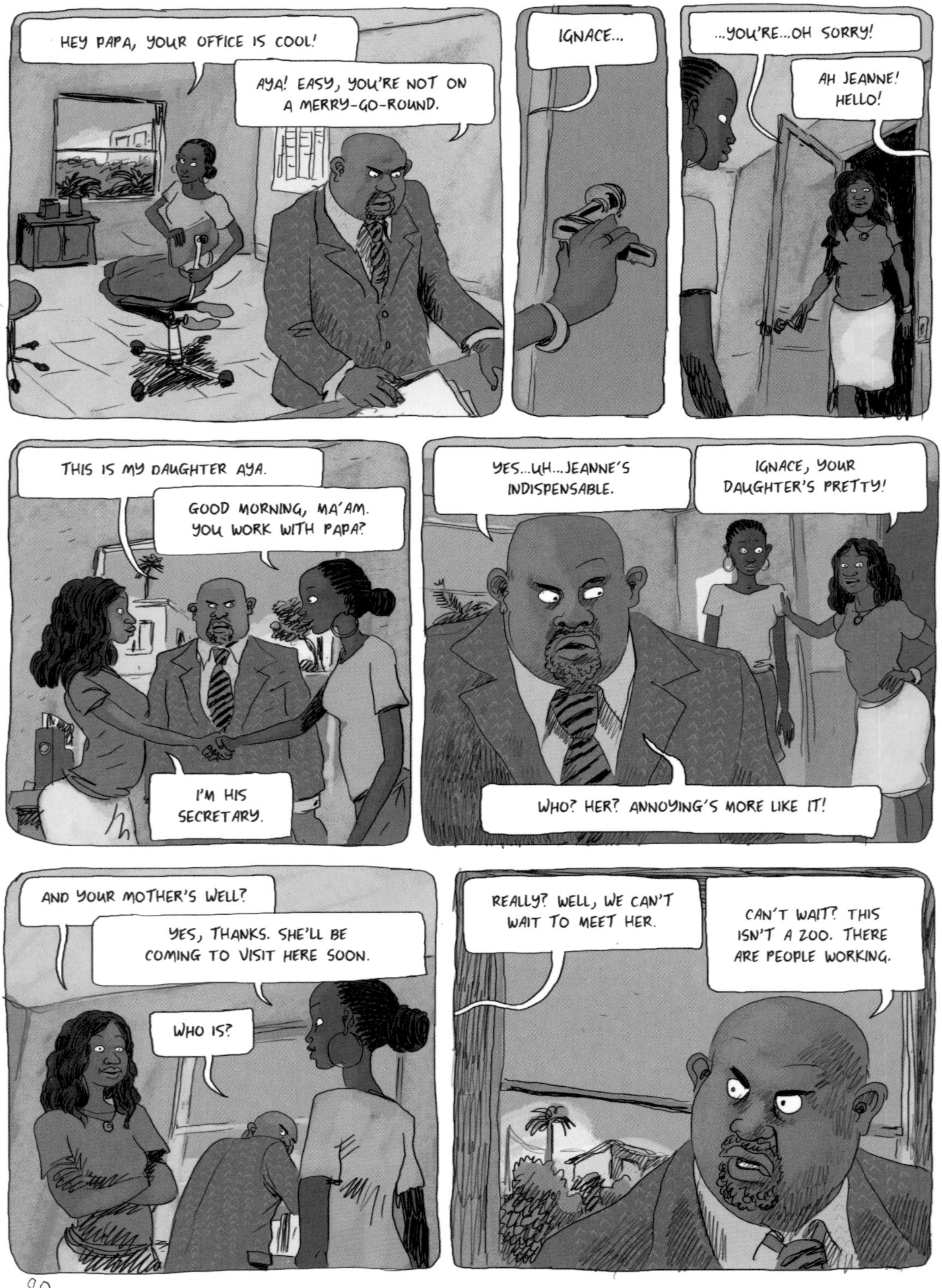
HEY PAPA, YOUR OFFICE IS COOL!
AYA! EASY, YOU'RE NOT ON A MERRY-GO-ROUND.
IGNACE...
...YOU'RE...OH SORRY!
AH JEANNE! HELLO!
THIS IS MY DAUGHTER AYA.
GOOD MORNING, MA'AM. YOU WORK WITH PAPA?
I'M HIS SECRETARY.
YES...UH...JEANNE'S INDISPENSABLE.
IGNACE, YOUR DAUGHTER'S PRETTY!
WHO? HER? ANNOYING'S MORE LIKE IT!
AND YOUR MOTHER'S WELL?
YES, THANKS. SHE'LL BE COMING TO VISIT HERE SOON.
WHO IS?
REALLY? WELL, WE CAN'T WAIT TO MEET HER.
CAN'T WAIT? THIS ISN'T A ZOO. THERE ARE PEOPLE WORKING.

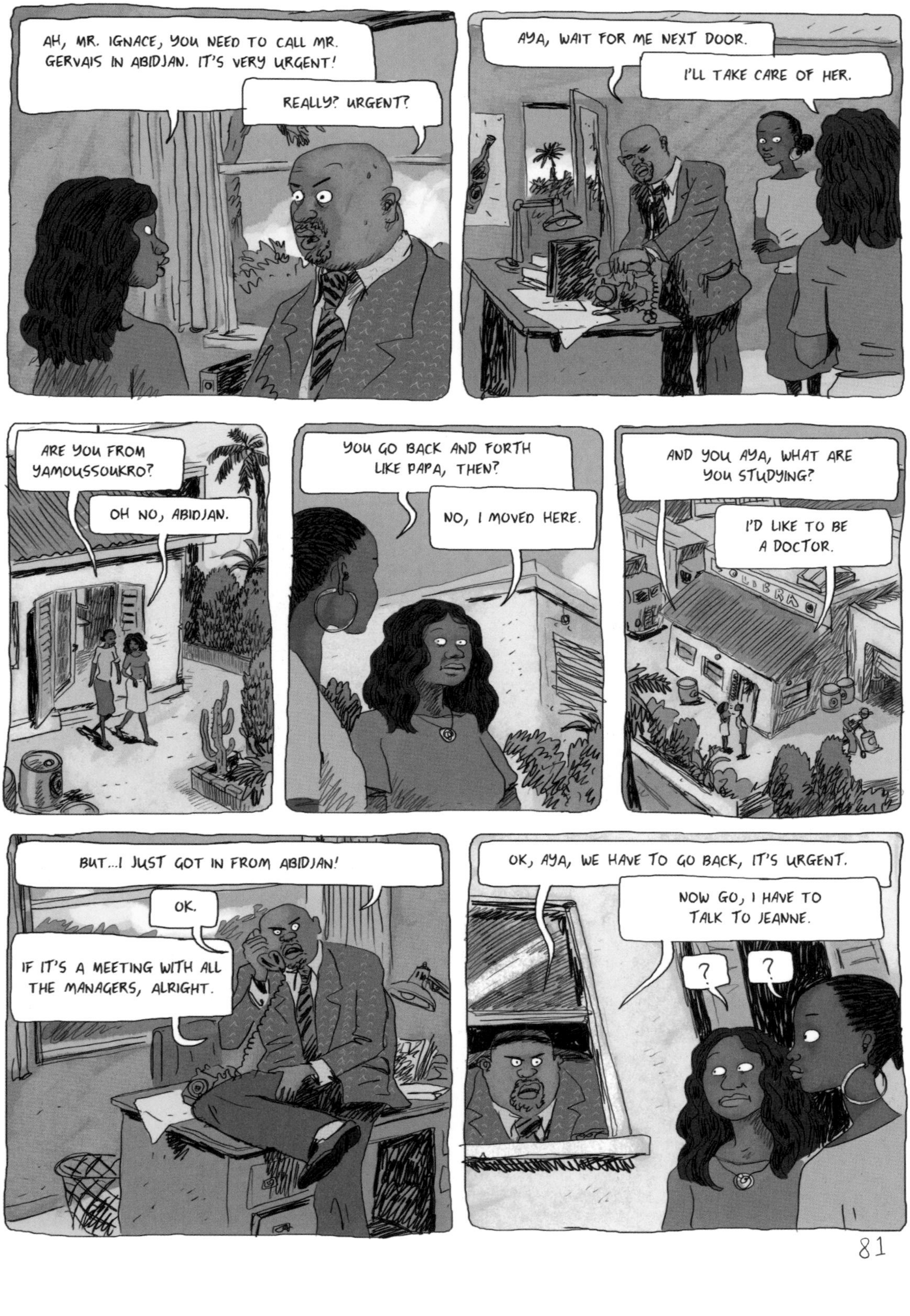
AH, MR. IGNACE, YOU NEED TO CALL MR. GERVAIS IN ABIDJAN. IT'S VERY URGENT!
REALLY? URGENT?
AYA, WAIT FOR ME NEXT DOOR.
I'LL TAKE CARE OF HER.
ARE YOU FROM YAMOUSSOUKRO?
OH NO, ABIDJAN.
YOU GO BACK AND FORTH LIKE PAPA, THEN?
NO, I MOVED HERE.
AND YOU AYA, WHAT ARE YOU STUDYING?
I'D LIKE TO BE A DOCTOR.
BUT...I JUST GOT IN FROM ABIDJAN!
OK.
IF IT'S A MEETING WITH ALL THE MANAGERS, ALRIGHT.
OK, AYA, WE HAVE TO GO BACK, IT'S URGENT.
NOW GO, I HAVE TO TALK TO JEANNE.
?
?

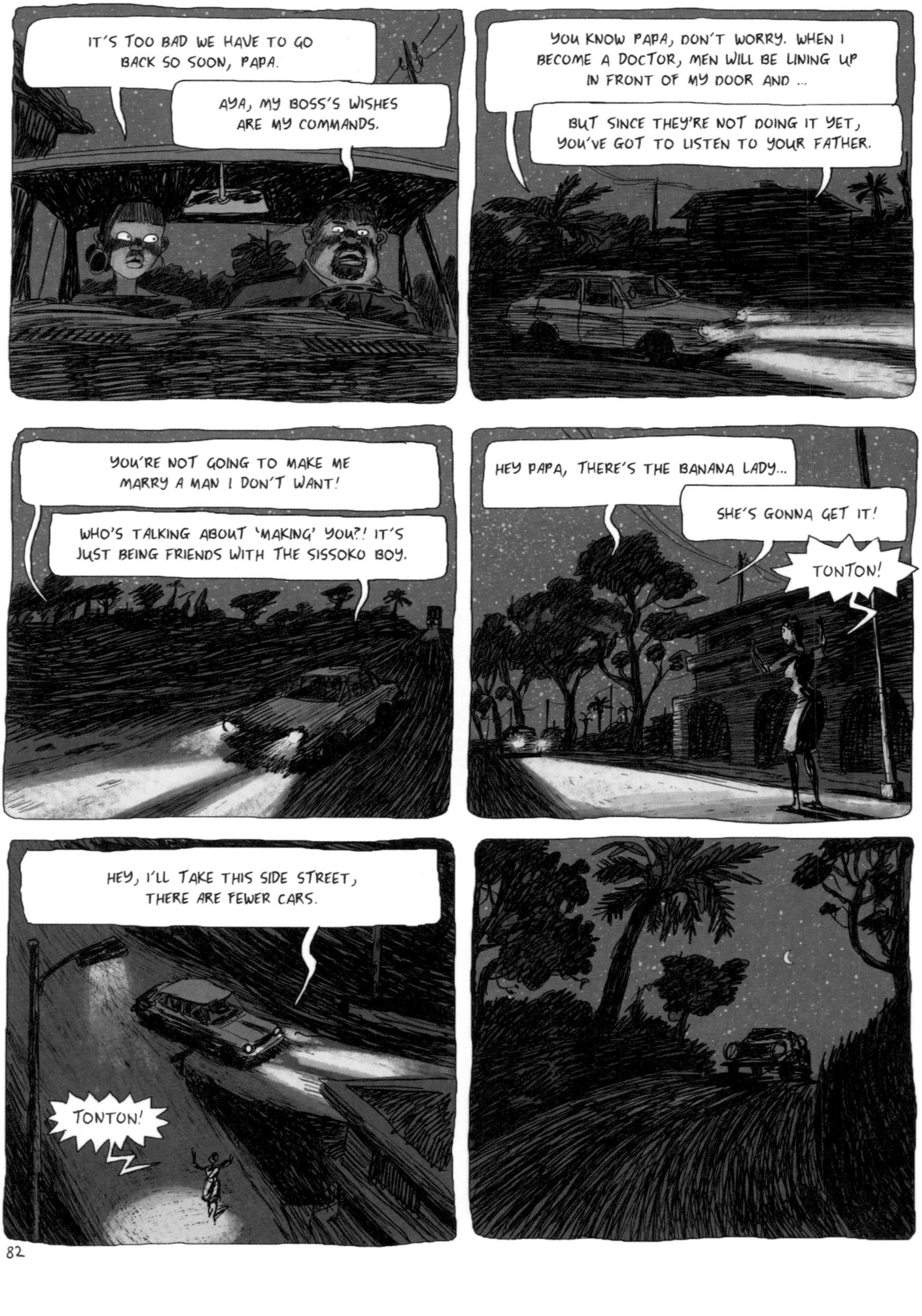
IT'S TOO BAD WE HAVE TO GO BACK SO SOON, PAPA.
AYA, MY BOSS'S WISHES ARE MY COMMANDS.
YOU KNOW PAPA, DON'T WORRY. WHEN I BECOME A DOCTOR, MEN WILL BE LINING UP IN FRONT OF MY DOOR AND ...
BUT SINCE THEY'RE NOT DOING IT YET, YOU'VE GOT TO LISTEN TO YOUR FATHER.
YOU'RE NOT GOING TO MAKE ME MARRY A MAN I DON'T WANT!
WHO'S TALKING ABOUT 'MAKING' YOU?! IT'S JUST BEING FRIENDS WITH THE SISSOKO BOY.
HEY PAPA, THERE'S THE BANANA LADY...
SHE'S GONNA GET IT!
TONTON!
HEY, I'LL TAKE THIS SIDE STREET, THERE ARE FEWER CARS.
TONTON!

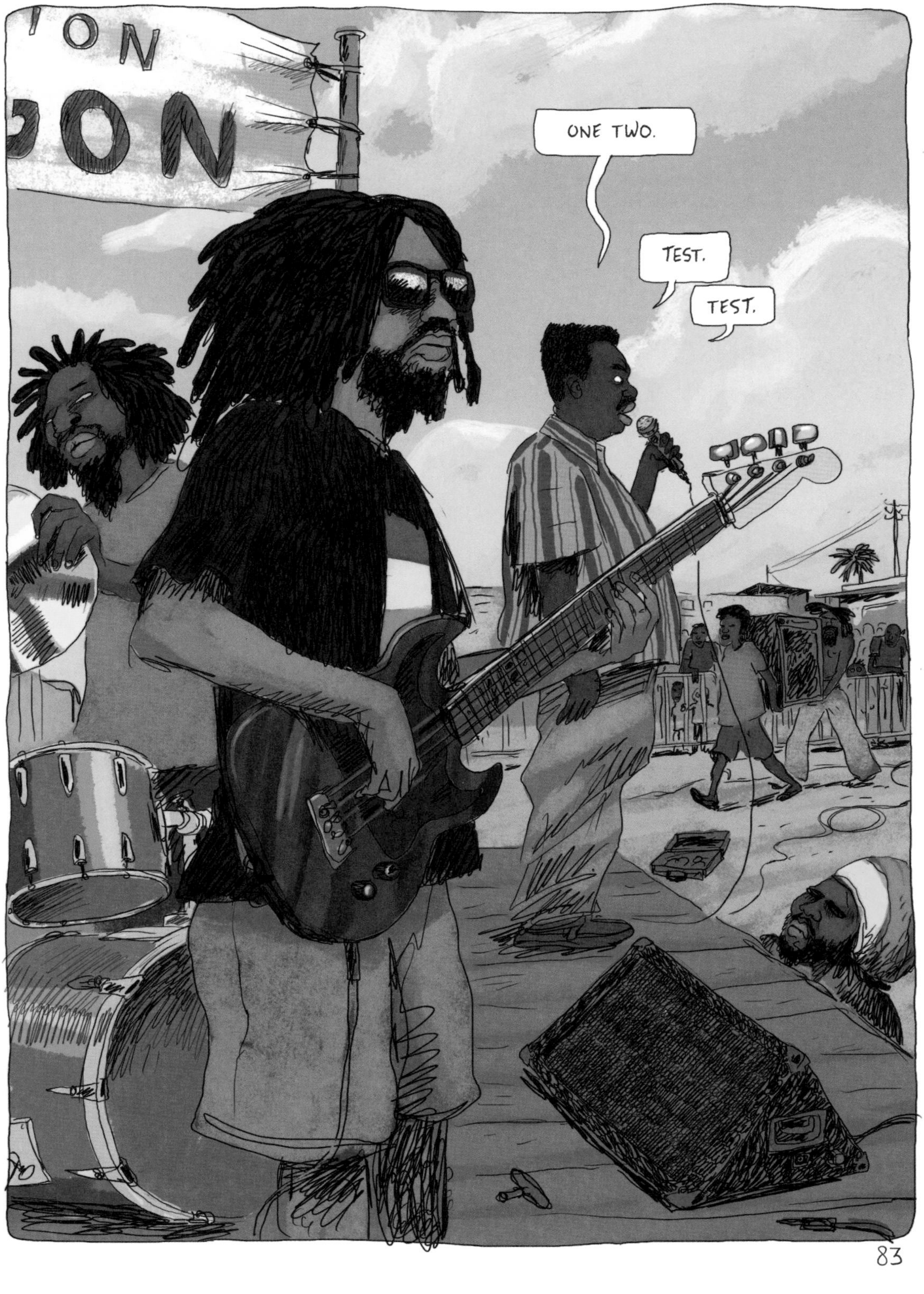
ION
ON
ONE TWO.
TEST.
TEST.

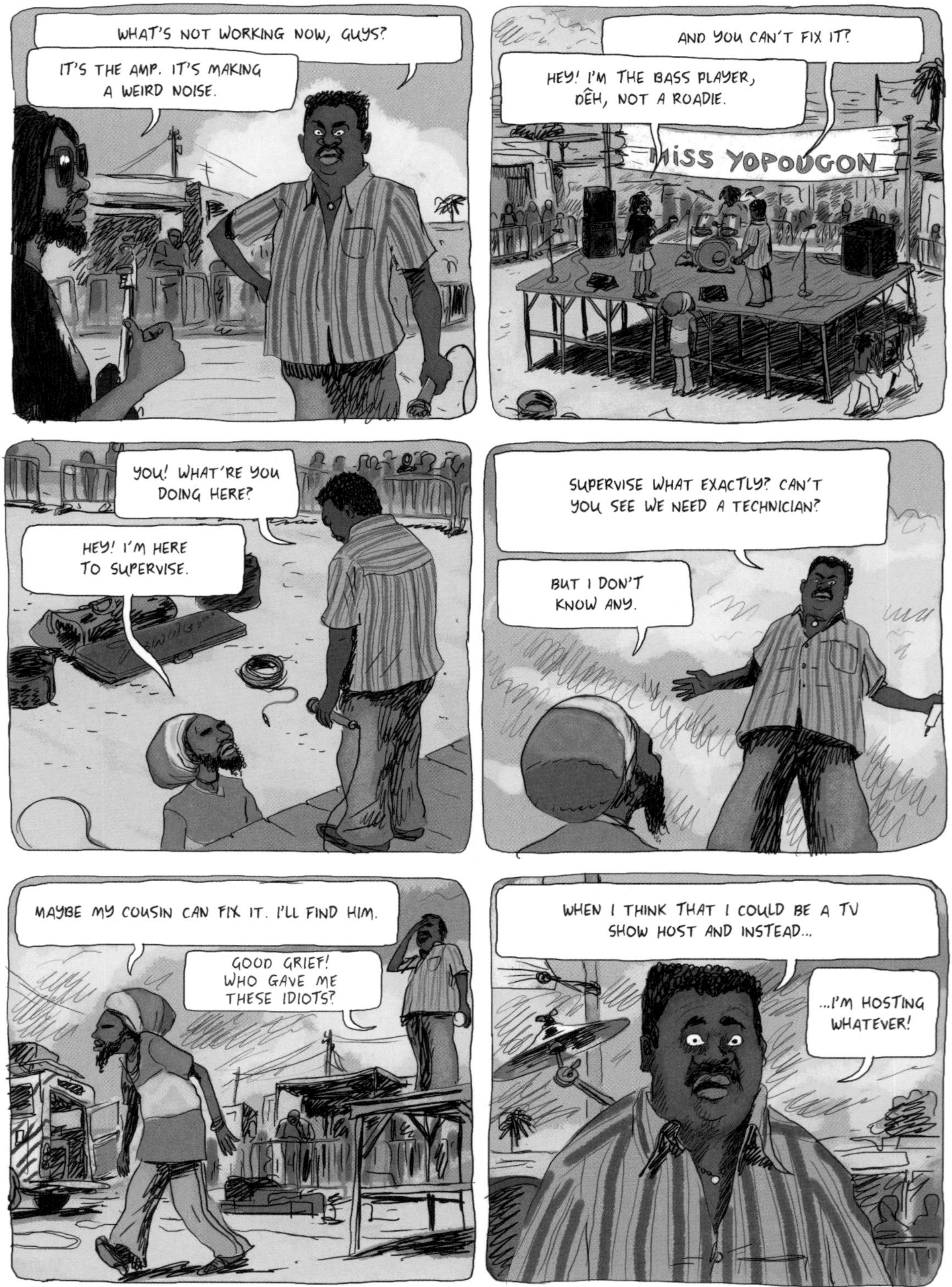
WHAT'S NOT WORKING NOW, GUYS?
IT'S THE AMP. IT'S MAKING A WEIRD NOISE.
AND YOU CAN'T FIX IT?
HEY! I'M THE BASS PLAYER, DÊH, NOT A ROADIE.
MISS YOPOUGON
YOU! WHAT'RE YOU DOING HERE?
HEY! I'M HERE TO SUPERVISE.
SUPERVISE WHAT EXACTLY? CAN'T YOU SEE WE NEED A TECHNICIAN?
BUT I DON'T KNOW ANY.
MAYBE MY COUSIN CAN FIX IT. I'LL FIND HIM.
GOOD GRIEF! WHO GAVE ME THESE IDIOTS?
WHEN I THINK THAT I COULD BE A TV SHOW HOST AND INSTEAD...
...I'M HOSTING WHATEVER!

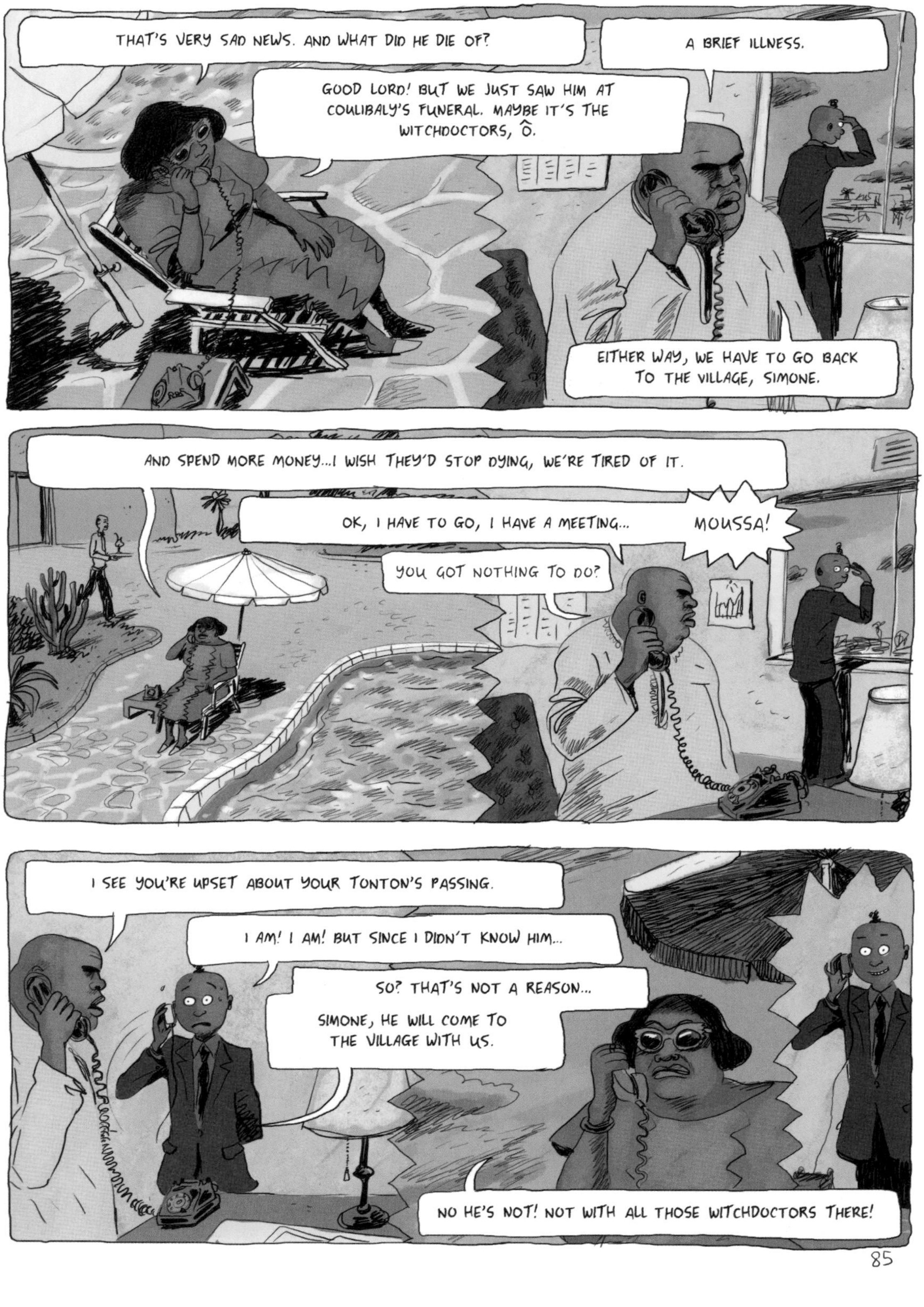

THAT'S VERY SAD NEWS. AND WHAT DID HE DIE OF?
A BRIEF ILLNESS.
GOOD LORD! BUT WE JUST SAW HIM AT COULIBALY'S FUNERAL. MAYBE IT'S THE WITCHDOCTORS, Ô.
EITHER WAY, WE HAVE TO GO BACK TO THE VILLAGE, SIMONE.
AND SPEND MORE MONEY...I WISH THEY'D STOP DYING, WE'RE TIRED OF IT.
OK, I HAVE TO GO, I HAVE A MEETING...
MOUSSA!
YOU GOT NOTHING TO DO?
I SEE YOU'RE UPSET ABOUT YOUR TONTON'S PASSING.
I AM! I AM! BUT SINCE I DIDN'T KNOW HIM...
SO? THAT'S NOT A REASON...
SIMONE, HE WILL COME TO THE VILLAGE WITH US.
NO HE'S NOT! NOT WITH ALL THOSE WITCHDOCTORS THERE!

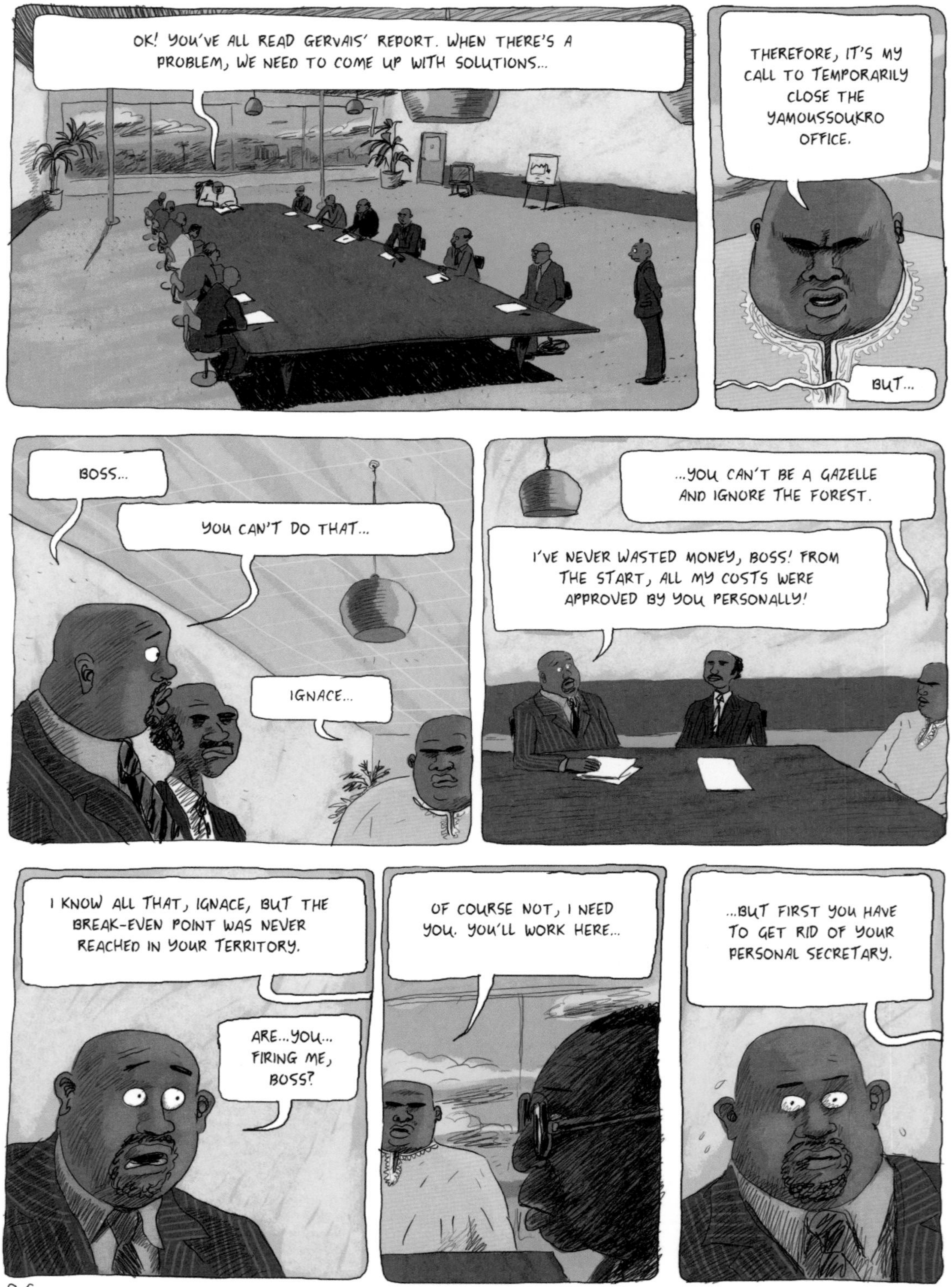
OK! YOU'VE ALL READ GERVAIS' REPORT. WHEN THERE'S A PROBLEM, WE NEED TO COME UP WITH SOLUTIONS...
THEREFORE, IT'S MY CALL TO TEMPORARILY CLOSE THE YAMOUSSOUKRO OFFICE.
BUT...
BOSS...
YOU CAN'T DO THAT...
IGNACE...
...YOU CAN'T BE A GAZELLE AND IGNORE THE FOREST.
I'VE NEVER WASTED MONEY, BOSS! FROM THE START, ALL MY COSTS WERE APPROVED BY YOU PERSONALLY!
I KNOW ALL THAT, IGNACE, BUT THE BREAK-EVEN POINT WAS NEVER REACHED IN YOUR TERRITORY.
ARE...YOU... FIRING ME, BOSS?
OF COURSE NOT, I NEED YOU. YOU'LL WORK HERE...
...BUT FIRST YOU HAVE TO GET RID OF YOUR PERSONAL SECRETARY.

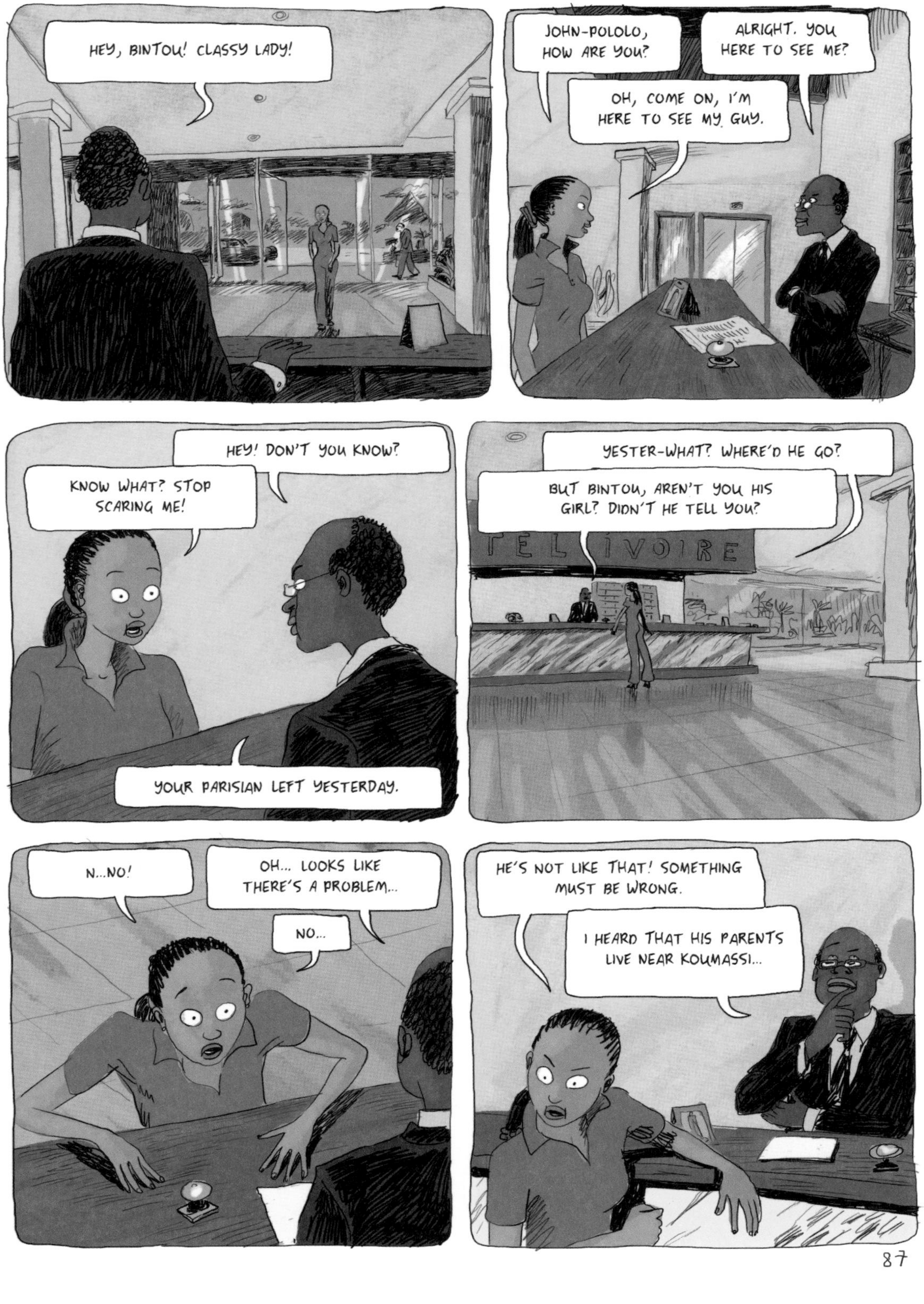
HEY, BINTOU! CLASSY LADY!
JOHN-POLOLO, HOW ARE YOU?
ALRIGHT. YOU HERE TO SEE ME?
OH, COME ON, I'M HERE TO SEE MY GUY.
HEY! DON'T YOU KNOW?
KNOW WHAT? STOP SCARING ME!
YOUR PARISIAN LEFT YESTERDAY.
YESTER-WHAT? WHERE'D HE GO?
BUT BINTOU, AREN'T YOU HIS GIRL? DIDN'T HE TELL YOU?
N...NO!
OH... LOOKS LIKE THERE'S A PROBLEM...
NO...
HE'S NOT LIKE THAT! SOMETHING MUST BE WRONG.
I HEARD THAT HIS PARENTS LIVE NEAR KOUMASSI...

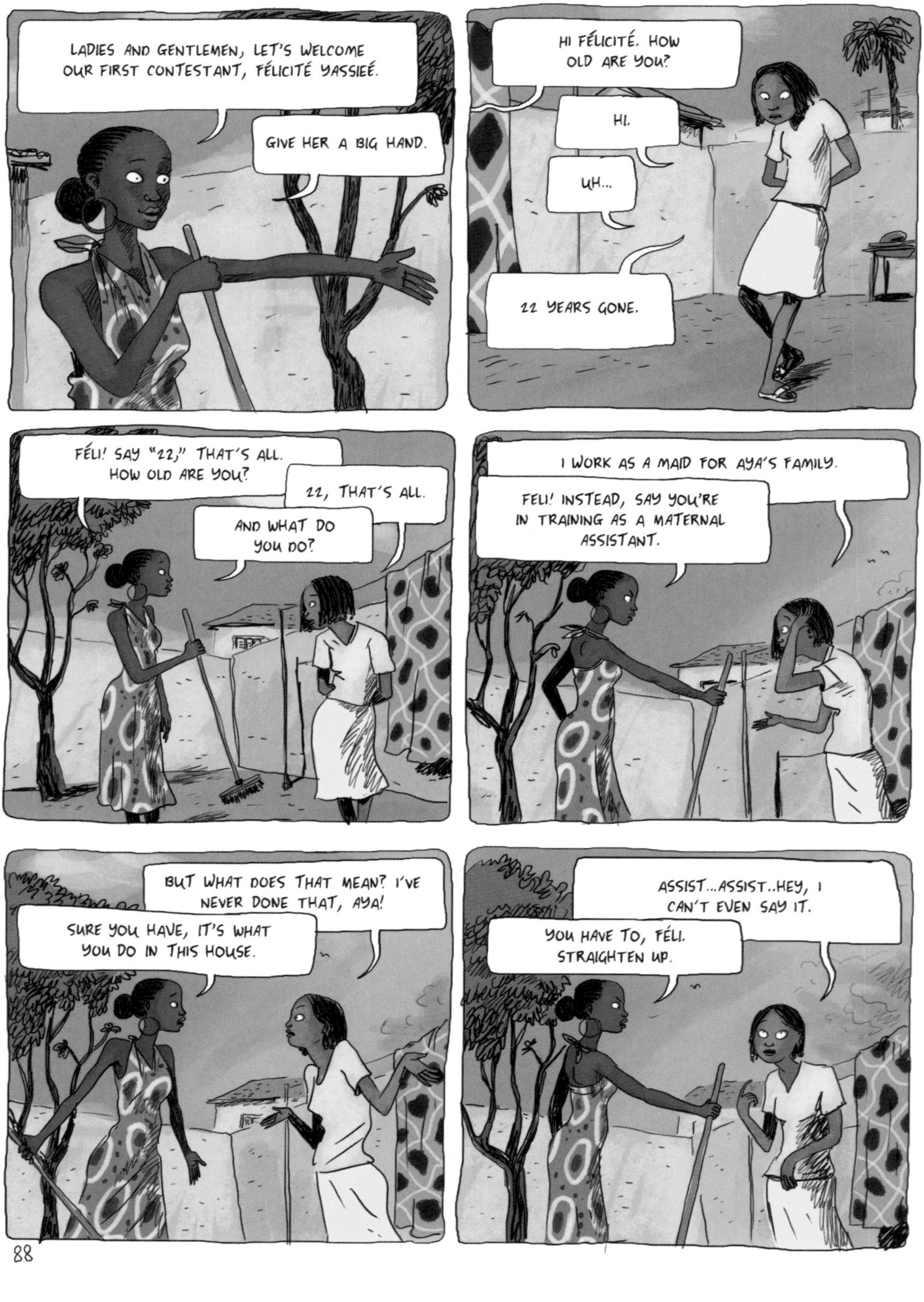
LADIES AND GENTLEMEN, LET'S WELCOME OUR FIRST CONTESTANT, FÉLICITÉ YASSIEÉ.
GIVE HER A BIG HAND.
HI FÉLICITÉ. HOW OLD ARE YOU?
HI.
UH...
22 YEARS GONE.
FÉLI! SAY "22," THAT'S ALL. HOW OLD ARE YOU?
22, THAT'S ALL.
AND WHAT DO YOU DO?
I WORK AS A MAID FOR AYA'S FAMILY.
FÉLI! INSTEAD, SAY YOU'RE IN TRAINING AS A MATERNAL ASSISTANT.
BUT WHAT DOES THAT MEAN? I'VE NEVER DONE THAT, AYA!
SURE YOU HAVE, IT'S WHAT YOU DO IN THIS HOUSE.
ASSIST...ASSIST..HEY, I CAN'T EVEN SAY IT.
YOU HAVE TO, FÉLI. STRAIGHTEN UP.

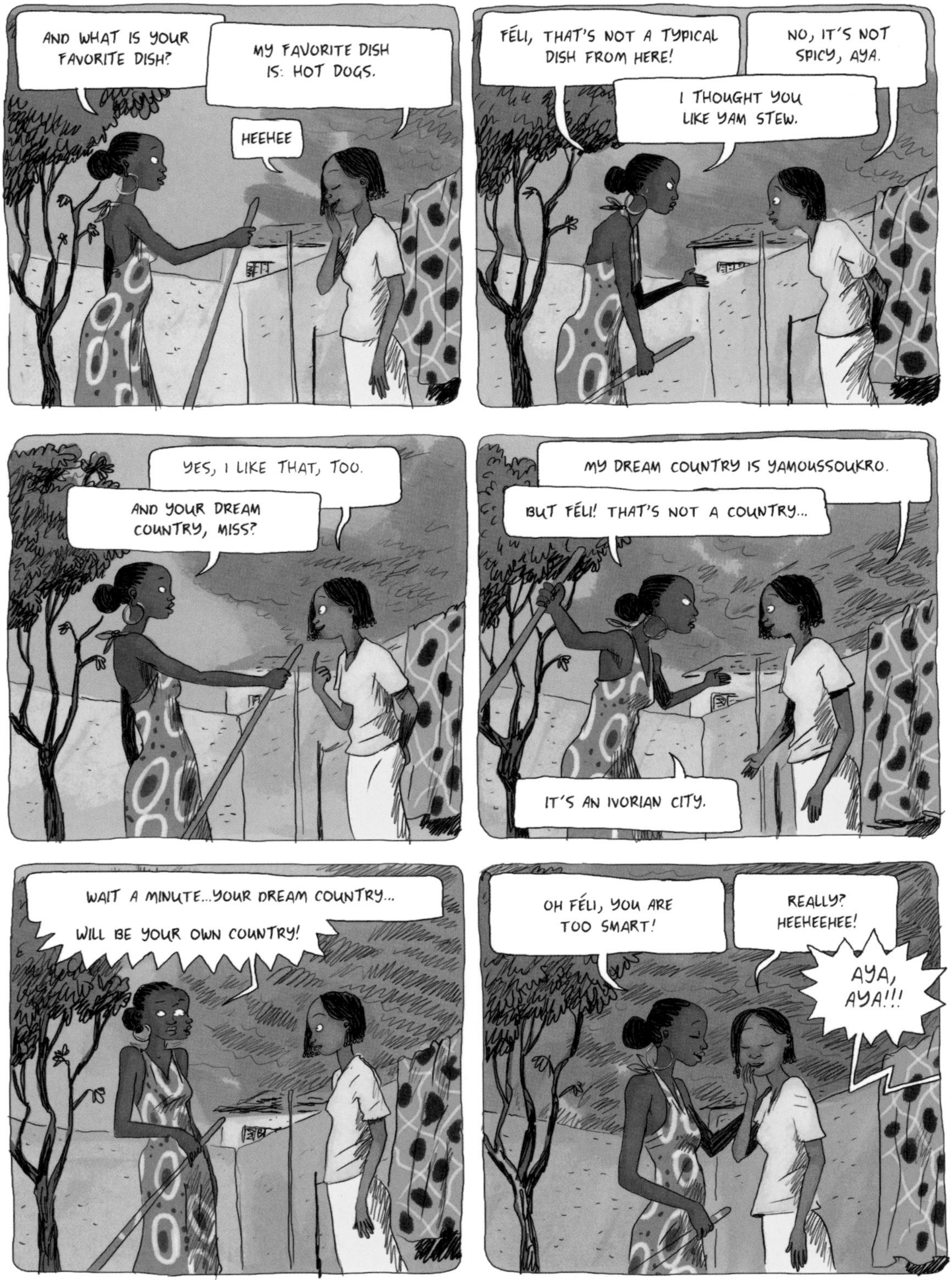
AND WHAT IS YOUR FAVORITE DISH?
MY FAVORITE DISH IS: HOT DOGS.
HEEHEE
FÉLI, THAT'S NOT A TYPICAL DISH FROM HERE!
I THOUGHT YOU LIKE YAM STEW.
NO, IT'S NOT SPICY, AYA.
YES, I LIKE THAT, TOO.
AND YOUR DREAM COUNTRY, MISS?
MY DREAM COUNTRY IS YAMOUSSOUKRO.
BUT FÉLI! THAT'S NOT A COUNTRY...
IT'S AN IVORIAN CITY.
WAIT A MINUTE...YOUR DREAM COUNTRY...
WILL BE YOUR OWN COUNTRY!
OH FÉLI, YOU ARE TOO SMART!
REALLY? HEEHEEHEE!
AYA, AYA!!!

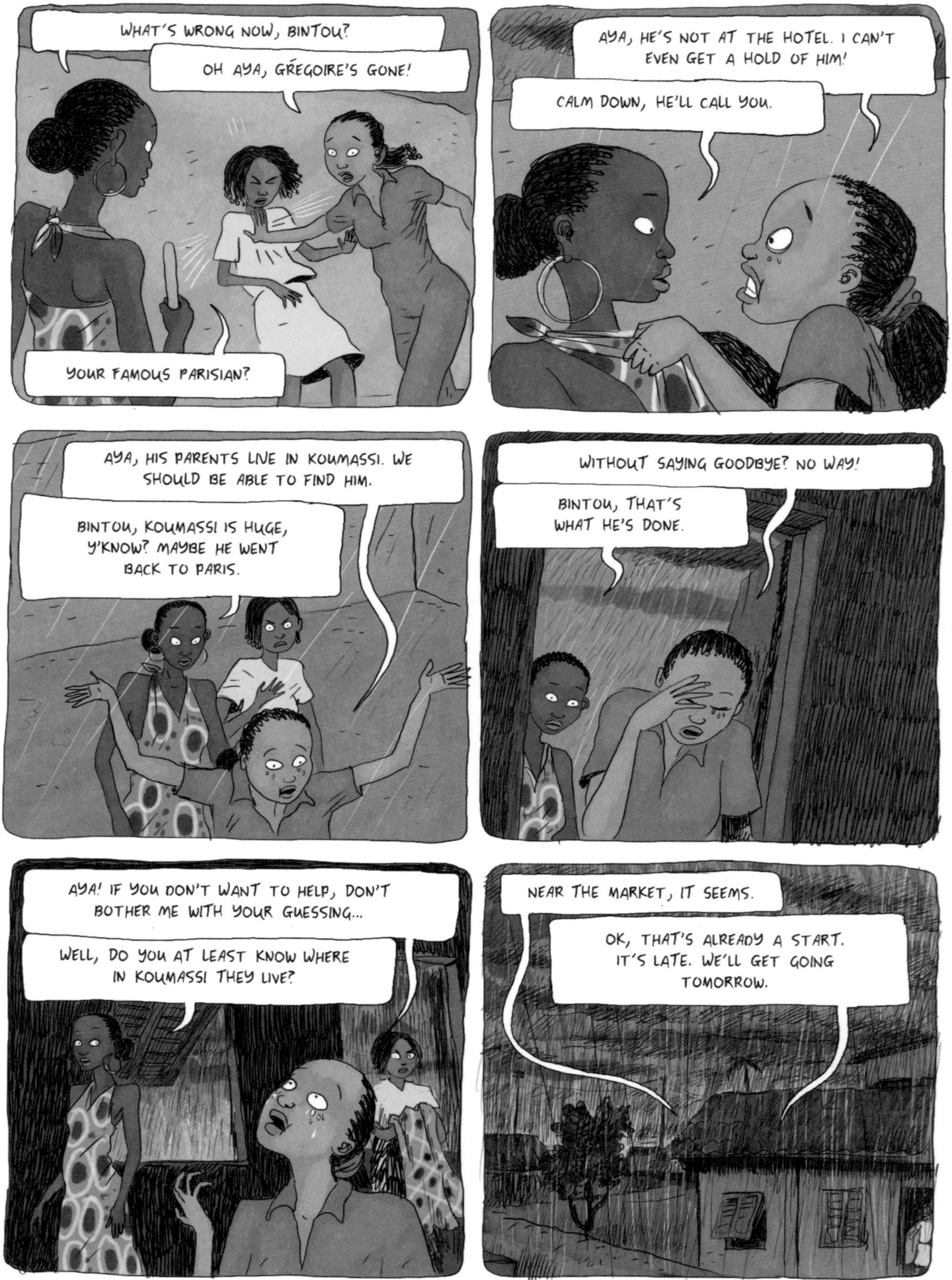
WHAT'S WRONG NOW, BINTOU?
OH AYA, GRÉGOIRE'S GONE!
YOUR FAMOUS PARISIAN?
AYA, HE'S NOT AT THE HOTEL. I CAN'T EVEN GET A HOLD OF HIM!
CALM DOWN, HE'LL CALL YOU.
AYA, HIS PARENTS LIVE IN KOUMASSI. WE SHOULD BE ABLE TO FIND HIM.
BINTOU, KOUMASSI IS HUGE, Y'KNOW? MAYBE HE WENT BACK TO PARIS.
WITHOUT SAYING GOODBYE? NO WAY!
BINTOU, THAT'S WHAT HE'S DONE.
AYA! IF YOU DON'T WANT TO HELP, DON'T BOTHER ME WITH YOUR GUESSING...
WELL, DO YOU AT LEAST KNOW WHERE IN KOUMASSI THEY LIVE?
NEAR THE MARKET, IT SEEMS.
OK, THAT'S ALREADY A START. IT'S LATE. WE'LL GET GOING TOMORROW.

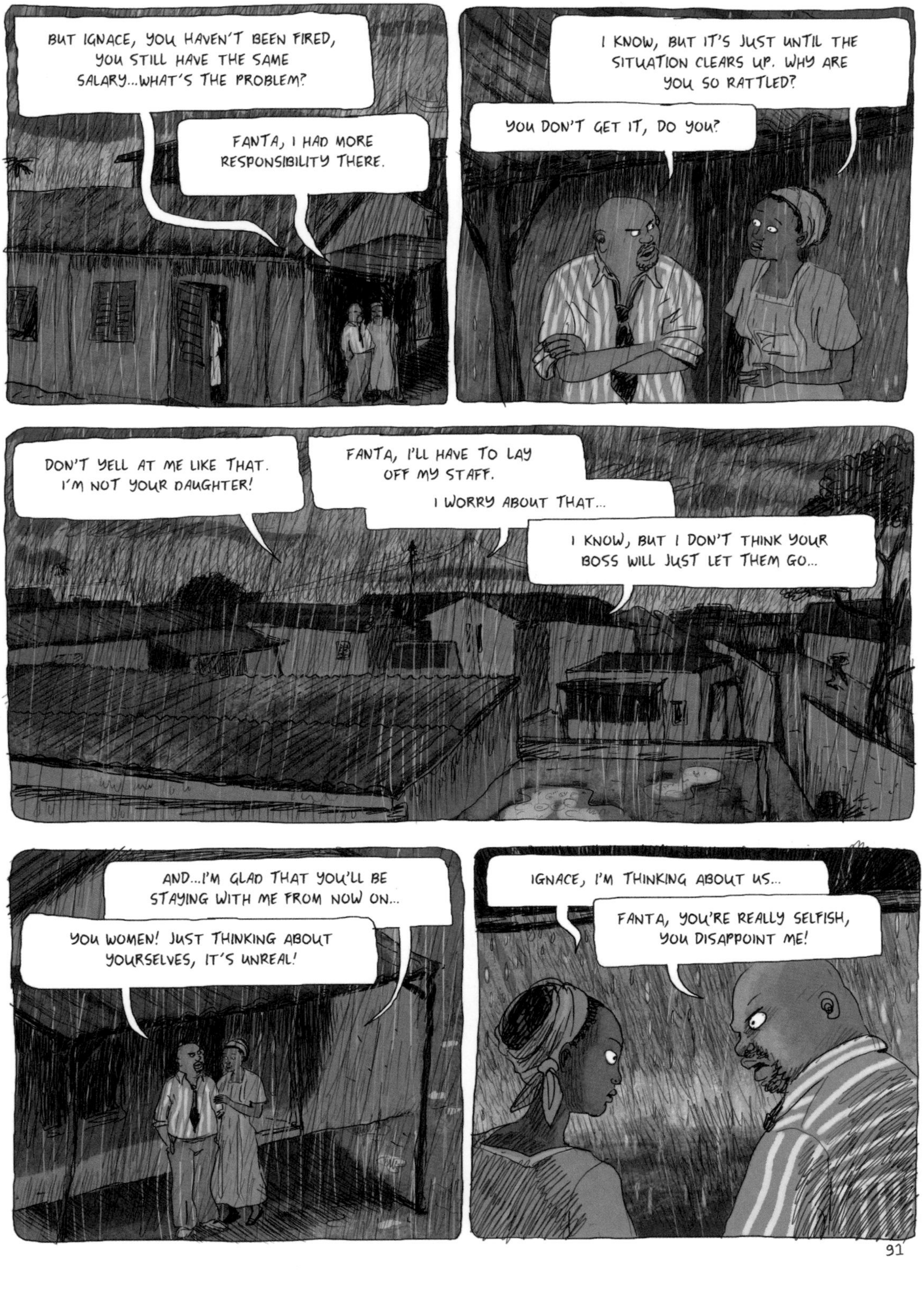
BUT IGNACE, YOU HAVEN'T BEEN FIRED, YOU STILL HAVE THE SAME SALARY...WHAT'S THE PROBLEM?
FANTA, I HAD MORE RESPONSIBILITY THERE.
I KNOW, BUT IT'S JUST UNTIL THE SITUATION CLEARS UP. WHY ARE YOU SO RATTLED?
YOU DON'T GET IT, DO YOU?
DON'T YELL AT ME LIKE THAT. I'M NOT YOUR DAUGHTER!
FANTA, I'LL HAVE TO LAY OFF MY STAFF.
I WORRY ABOUT THAT...
I KNOW, BUT I DON'T THINK YOUR BOSS WILL JUST LET THEM GO...
AND...I'M GLAD THAT YOU'LL BE STAYING WITH ME FROM NOW ON...
YOU WOMEN! JUST THINKING ABOUT YOURSELVES, IT'S UNREAL!
IGNACE, I'M THINKING ABOUT US...
FANTA, YOU'RE REALLY SELFISH, YOU DISAPPOINT ME!

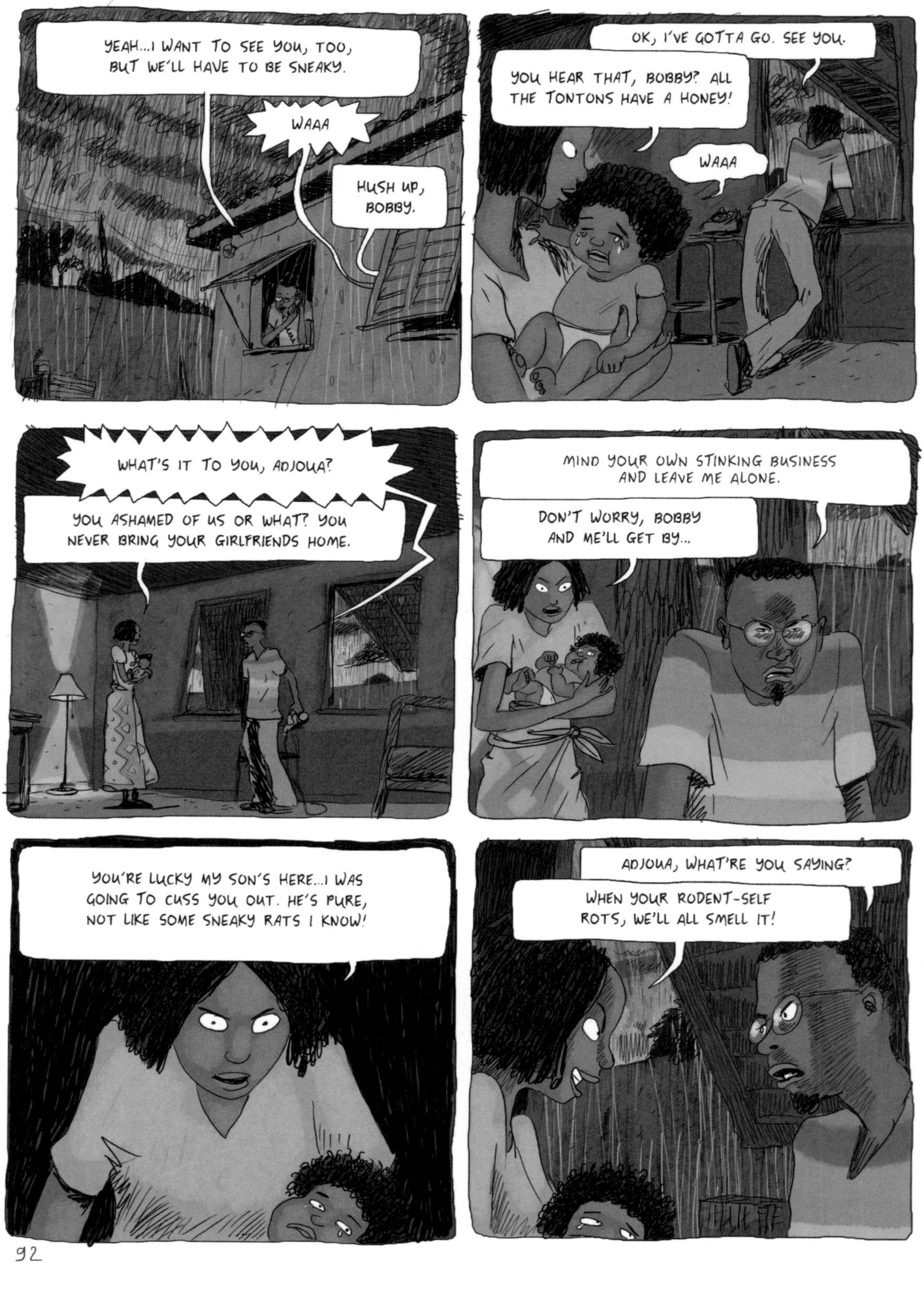
YEAH...I WANT TO SEE YOU, TOO, BUT WE'LL HAVE TO BE SNEAKY.
WAAA
HUSH UP, BOBBY.
OK, I'VE GOTTA GO. SEE YOU.
YOU HEAR THAT, BOBBY? ALL THE TONTONS HAVE A HONEY!
WAAA
WHAT'S IT TO YOU, ADJOUA?
YOU ASHAMED OF US OR WHAT? YOU NEVER BRING YOUR GIRLFRIENDS HOME.
MIND YOUR OWN STINKING BUSINESS AND LEAVE ME ALONE.
DON'T WORRY, BOBBY AND ME'LL GET BY...
YOU'RE LUCKY MY SON'S HERE...I WAS GOING TO CUSS YOU OUT. HE'S PURE, NOT LIKE SOME SNEAKY RATS I KNOW!
ADJOUA, WHAT'RE YOU SAYING?
WHEN YOUR RODENT-SELF ROTS, WE'LL ALL SMELL IT!

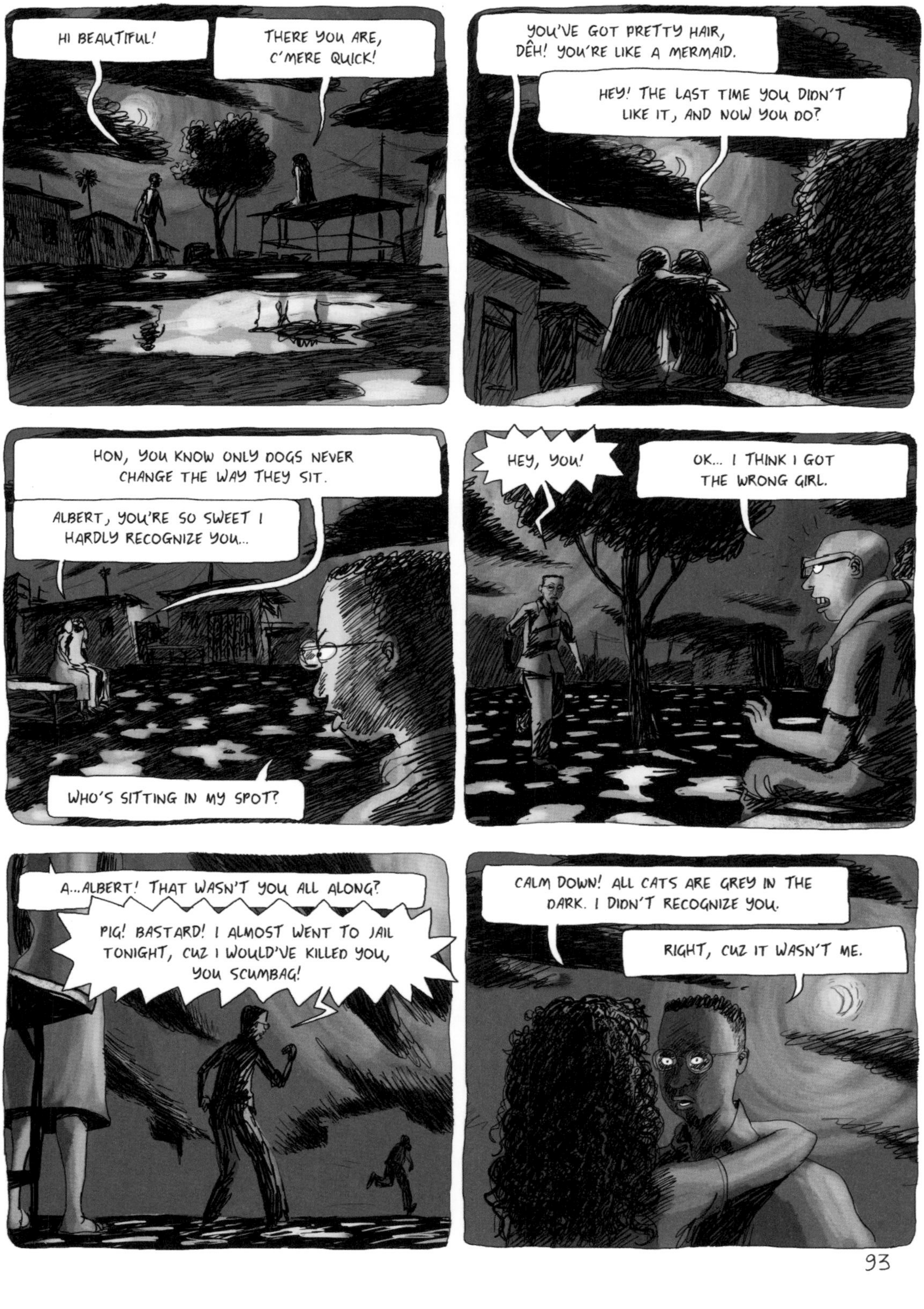
HI BEAUTIFUL!
THERE YOU ARE, C'MERE QUICK!
YOU'VE GOT PRETTY HAIR, DÊH! YOU'RE LIKE A MERMAID.
HEY! THE LAST TIME YOU DIDN'T LIKE IT, AND NOW YOU DO?
HON, YOU KNOW ONLY DOGS NEVER CHANGE THE WAY THEY SIT.
ALBERT, YOU'RE SO SWEET I HARDLY RECOGNIZE YOU...
WHO'S SITTING IN MY SPOT?
HEY, YOU!
OK... I THINK I GOT THE WRONG GIRL.
A...ALBERT! THAT WASN'T YOU ALL ALONG?
PIG! BASTARD! I ALMOST WENT TO JAIL TONIGHT, CUZ I WOULD'VE KILLED YOU, YOU SCUMBAG!
CALM DOWN! ALL CATS ARE GREY IN THE DARK. I DIDN'T RECOGNIZE YOU.
RIGHT, CUZ IT WASN'T ME.

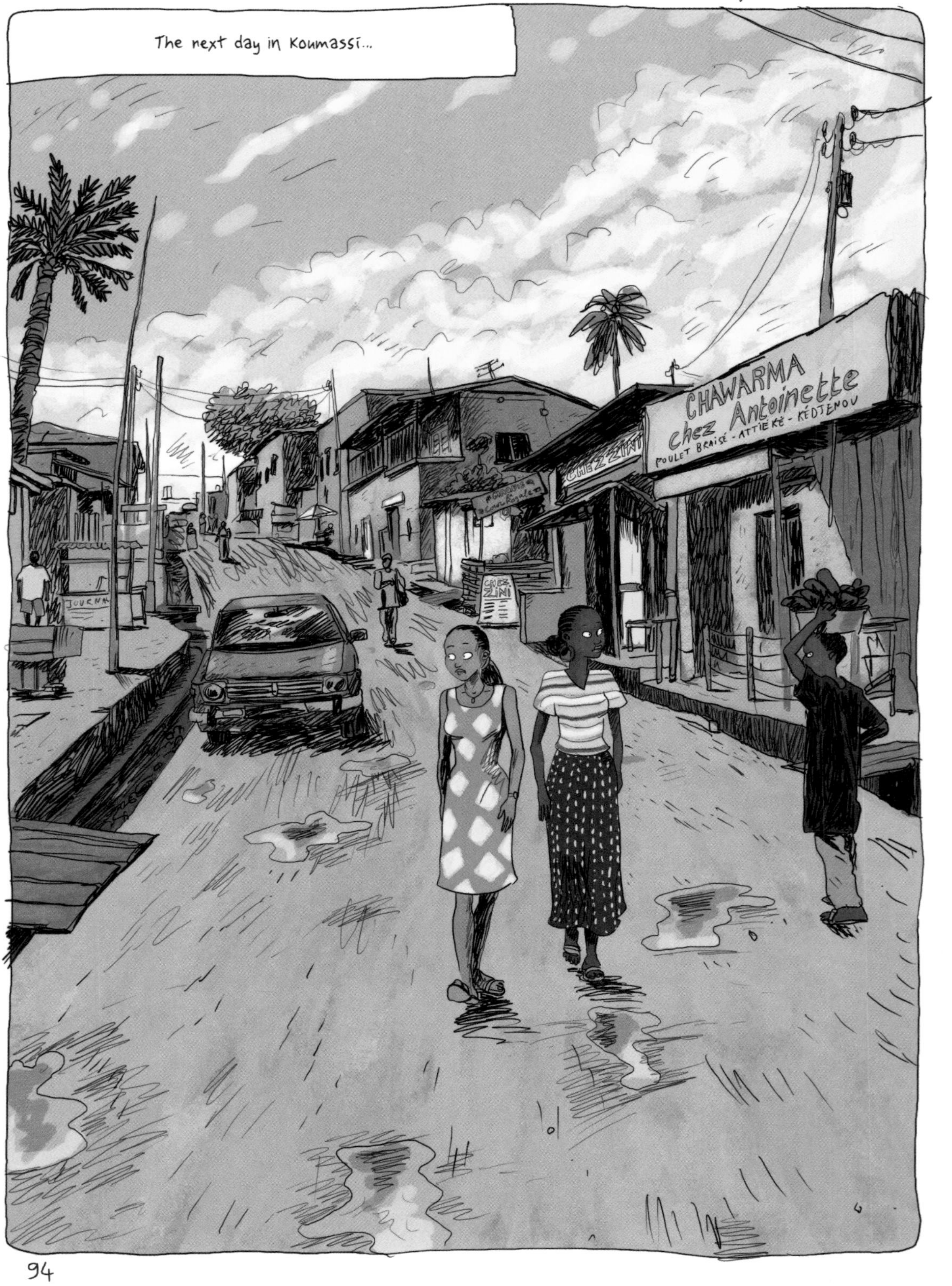
The next day in Koumassi...
CHAWARMA
Chez Antoinette
POULET BRAISÉ - ATTIÉKÉ - KÉDJENOU
CHEZ ZINI

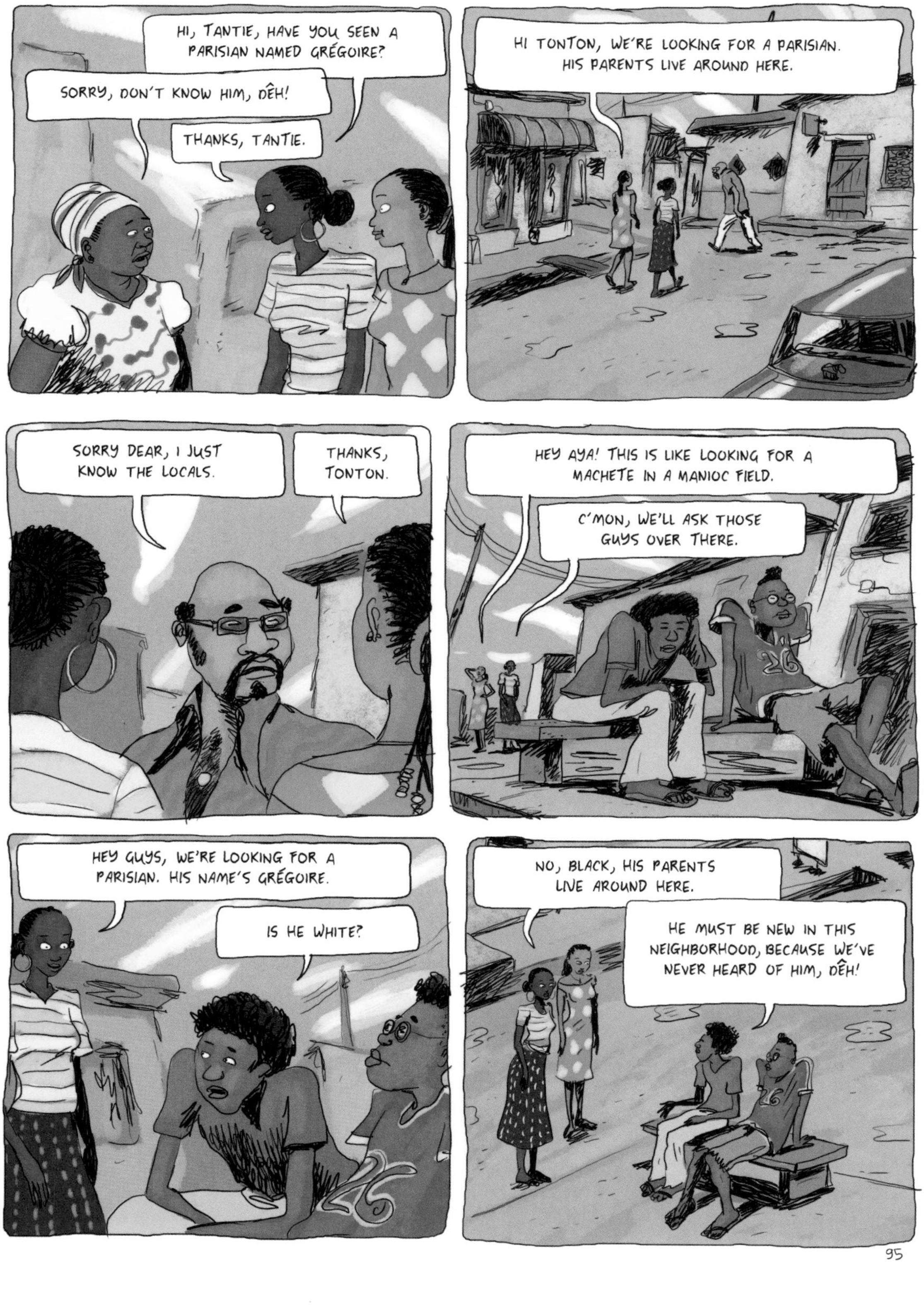
HI, TANTIE, HAVE YOU SEEN A PARISIAN NAMED GRÉGOIRE?
SORRY, DON'T KNOW HIM, DÊH!
THANKS, TANTIE.
HI TONTON, WE'RE LOOKING FOR A PARISIAN. HIS PARENTS LIVE AROUND HERE.
SORRY DEAR, I JUST KNOW THE LOCALS.
THANKS, TONTON.
HEY AYA! THIS IS LIKE LOOKING FOR A MACHETE IN A MANIOC FIELD.
C'MON, WE'LL ASK THOSE GUYS OVER THERE.
HEY GUYS, WE'RE LOOKING FOR A PARISIAN. HIS NAME'S GRÉGOIRE.
IS HE WHITE?
NO, BLACK, HIS PARENTS LIVE AROUND HERE.
HE MUST BE NEW IN THIS NEIGHBORHOOD, BECAUSE WE'VE NEVER HEARD OF HIM, DÊH!

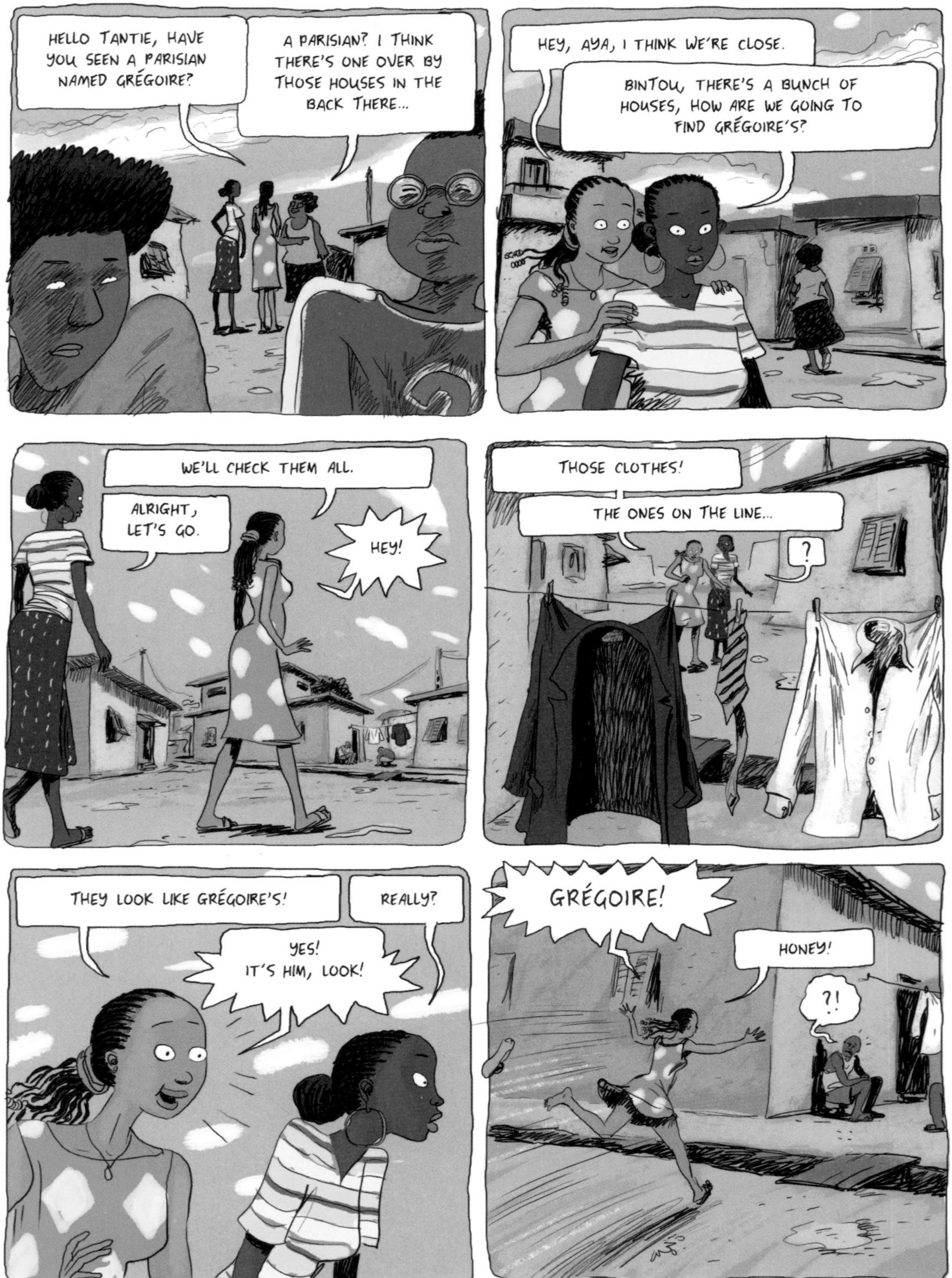
HELLO TANTIE, HAVE YOU SEEN A PARISIAN NAMED GRÉGOIRE?
A PARISIAN? I THINK THERE'S ONE OVER BY THOSE HOUSES IN THE BACK THERE...
HEY, AYA, I THINK WE'RE CLOSE.
BINTOU, THERE'S A BUNCH OF HOUSES, HOW ARE WE GOING TO FIND GRÉGOIRE'S?
WE'LL CHECK THEM ALL.
ALRIGHT, LET'S GO.
HEY!
THOSE CLOTHES!
THE ONES ON THE LINE...
?
THEY LOOK LIKE GRÉGOIRE'S!
REALLY?
YES! IT'S HIM, LOOK!
GRÉGOIRE!
HONEY!
?!

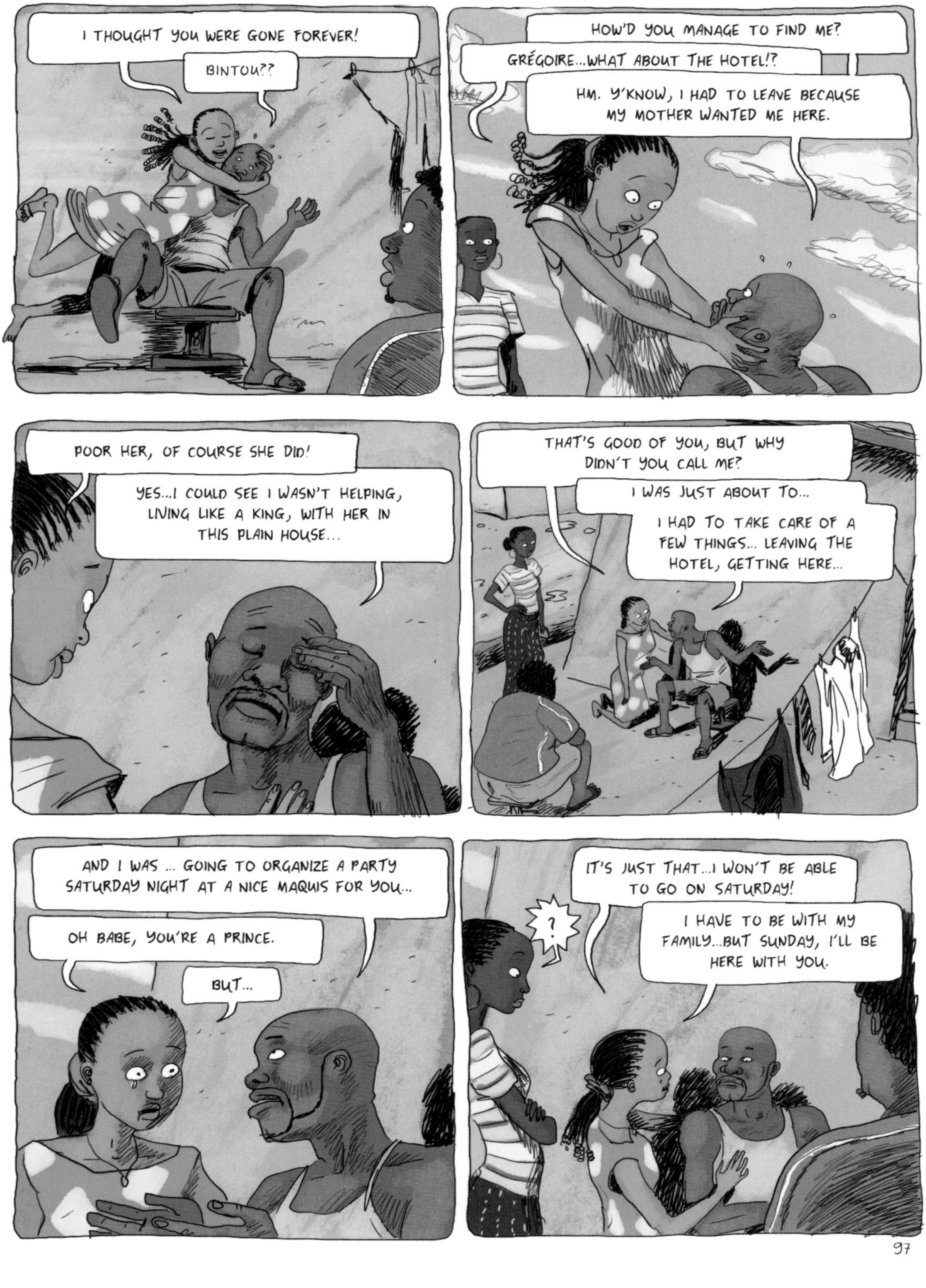
I THOUGHT YOU WERE GONE FOREVER!
BINTOU??
HOW'D YOU MANAGE TO FIND ME?
GRÉGOIRE...WHAT ABOUT THE HOTEL!?
HM. Y'KNOW, I HAD TO LEAVE BECAUSE MY MOTHER WANTED ME HERE.
POOR HER, OF COURSE SHE DID!
YES...I COULD SEE I WASN'T HELPING, LIVING LIKE A KING, WITH HER IN THIS PLAIN HOUSE...
THAT'S GOOD OF YOU, BUT WHY DIDN'T YOU CALL ME?
I WAS JUST ABOUT TO...
I HAD TO TAKE CARE OF A FEW THINGS... LEAVING THE HOTEL, GETTING HERE...
AND I WAS ... GOING TO ORGANIZE A PARTY SATURDAY NIGHT AT A NICE MAQUIS FOR YOU...
OH BABE, YOU'RE A PRINCE.
BUT...
IT'S JUST THAT...I WON'T BE ABLE TO GO ON SATURDAY!
?
I HAVE TO BE WITH MY FAMILY...BUT SUNDAY, I'LL BE HERE WITH YOU.

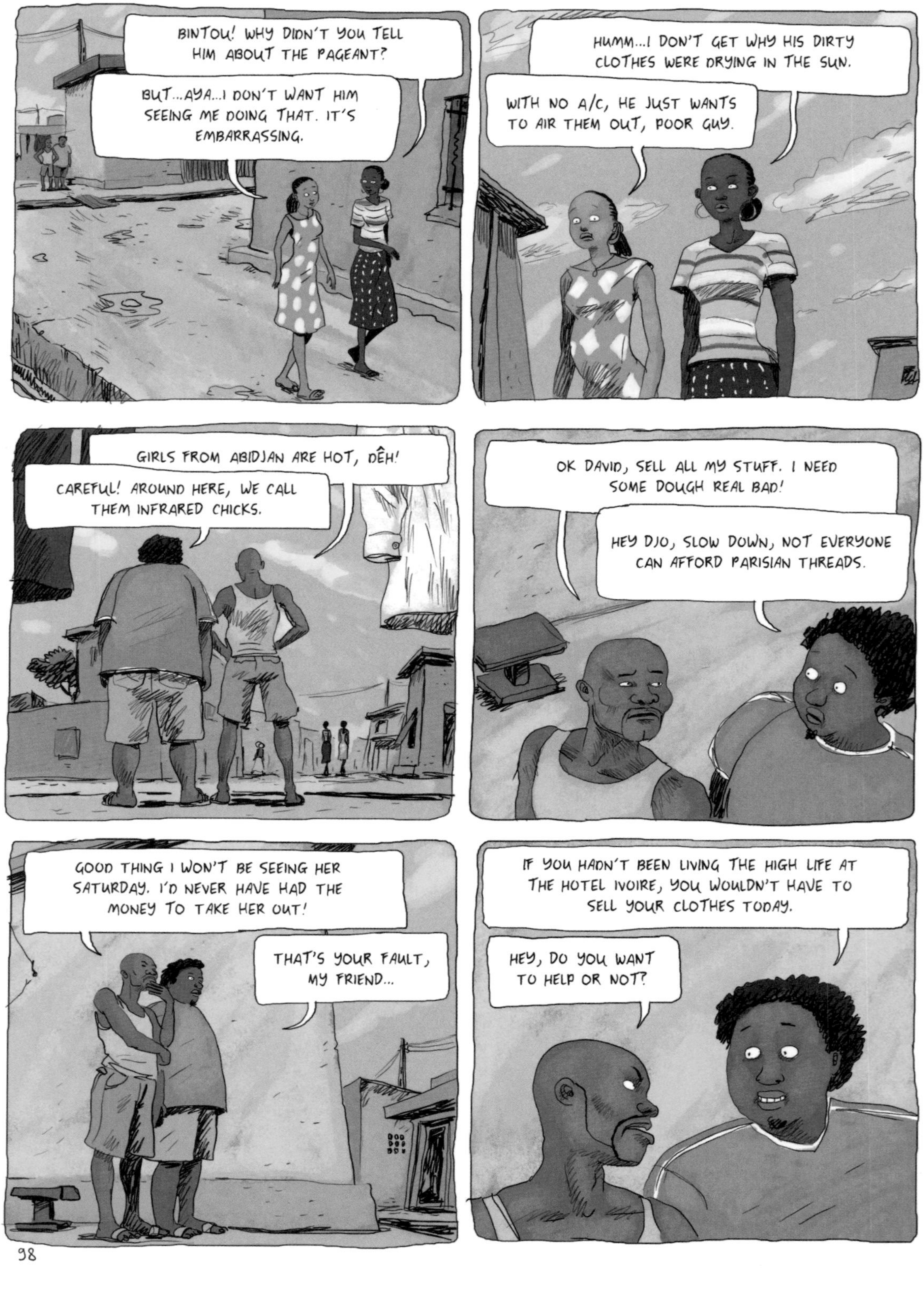
BINTOU! WHY DIDN'T YOU TELL HIM ABOUT THE PAGEANT?
BUT...AYA...I DON'T WANT HIM SEEING ME DOING THAT. IT'S EMBARRASSING.
HUMM...I DON'T GET WHY HIS DIRTY CLOTHES WERE DRYING IN THE SUN.
WITH NO A/C, HE JUST WANTS TO AIR THEM OUT, POOR GUY.
GIRLS FROM ABIDJAN ARE HOT, DÊH!
CAREFUL! AROUND HERE, WE CALL THEM INFRARED CHICKS.
OK DAVID, SELL ALL MY STUFF. I NEED SOME DOUGH REAL BAD!
HEY DJO, SLOW DOWN, NOT EVERYONE CAN AFFORD PARISIAN THREADS.
GOOD THING I WON'T BE SEEING HER SATURDAY. I'D NEVER HAVE HAD THE MONEY TO TAKE HER OUT!
THAT'S YOUR FAULT, MY FRIEND...
IF YOU HADN'T BEEN LIVING THE HIGH LIFE AT THE HOTEL IVOIRE, YOU WOULDN'T HAVE TO SELL YOUR CLOTHES TODAY.
HEY, DO YOU WANT TO HELP OR NOT?

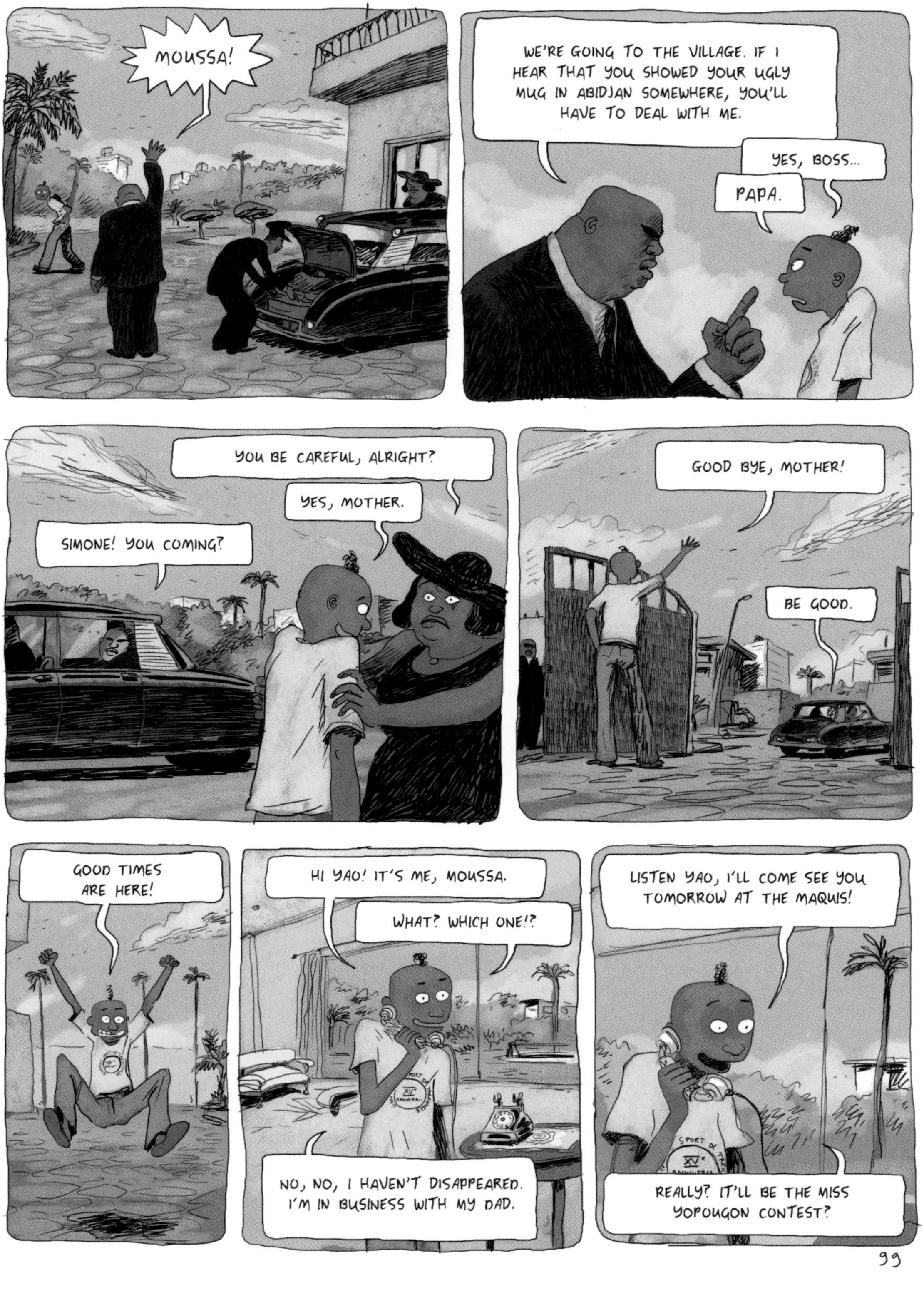
MOUSSA!
WE'RE GOING TO THE VILLAGE. IF I HEAR THAT YOU SHOWED YOUR UGLY MUG IN ABIDJAN SOMEWHERE, YOU'LL HAVE TO DEAL WITH ME.
YES, BOSS...
PAPA.
YOU BE CAREFUL, ALRIGHT?
YES, MOTHER.
SIMONE! YOU COMING?
GOOD BYE, MOTHER!
BE GOOD.
GOOD TIMES ARE HERE!
HI YAO! IT'S ME, MOUSSA.
WHAT? WHICH ONE!?
NO, NO, I HAVEN'T DISAPPEARED. I'M IN BUSINESS WITH MY DAD.
LISTEN YAO, I'LL COME SEE YOU TOMORROW AT THE MAQUIS!
REALLY? IT'LL BE THE MISS YOPOUGON CONTEST?

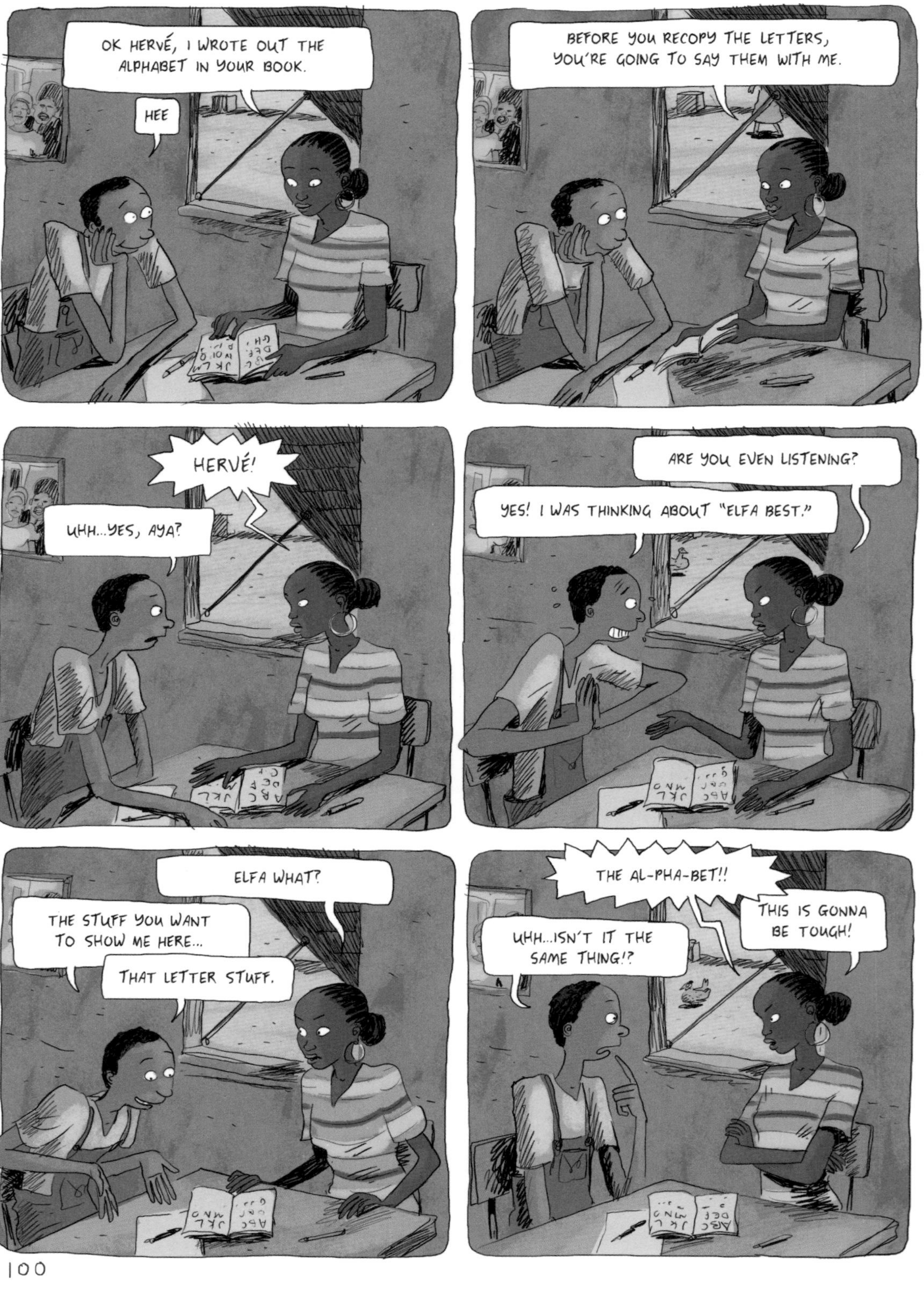
OK HERVÉ, I WROTE OUT THE ALPHABET IN YOUR BOOK.
HEE
BEFORE YOU RECOPY THE LETTERS, YOU'RE GOING TO SAY THEM WITH ME.
HERVÉ!
UHH...YES, AYA?
ARE YOU EVEN LISTENING?
YES! I WAS THINKING ABOUT "ELFA BEST."
ELFA WHAT?
THE STUFF YOU WANT TO SHOW ME HERE...
THAT LETTER STUFF.
THE AL-PHA-BET!!
UHH...ISN'T IT THE SAME THING!?
THIS IS GONNA BE TOUGH!

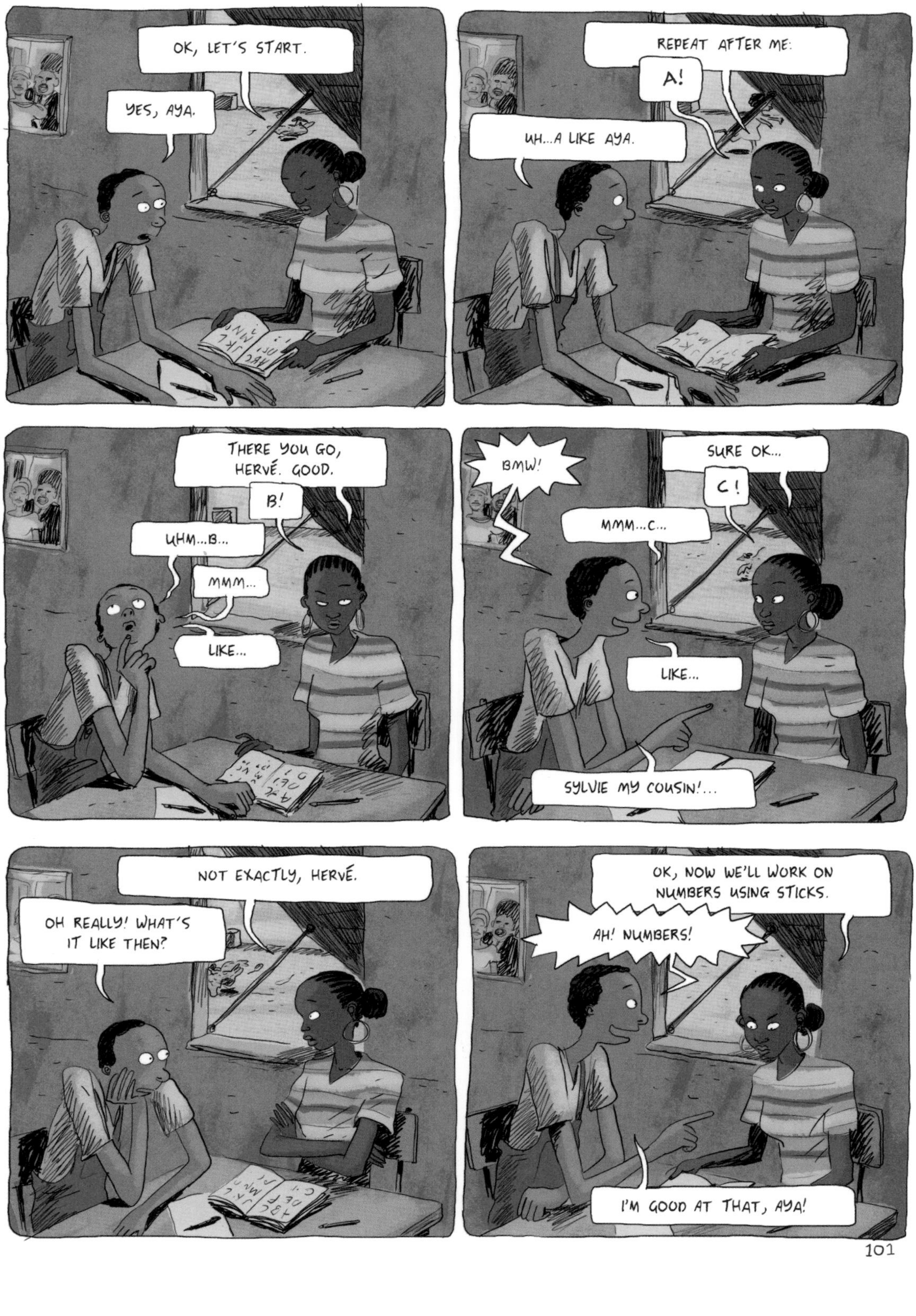
OK, LET'S START.
YES, AYA.
REPEAT AFTER ME:
A!
UH...A LIKE AYA.
THERE YOU GO, HERVÉ. GOOD.
B!
UHM...B...
MMM...
LIKE...
BMW!
SURE OK...
C!
MMM...C...
LIKE...
SYLVIE MY COUSIN!...
NOT EXACTLY, HERVÉ.
OH REALLY! WHAT'S IT LIKE THEN?
OK, NOW WE'LL WORK ON NUMBERS USING STICKS.
AH! NUMBERS!
I'M GOOD AT THAT, AYA!

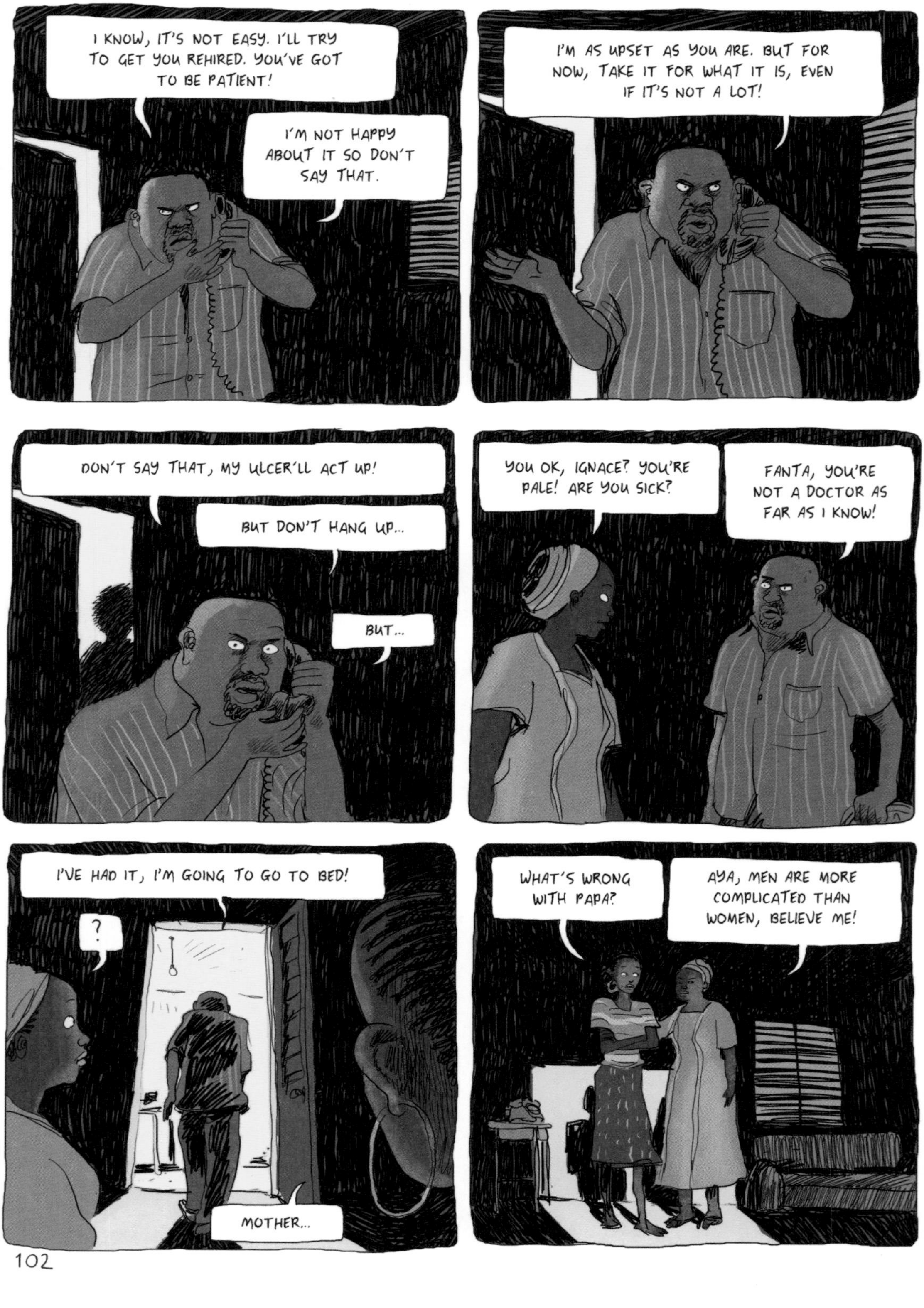
I KNOW, IT'S NOT EASY. I'LL TRY TO GET YOU REHIRED. YOU'VE GOT TO BE PATIENT!
I'M NOT HAPPY ABOUT IT SO DON'T SAY THAT.
I'M AS UPSET AS YOU ARE. BUT FOR NOW, TAKE IT FOR WHAT IT IS, EVEN IF IT'S NOT A LOT!
DON'T SAY THAT, MY ULCER'LL ACT UP!
BUT DON'T HANG UP...
BUT...
YOU OK, IGNACE? YOU'RE PALE! ARE YOU SICK?
FANTA, YOU'RE NOT A DOCTOR AS FAR AS I KNOW!
I'VE HAD IT, I'M GOING TO GO TO BED!
?
MOTHER...
WHAT'S WRONG WITH PAPA?
AYA, MEN ARE MORE COMPLICATED THAN WOMEN, BELIEVE ME!

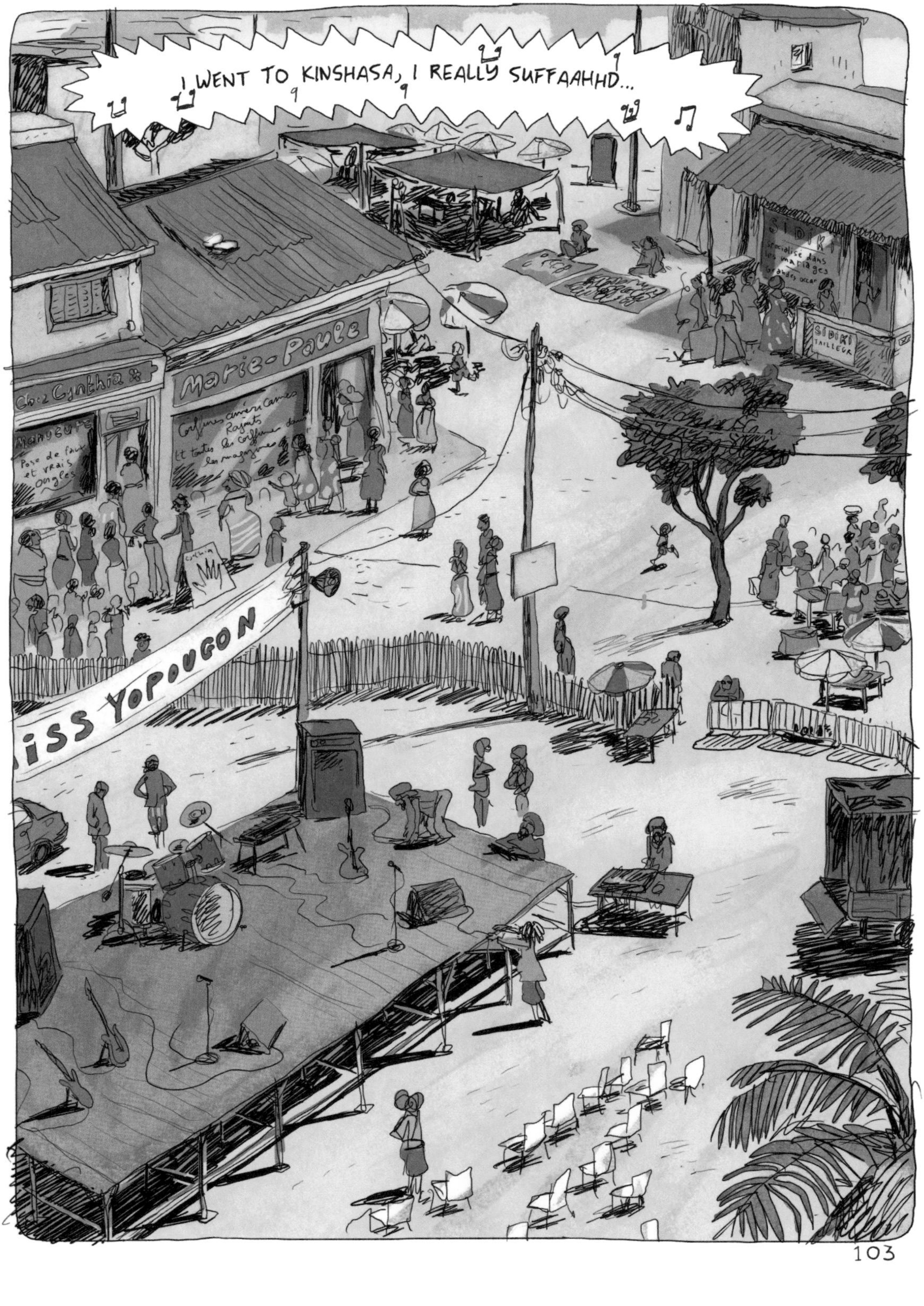
I WENT TO KINSHASA, I REALLY SUFFAAHHD...
Chez Cynthia
Manucure
Pose de faux et vrais ongles
Marie-Paule
Coiffures américaines
Rajouts
Et toutes les coiffures dans les magazines
SIDIKI
spécialisé dans les mariages grandes occa
SIDIKI TAILLEUR
ISS YOPOUGON

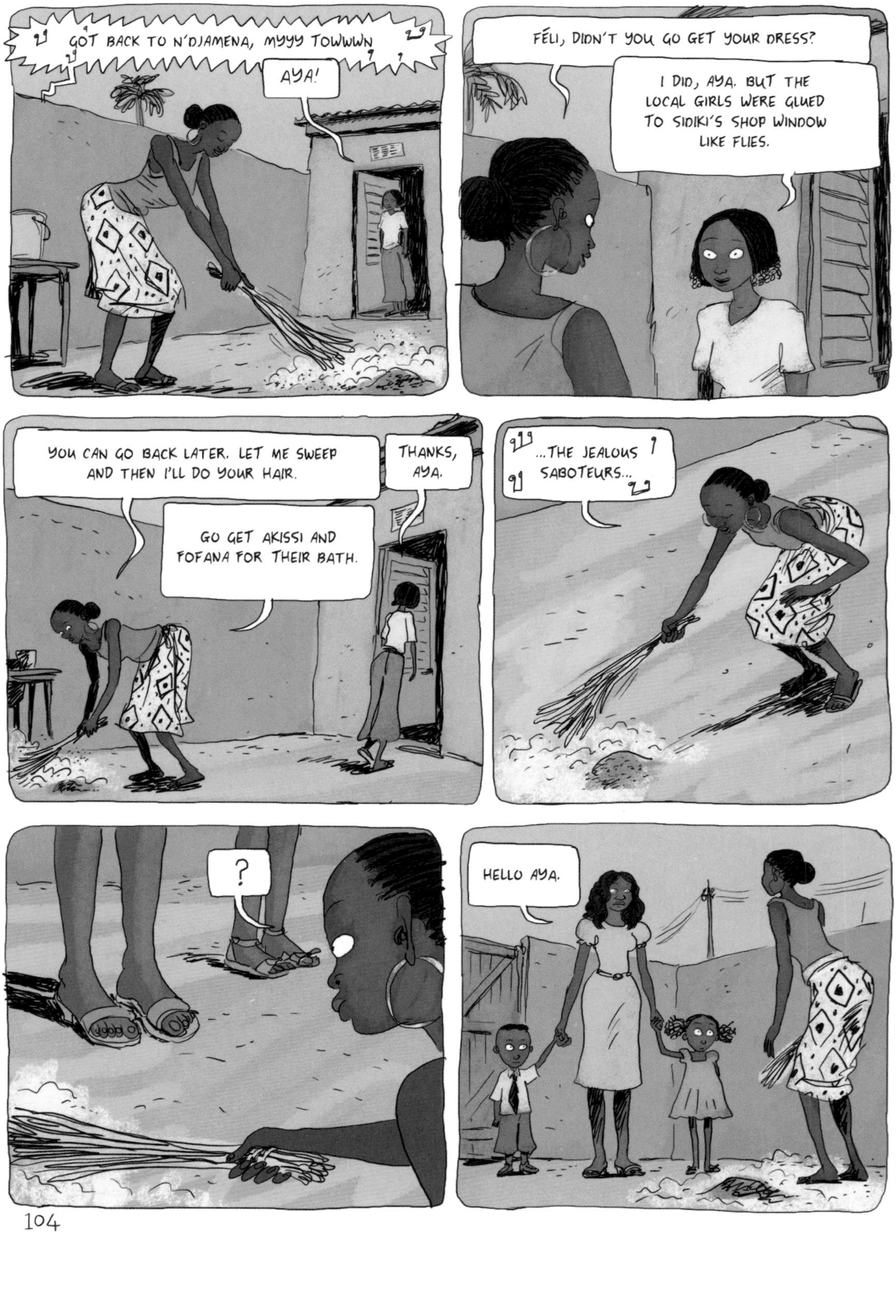
GOT BACK TO N'DJAMENA, MYYY TOWWWN
AYA!
FÉLI, DIDN'T YOU GO GET YOUR DRESS?
I DID, AYA. BUT THE LOCAL GIRLS WERE GLUED TO SIDIKI'S SHOP WINDOW LIKE FLIES.
YOU CAN GO BACK LATER. LET ME SWEEP AND THEN I'LL DO YOUR HAIR.
GO GET AKISSI AND FOFANA FOR THEIR BATH.
THANKS, AYA.
...THE JEALOUS SABOTEURS...
?
HELLO AYA.

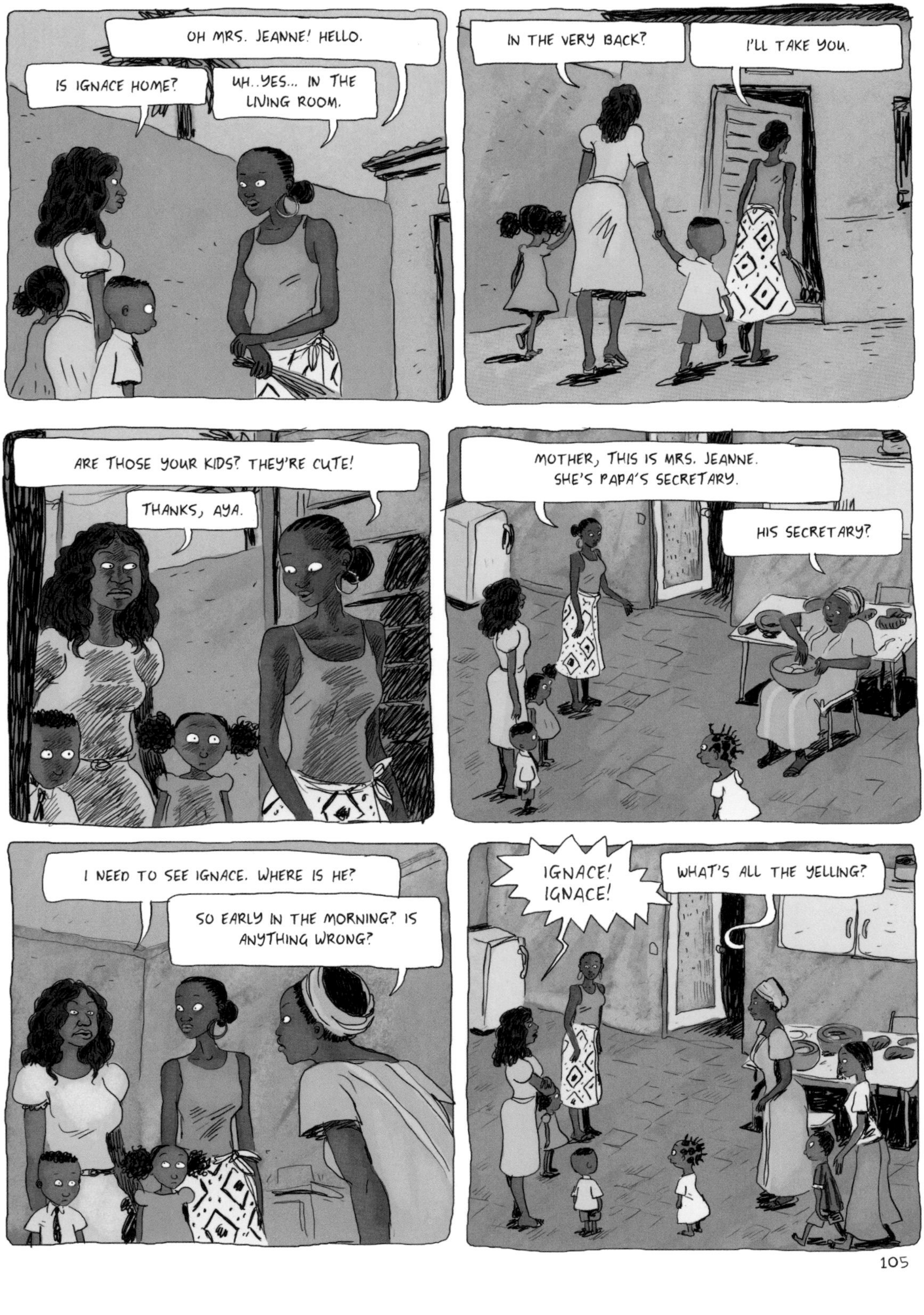
OH MRS. JEANNE! HELLO.
IS IGNACE HOME?
UH..YES... IN THE LIVING ROOM.
IN THE VERY BACK?
I'LL TAKE YOU.
ARE THOSE YOUR KIDS? THEY'RE CUTE!
THANKS, AYA.
MOTHER, THIS IS MRS. JEANNE. SHE'S PAPA'S SECRETARY.
HIS SECRETARY?
I NEED TO SEE IGNACE. WHERE IS HE?
SO EARLY IN THE MORNING? IS ANYTHING WRONG?
IGNACE! IGNACE!
WHAT'S ALL THE YELLING?

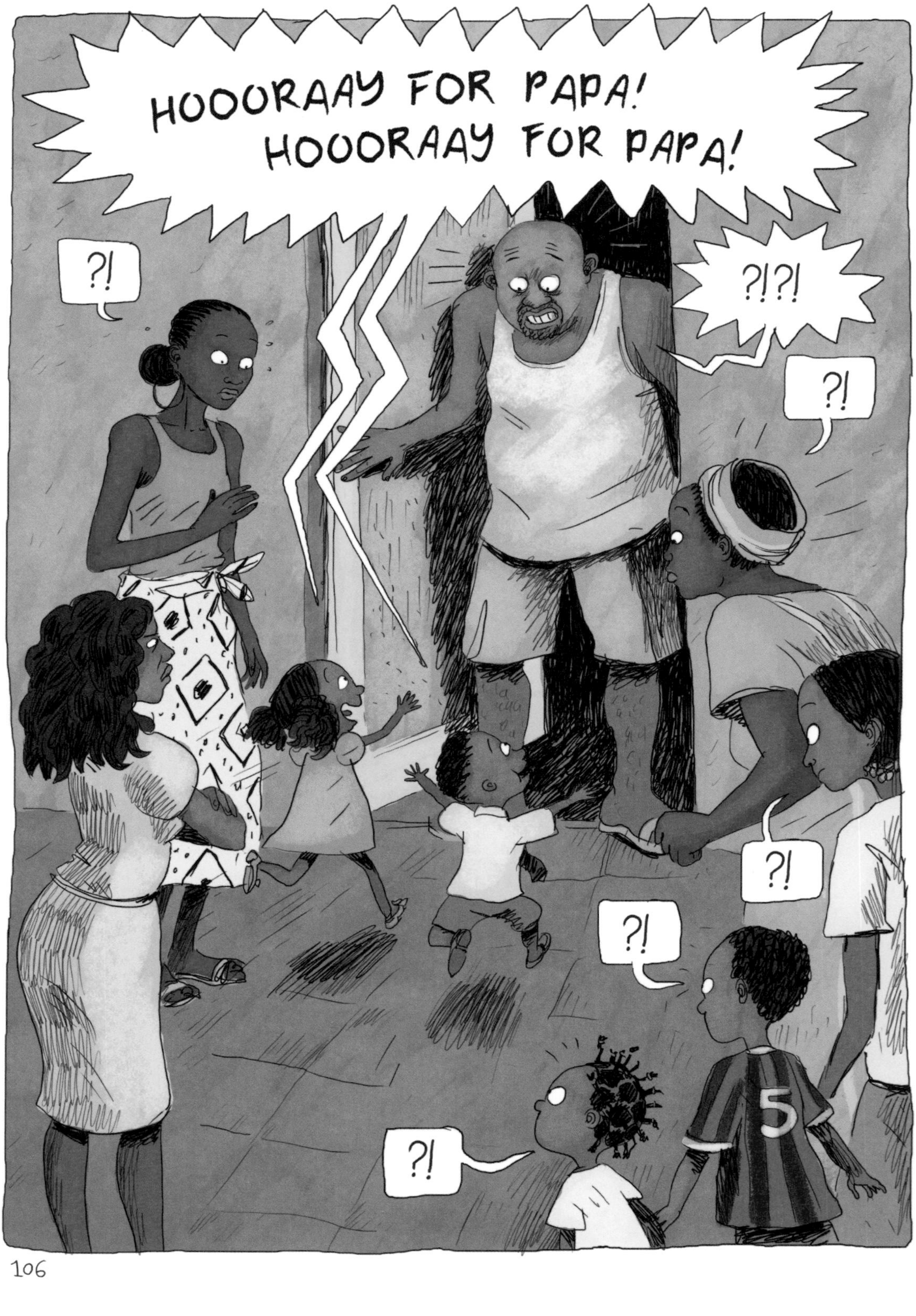
HOOORAAY FOR PAPA!
HOOORAAY FOR PAPA!
?!
?!?!
?!
?!
?!
?!
5

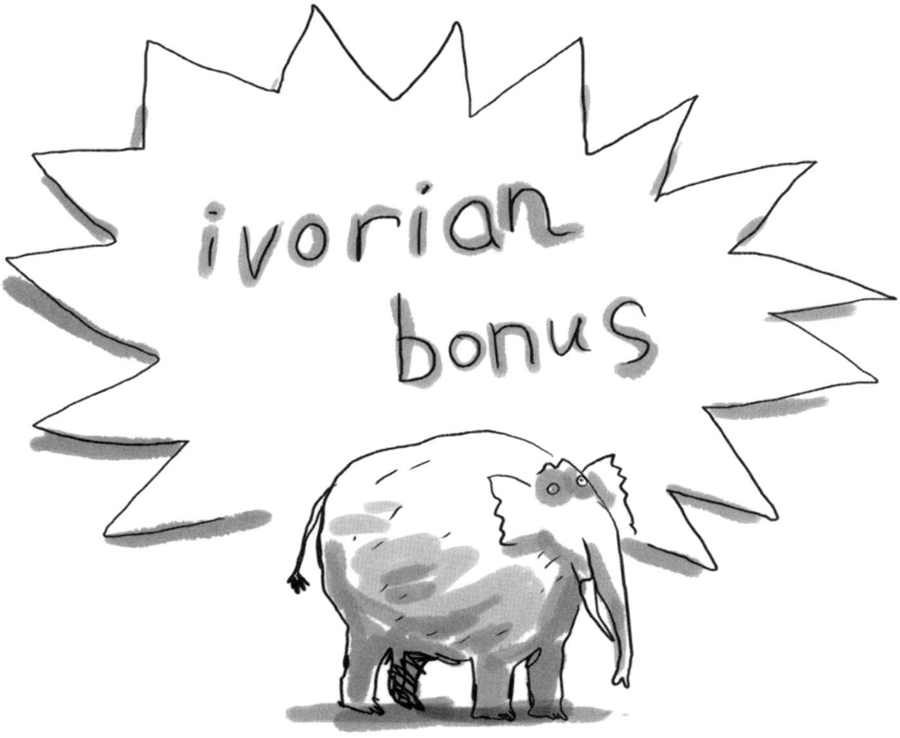
ivorian bonus

HERE'S A **LITTLE GLOSSARY**
TO HELP YOU BETTER UNDERSTAND
THE STORY

- CHOCODI: BRAND OF IVORIAN CHOCOLATE.

- CLACLOS: SMALL DUMPLING MADE OF RIPE PLANTAINS MIXED WITH FLOUR, ONIONS AND SALT, WITH OR WITHOUT A LITTLE CHILI PEPPER, AND THEN FRIED.

- DÊH!: EXCLAMATORY EXPRESSION.

- DJO: A GUY, DUDE.

- KÊH: EXCLAMATORY EXPRESSION.

- KOUTOUKOU: A POTENT ALCOHOLIC BEVERAGE DISTILLED FROM PALM WINE AND HAVING AN ALCOHOL CONTENT OF AT LEAST 40%.

- MAMAN: INFORMAL, MOTHER.

- MAQUIS: AN INEXPENSIVE OPEN-AIR RESTAURANT WHERE PEOPLE CAN DANCE.

- PALU: SHORT FOR PALLUDISM (MALARIA).

- TANTIE: INFORMAL, AUNT. ALSO USED TO SHOW RESPECT OR AFFECTION WHEN TALKING TO AN OLDER WOMAN.

- TONTON: INFORMAL, UNCLE. USED IN THE SAME WAY AS "TANTIE."

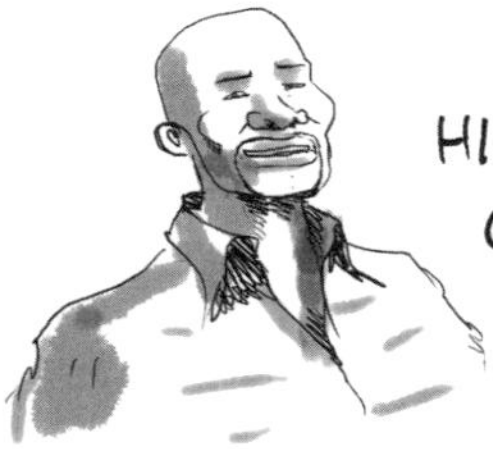

HI FRIENDS! ONE OF MY SECRETS (AMONG MANY OTHERS) THAT LETS ME SCORE WITH WOMEN IN PARIS AND ELSEWHERE IS MY DELICIOUS

CHICKEN KÉDJÉNOU.

IT'S VERY SIMPLE TO MAKE AND IT WILL POSITIVELY FLOOR THEM (PROBABLY THANKS TO THE CHICKEN). HERE'S THE RECIPE:

SERVES 2:

- 1 CHICKEN

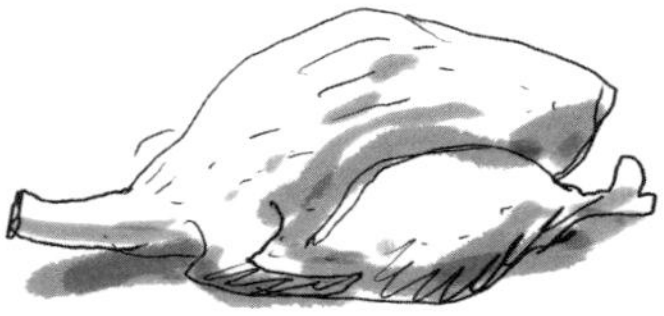

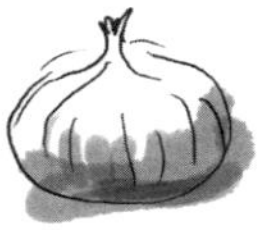

- 1 LARGE ONION
- 2 TOMATOES

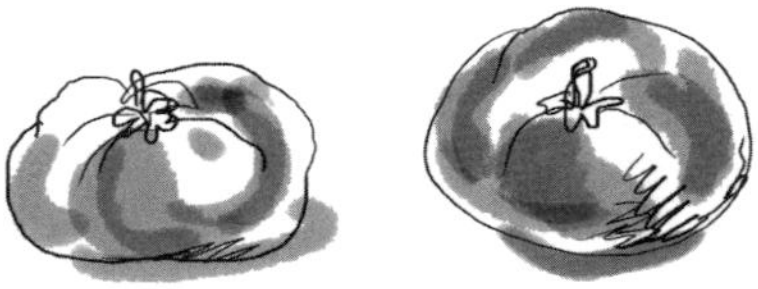

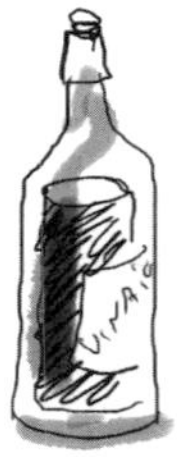

- 1 TABLESPOON OF VINEGAR

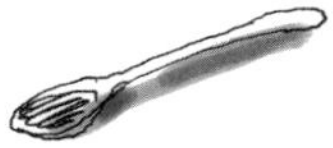

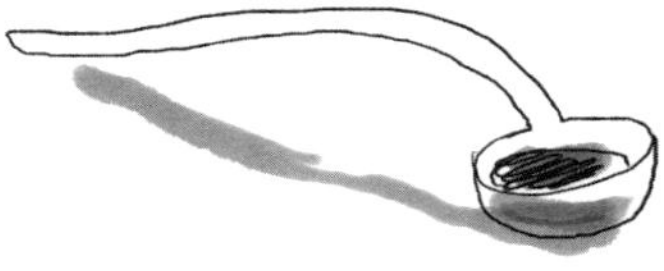

- 1 LADLE OF RED WINE
- SALT

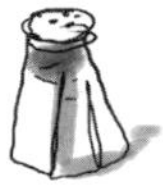

- 1 BOUILLON CUBE (MAGGI BRAND)

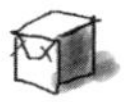

- 1 CHILI PEPPER (NOT REQUIRED, ONLY FOR THE BRAVE)

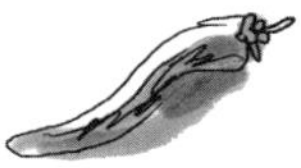

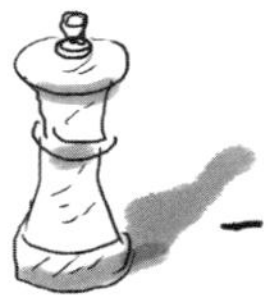

- PEPPER

1) WASH AND CUT UP THE CHICKEN, ONION, AND TOMATOES.

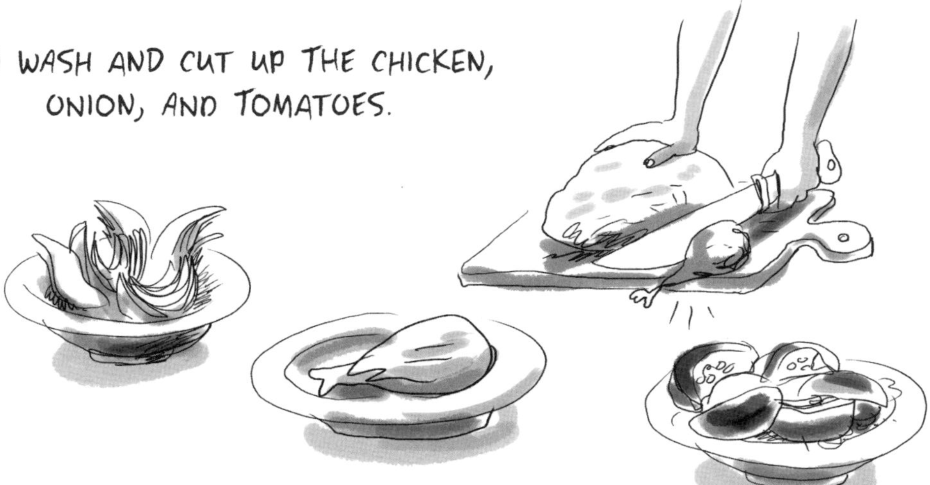

2) PLACE THE CHICKEN PIECES, CHOPPED ONION, QUARTERED TOMATOES, SALT, MAGGI CUBES, CHILI PEPPER, PEPPER, VINEGAR, AND RED WINE IN A LARGE POT, AND LET YOUR STEW COOK WITH THE LID ON FOR ONE HOUR.

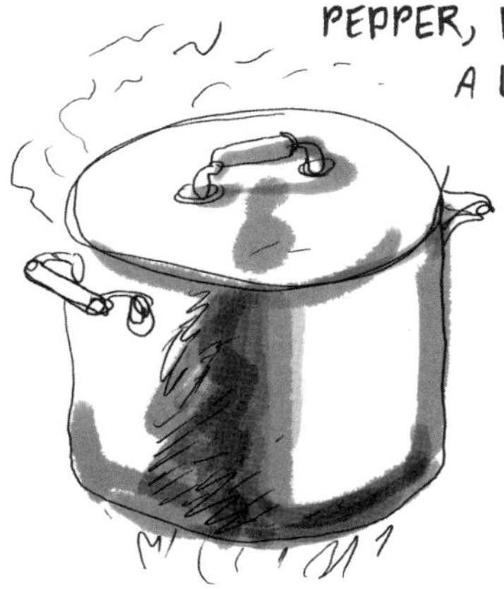

THAT'S IT, IT'S READY TO SERVE!

YOU CAN ACCOMPANY THIS DISH WITH RICE, ATTIÉKÉ (GROUND CASSAVA), CORN, COUSCOUS, YAMS OR POTATOES...

IT'S A WINNER EVERY TIME!

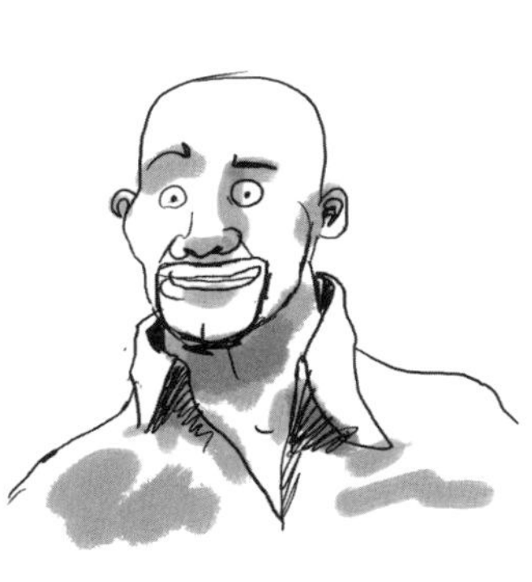

 GIRLFRIENDS, IT'S NOT EASY LOOKING AFTER A BABY, ESPECIALLY WHEN THERE'S NO TANTIES OR YOUNG GIRLS IN THE NEIGHBORHOOD TO HELP OUT.

SO HOW DOES ONE RUN ERRANDS, DO HOUSEWORK, AND COOK WITH A BABY THAT'S CRYING ALL THE TIME (ESPECIALLY IF IT'S COLICKY)?

I'M GOING TO HELP YOU BY TELLING YOU MY SECRET (WHICH IS KNOWN THROUGHOUT AFRICA BY THE WAY):

YOU CARRY YOUR BABY ON YOUR BACK.

NO MORE STROLLERS THAT GET IN THE WAY, NO MORE LATE DINNERS. YOUR LIFE WILL CHANGE! THE HARDEST THING IS FINDING A PAGNE (A PIECE OF BRIGHTLY COLORED, WAX-PRINTED CLOTH).

① WRAP THE PAGNE AROUND YOUR WAIST BEFORE PICKING UP THE BABY.

② PLACE THE BABY ON YOUR HIP.

③ MOVE IT TOWARDS YOUR BACK AS YOU BEND OVER (WITHOUT LETTING GO OF THE BABY).

④ THE BABY IS NOW ON YOUR BACK, YOU'RE STILL BENT OVER, AND YOU SQUEEZE THE BABY'S ARMS UNDER YOUR ARMPITS.

⑤ STILL BENT OVER, YOU NOW LIFT THE UNWRAPPED PAGNE OVER THE BABY UP TO ITS NECK TO HOLD ITS HEAD UP (IF THE BABY IS SMALL) OR UNDER ITS ARMPITS (FOR A BIGGER BABY).

⑥ YOU STAND UP STRAIGHT AND FASTEN THE PAGNE AROUND YOUR CHEST BY ROLLING IT OR MAKING A KNOT.

⑦ THEN, YOU RAISE THE BOTTOM OF THE PAGNE UP TO THE BABY, AND YOU MAKE A KNOT.

THERE YOU GO, NOW YOU CAN TEND TO WHATEVER NEEDS TO BE DONE.
OBVIOUSLY, IT LOOKS COMPLICATED, BUT WITH A LITTLE PRACTICE, YOU'LL MANAGE...
JUST TO PLAY IT SAFE, YOU MIGHT WANT TO PRACTICE FIRST ON A TEDDY BEAR OR A DOLL.

In our country, we have a famous proverb that goes like this:

"When a baby is in the belly, it belongs to its mother. When it's born, it belongs to everyone."

The "it belongs to everyone" part is really great, believe me. And here's why:

First, when you give birth, you only stay in the maternity ward for a day, unless you have a caesarian, in which case you go home the day after (not enough room and it's expensive).
But that doesn't matter because as soon as you get home, you are welcomed like a "queen" by everyone.
(Your family will take care of you and your baby for a while, and that's great, because you won't have time to get those famous postpartum blues.)
The baby and you are promptly looked after.
Your mother heats some water and massages your whole body, especially the belly. Next she slathers you in shea butter and you go shower. Then she slathers you in shea butter again and wraps your belly (if you haven't had a caesarian, of course). Afterward, she dresses you and does your hair (you couldn't get better treatment at a spa).

During this time, a team made up of your grandmother (if you still have one) and great-aunts takes care of your baby. They massage its head with a warm washcloth (so that its head becomes nice and round) and then its whole body (to make it nice and firm). When that's done, the baby is washed, slathered in lotion and dusted with "Bébé d'or" talcum powder or other things, then dressed in pretty clothes.

Meanwhile, another team made up of female cousins, sisters-in-law and tanties makes a delicious meal, and then it's time to sit down to eat! You come out of your room beautiful and glowing (thanks to the shea butter) and you enjoy the special meal (that you requested) under the happy gaze of your whole family.

When you have finished your meal, your beautiful baby is returned to you so you can nurse it (yup, that's right, you've got to work just a little bit). After it burps, you put it down to sleep, and you can take a well-deserved nap and rest easy because your baby is being watched over by dozens of people.

And what does the father do in all of this? Don't think he's excluded. On the contrary, he's got a ton of things to do. He can carry his baby (if he's not too scared about crushing it), or hug his wife (if he's not too embarrassed in front of everyone). But most of the time, he's busy serving drinks to all the friends and neighbors who've come to congratulate him. He's proud and happy to tell anyone who'll listen that he's a father, and spends his evenings at the maquis celebrating, and when he comes home late and tipsy, you listen to him saying how happy he is to be a father, and you curl up with him because you're rested enough to do so, and especially so you don't get riled up about his antics.

You're helped in this way for some time. A few days before the aunts, female cousins, and sisters-in-law leave (your mother and grandmother can stay much longer), you introduce your baby to all the people in your neighborhood (even though they've all come by your house already to see you). This ritual is very important because you bring them your baby as a sign of respect and consideration. That's how you get everyone to adopt your baby.

That's how children grow up in this community. When your children are old enough to play outside, they'll always be watched by someone and they'll get scolded by a tantie or tonton the minute they're up to some mischief.

Your children will invite other neighbor kids to come eat at your house because your children have had meals at theirs.
They'll learn about sharing and life as part of a community.
You're probably wondering about the "mother-father-child" bond. Don't worry, the others will never get in the way of that bond. Just because you give your children to others for a short time, doesn't mean they'll love you any less.

In any event, in our country, we don't have to deal with those kinds of questions, because we don't even think about them, and everything goes really well.

After all, we all want our children to be happy.

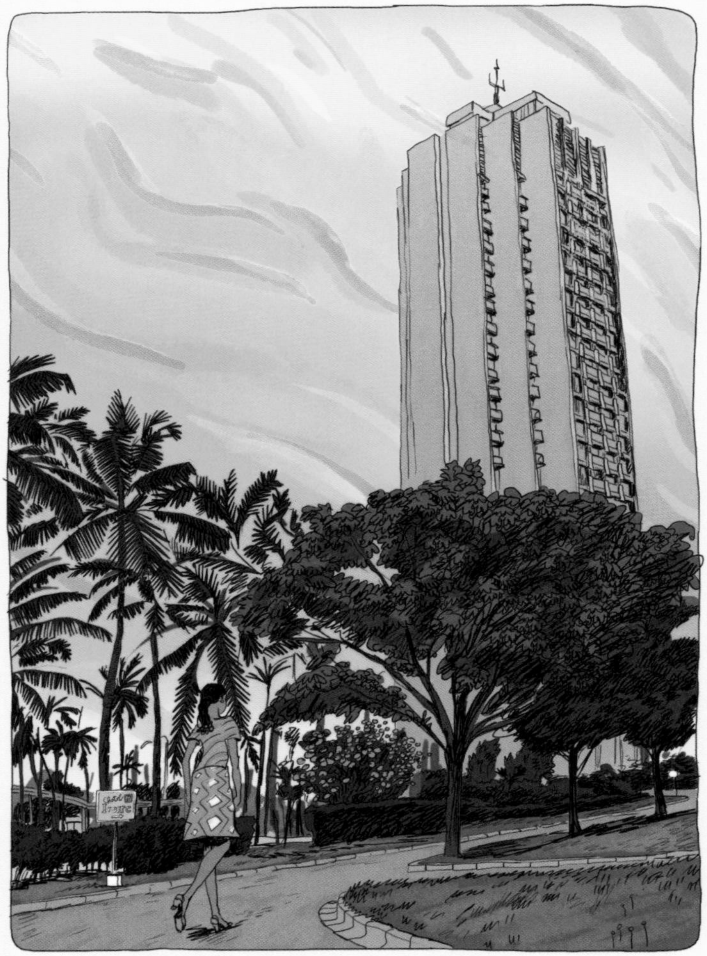

DRAWING ON THE UNIVERSAL IN AFRICA

An Interview with Marguerite Abouet

BY ANGELA AJAYI

Reprinted with permission of the *Wild River Review.*

Too often, it is easier than we realize to forget the intimate details of a childhood, especially one lived thousands of miles away in a different country. As the years pass by, distance and time make fading memories more difficult to recall. Slowly, a new—and hopefully better—life takes over our days, making it even harder to remember little details.

Like Marguerite Abouet, I left West Africa at an early age. And like her, I too, long to remember and write about what it was like then, for in the back of my mind West Africa is always present. It comes as no surprise to me that Abouet's only comic book in English, Aya, *is her very powerful visual and literary expression of this longing, this deep need to hold onto childhood memories filled with "unbelievable" stories about neighbors, families, friends—all in an Ivory Coast that had recently gained independence from France and was enjoying a new middle class society.*

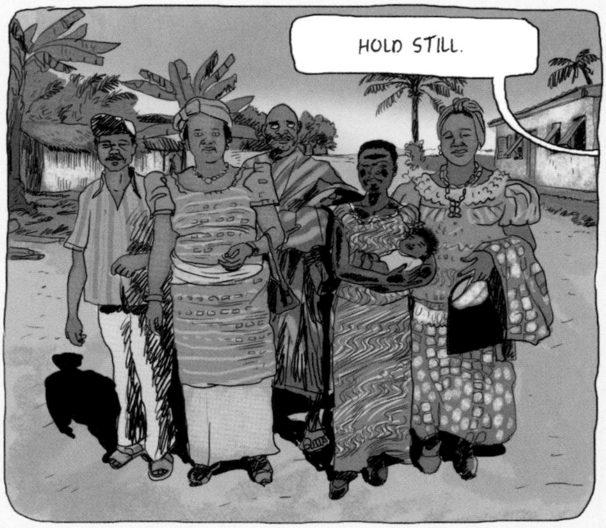
HOLD STILL.

Set in a bustling city in Ivory Coast, Aya *is a witty, urban story. One that, Abouet says, could have taken place anywhere in the world. She is right, in theory, for there is a universalizing force that seems to drive Marguerite Abouet, the writer.*

So come along and let her show you why, and literally through pictures, how, just as they might do in Europe or America, young girls sneak out to meet guys at night—or go to a party and flirt with the most attractive guy there. Around the world, it's really all the same.

And yet, Aya *is also an urban story that takes place, specifically, in Ivory Coast—a country which is now experiencing what many other African countries have faced after decades of colonial rule: political corruption, disease, civil strife, and staggering poverty.*

Days after I finished this interview with Abouet, I realized that in it I had brought attention to the current harsh realities for Africans in Ivory Coast, and for those who migrated to Europe. Perhaps, as someone who was raised in Africa, I felt I had to...and it was the responsible thing to do. Perhaps it may always remain so; I don't know. Thankfully, Abouet was generous and warm in her response to my questions, always unapologetically reaching for honesty in her own reflections.

At a panel discussion at the 2007 PEN World Voices Festival in New York City, Abouet spoke of how she often feels a certain responsibility as an African writer because she wrote the book Aya. *It was unclear to me whether this feeling of responsibility, like mine, had everything to do with addressing the current crisis in many parts of Africa. But I secretly wished it didn't, and that part of it also meant continuously drawing attention to the universal and relatable aspects of Africa, which Abouet has indeed successfully done in her engaging work,* Aya*—and in her interview with me.*

ANGELA AJAYI: *Tell me about moving from Ivory Coast to France at a very young age (seven?)—and how this experience, coupled with living in France from thereon, might have influenced the course of your life and your writing of* Aya *(if at all).*

MARGUERITE ABOUET: I came to France at the age of twelve. Because the Ivory Coast is an old French colony, I spoke French very well—obviously with an accent! Culturally speaking, I also did not have great difficulty integrating into the society.

Then, as the years went by, I had the desire to write *Aya*. I had always felt the need to recollect my youth down there, the mischief I got into, the unbelievable stories about the quartier (neighborhood), the families, the neighbors. I did not want to forget that part of my life. I wanted to hold on to those memories, and the desire to recount them got stronger with age. I felt a little guilty for being content in another country, far away from my family; in addition, I got so annoyed at the way in which the media systematically showed the bad side of the African continent, habitual litanies of wars, famine, of the 'sida,' (AIDS) and other disasters, that I wished to show the other side, to tell about daily modern life that also exists in Africa. *Aya* is therefore an urban story which could have taken place anywhere in the world.

AJAYI: *Ivory Coast enjoyed what some have called la belle époque in the 1970s when President Houphouet-Boigny's free land policies brought about an economic boom — and thus the emergence of a middle class was possible. This is indeed something that is sorely lacking in many African countries today. In Aya you capture the middle class society so well that I wondered if your family was part of it. If yes, what were some of its societal norms at that time? I ask this because in* Aya, *there is a focus on societal norms and a testing of them by some of the main characters like Bintou, Adjoua, and even Aya herself. For instance, in the book, Aya tells her father she wants to become a doctor and he discourages her because "university is for men, not girls."*

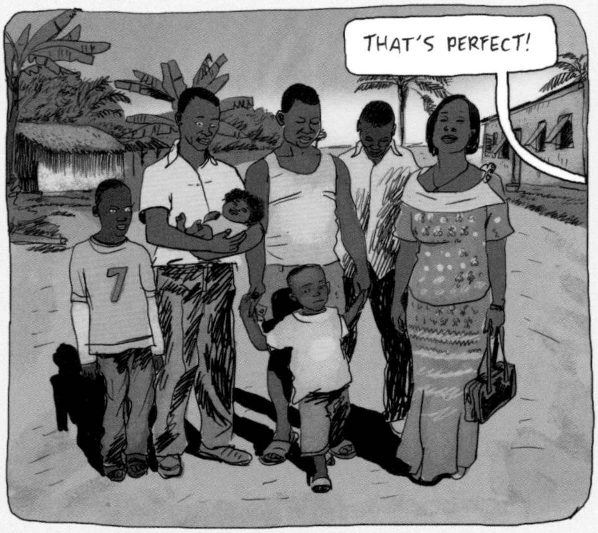
THAT'S PERFECT!

ABOUET: After gaining independence, a new middle class appeared on the Ivory Cost. Many peasants' children had the opportunity to study in the city. Thus it was necessary to provide housing for these young people, and new additions and areas began to crowd Abidjan. Helped along by the economy of the time, all these new graduates found jobs. For relaxation, they formed clubs where they met after work or on weekends. That is also where they socialized and married. Their parents no longer had much influence on their life choices; they had been surpassed by the changes in the country and by this new freedom brought about by the "Ivorian miracle."

Women above all were influenced by the Western media and were emancipated. They no longer yielded to their parents' authority in choosing a husband. Their level of education made them aware of their rights: the right to divorce, access to the pill, opportunities for professional careers.

It is true that Africans had a strong desire for a male as the eldest child. It is he who would carry on the family name and would contribute to the support of the family by caring for aging parents. As far as a girl was concerned, she was often a liability and was married very quickly, mostly to the advantage of the parents.

But here, as in the Ivory miracle, men justifiably chose women from these clubs; they knew that they were very modern and cultivated, and financially independent. My parents were a part of that middle class. They were well off before they met. When they decided to get married, their parents both approved the match because their children already had a place to live and a job. It is true that in *Aya* the father tells his daughter that great accomplishments are made by men. This comment must be taken in context: this is only fiction, and fortunately not all African fathers are like Ignace. His only goal is to marry his daughter to the son of his boss. He is so intent on this that he urges her not to go too far in her studies.

AJAYI: *In* Aya, *the modern (telephones, fancy dresses, and cars from Paris, etc.) and the traditional (wearing of traditional waxed cloth-like pagne, etc) seem to coexist well and without much friction (except perhaps when norms are obviously challenged). You seem to be saying something about the impact of modernity on women in African society in the book though,* *both good and bad. Please elaborate more on this if you can.*

ABOUET: It is true: Africa is torn between tradition and modern times. That is the logical result of the meeting between Africa and the West in the media where many European and Brazilian programs are replayed. Actually, the women in *Aya* avail themselves of certain rights, even though they are subject to numerous patriarchal dictates: the right and choice of working (that is true for all yopoupan mothers), control over household funds, also the choice to have fewer children (true for Bintou's mother), the right not to accept polygamy, access to a basic level of education (true for Aya's mother), also the right to divorce.

It is the good side of modern times that can coexist well with tradition. The tradition of Ivorian hospitality that is characteristic to young and old is one of respect for family environments and for the aged. That is why girls adhere to traditional values in *Aya,* in spite of the freedoms they have.

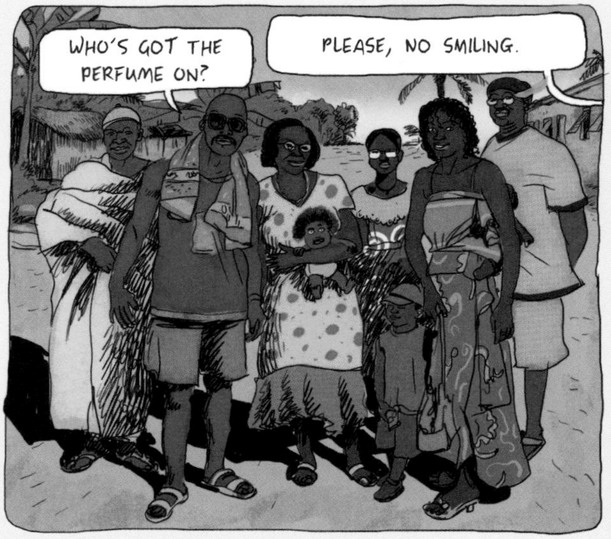
WHO'S GOT THE PERFUME ON?
PLEASE, NO SMILING.

AJAYI: *You've chosen the comic book to convey your story. Is there a specific reason for this or was it coincidental? I read that you are currently working on some novels. Do you find the creative process different from when you wrote a comic book like* Aya*? Harder? Easier? Not comparable at all?*

ABOUET: Novels written for young people are subject to a host of commercial constraints such as age, purpose, themes, and editors who do not shy away from endless correcting and reworking of the text. That is a problem that I did not face in *Aya*. By addressing adults as well as the young, I had great freedom to create.

AJAYI: *There is a lot of humor in* Aya*, even when the characters show questionable moral behavior like promiscuity and infidelity. It seems to me that humor could be the vehicle you've used to draw attention to these particular aspects of 1970s urban life in Ivory Coast. Please elaborate on your use of humor in the book.*

ABOUET: The people of the Ivory Coast are known for their sense of humor, particularly with regard to things that are not humorous. Their motto is: as long as no one has died, life continues. Whatever the conflicts or the problems, they will be resolved by following the advice of the sages at the foot of the talking tree (tree of advice), and then one can reconcile by celebrating with a feast.

The humor in *Aya* is not limited to the 70s; it is equally appropriate for today, because there are new sources of humor (all the coup d'états and their successive presidents, the unexpected fates of immigrants in Europe and the United States, escapades with hookers, brazen corruption, and so on.) Moreover, one need go no further than listening to the songs and reading the humor magazines like 'GBICH' to realize that Ivorian humor has grown. In *Aya* I only paid homage to the kind of humor that is part of me and with which I grew up.

AJAYI: *What is your life in France like at the moment? And as an African woman who immigrated to France, what do you think of the current socio-political situation in the country in regards to immigrants, especially North Africans?*

ABOUET: My life is quite normal. I live with my husband and our two-month-old son. I stopped working as a legal assistant and I am trying to write every day.

From the very beginning, I believed that the socio-political situation in North Africa and that in West Africa are totally different.

As an African from the West, I would like to point out that the French had the black Africans brought over to do the jobs that no one else wanted to do. As long as the Blacks stayed in their assigned place—as supermarket attendants, house maids, street sweepers, in child and geriatric care, or at most, as artists and athletes—all went very well. But now some of the offspring and young children of those first arrivals are doing more than that. At the price of a difficult struggle, they are becoming company owners, managers, intellectuals, and they are more visible. These Blacks sense more discrimination because they have abandoned their role. This kind of racism is more frequent when the economy is doing poorly.

Today's real danger is not idiotic racism and the increase in nationalists. We know how to deal with it—it is evident in ordinary attitudes which convey the worst paternalistic and condescending clichés that symbolically destroy Blacks even more surely than the overtly racist insults.

I believe that Blacks have just need for a Republic that is accessible to all and allows each one to find his place in society according to his talents.

ABOUET: We are often told that Africans live in famine, illness, tribal wars, poverty, with a hand extended, begging the West for aid.

It is interesting to confirm that the easygoing and careless impression of Africa that is found in Aya fortunately still exists, even today. It would be nice if the African continent were evoked dropping the stereotypes of suffering because Africa is really quite a large and diverse continent, and as everywhere else—particularly in the United States, there are enormous differences in social classes…

Paradoxically, it is a form of well-disposed racism when I hear some people say that they will never go to Africa for fear of seeing this suffering.

STOP SHAKING, PÉPÉ!

WAAH!

One needs to know that Africans are about more than the side of misery that is persistently shown of their continent. Africans have only had their independence for forty years, compared to a century for France; it seems fair to give Africans time to free themselves of old crocodiles in power and to evolve.

AJAYI: *Today, many people in Africa are obviously experiencing serious economic hardship and struggle to survive on a daily basis—and the American media via films such as* Blood Diamonds *and* The Constant Gardener *continuously portray an Africa that is wrought with violent civil war, corruption, etc. The post-colonial Ivory Coast in* Aya *is a totally different one— almost unrecognizable, especially given the media's images. Life was refreshingly simple, peaceful, and people were obviously enjoying themselves. What do you think of how the West (more so America, I think) portrays Africa in general nowadays—and was* Aya *an attempt to respond to that at all? If not, inadvertently, you have a portrayed an Africa that seems almost non-existent now, one that we really don't see or hear much of anymore. Wonderful, I think.*

I can assure you that the Ivory Coast remains a beautiful country with nice quartiers (neighborhoods), superb beaches, and a magnificent fauna and flora, despite its disasters. African women finally share the same dreams of other women on the planet, and all I want to do is show their daily lives along with their hopes and desires to find fulfillment as modern women in Africa.

BORN IN NIGERIA, ANGELA AJAYI CAME TO THE UNITED STATES TO ATTEND COLLEGE AND DISCOVERED AN UNDENIABLE LOVE FOR LITERATURE—AND BOOKS. AFTER COMPLETING A B.A. IN ENGLISH LITERATURE, SHE SPENT SIX WEEKS AT THE RADCLIFFE PUBLISHING COURSE IN CAMBRIDGE, MASSACHUSETTS, AND THEN MOVED TO NEW YORK CITY WHERE SHE WORKED IN SCHOLARLY PUBLISHING FOR A NUMBER OF YEARS AND COMPLETED AN M.A. IN COMPARATIVE LITERATURE AT COLUMBIA UNIVERSITY. SHE CURRENTLY WORKS FOR A PUBLISHING HOUSE IN NEW JERSEY AND EDITS MAINLY SCHOLARLY BOOKS ON AFRICA.

Marguerite Abouet was born in Abidjan in 1971. At the age of 12, she was sent with her older brother to study in France under the care of a great uncle. She now lives in Romainville, a suburb of Paris, where she works as a legal assistant and writes novels she has yet to show to publishers. *Aya* is her first graphic novel. It taps into Abouet's childhood memories of Ivory Coast in the 1970s, a prosperous, promising time in that country's history, to tell an unpretentious and gently humorous story of an Africa we rarely see—spirited, hopeful and resilient.

Clément Oubrerie was born in Paris in 1966. After a stint in art school he spent two years in the United States doing a variety of odd jobs, publishing his first children's books and serving jail time in New Mexico for working without papers. Back in France, he went on to a prolific career in illustration. With over 40 children's books to his credit, he is also co-founder of the 3-D animation studio, Station OMD. A drummer in a funk band in his spare time, he still travels frequently, especially to the Ivory Coast. In *Aya*, his first graphic novel, Oubrerie's warm colors and energetic, playful line connect expressively with Abouet's vibrant writing.

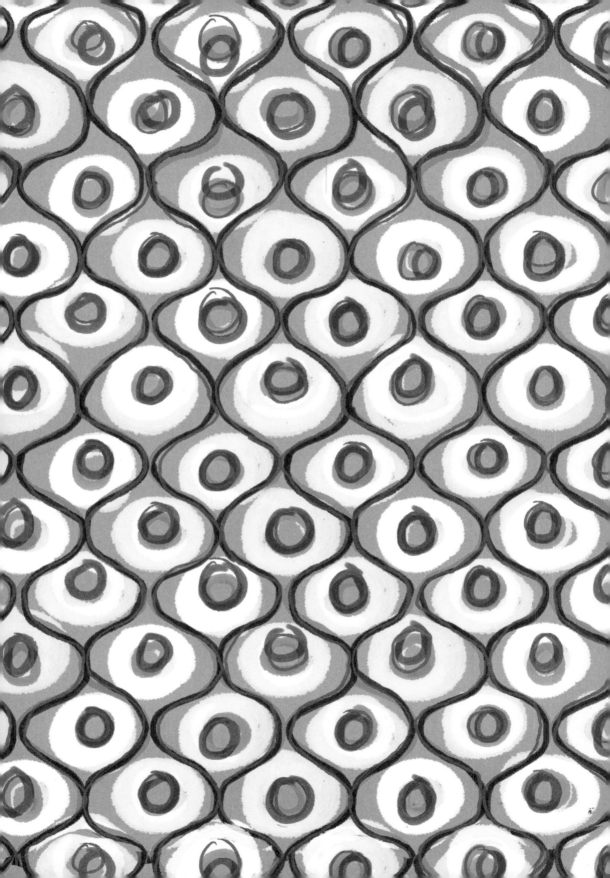